What Leaders Are Saying about Women's Bible Journals

"I'm touched and blessed by Lenya's and Penny's heart for His kingdom."
—Kay Arthur, Bible teacher and author of many best-selling Bible studies

"This Bible study will take you into a deeper relationship with Christ, bringing about transformation in your life."
—Ruth Bell Graham, speaker, poet, and author of *Footprints of a Pilgrim*

"Lenya's and Penny's love for the Lord and knowledge of His Word uniquely equip them to help other women discover the path ————————— *e in-depth Bible studies."*
—Kay Smith, wife of Chuck S

Ephesians

Women's Bible Journal

pathway to
God's Treasure

Lenya Heitzig | Penny Pierce Rose

TYNDALE HOUSE PUBLISHERS, INC • WHEATON, IL

Visit Tyndale's exciting Web site at www.tyndale.com

Pathway to God's Treasure: Ephesians

Copyright © 2001 by Lenya Heitzig and Penny Pierce Rose. All rights reserved.

Cover photograph © by Colin Hawkins/Getty Images. All rights reserved.

Authors' photos copyright © 2001 by Frank Frost Photography. All rights reserved.

Designed by Timothy R. Botts and Kelly Bennema

Edited by Lynn Vanderzalm and Mary Horner Collins

Bible Illustrator for Windows. Parsons Technology, 1997-1998. Illustrations copyright © 1998 by Christianity Today, Inc. All rights reserved. Portions copyright © 1984-1995 Faircom Corp.

Unless otherwise indicated, all Scripture quotations are taken from the New King James Version. Copyright © 1979, 1980, 1982 by Thomas Nelson, Inc. Used by permission. All rights reserved.

Scripture quotations marked NLT are taken from the *Holy Bible,* New Living Translation, copyright © 1996. Used by permission of Tyndale House Publishers, Inc., Wheaton, Illinois 60189. All rights reserved.

Scripture quotations marked NIV are taken from the *Holy Bible,* New International Version®. NIV®. Copyright © 1973, 1978, 1984 by International Bible Society. Used by permission of Zondervan Publishing House. All rights reserved.

Scripture quotations marked KJV are taken from the *Holy Bible,* King James Version.

Printed in the United States of America

06   05   04   03
8   7   6   5   4

Contents

There's a bit of explorer in all of us. Like Dorothy, some people may long to go "somewhere over the rainbow" instead of the flatlands of Kansas. Others dream of journeys aboard the Starship Enterprise, boldly going "where no one has gone before." Though none of us will ever make it to Oz or Deep Space Nine, it is within our reach to take a family vacation to Disneyland or perhaps travel to Paris for a romantic honeymoon. While these vacations take us across the globe for a short time, we can take spiritual journeys that are out of this world and will last a lifetime. Those are the trips worth taking!

Spiritual journeys have something in common with real travel—you have to experience them for yourself. Perusing travel guides about Paris doesn't come close to strolling along the Champs-Élysées. In the same way, reading books about God's grace can't compare with experiencing it in your own heart. Until you have reached a destination yourself, it is just secondhand knowledge—stimulating but not fulfilling.

Have *you* dreamed of taking spiritual journeys but didn't know where to start? The Women's Bible Study Journals are your ticket to exciting adventures in God's Word, helping you become an explorer instead of a bystander. Your journeys will take you on paths through the Bible and lead you into experiences with God that are up close and personal—no more secondhand knowledge! Whether you are doing this study in a small-group setting or alone for personal study, you will be able to bring home your own spiritual mementos from the journey of a lifetime.

On this particular trip we fully explore Paul's letter to the Ephesians, where you'll discover God's treasures—the rich inheritance He has bequeathed to *you*, His beloved daughter. God's purpose in sending the letter to the Ephesian Christians in the first century, and now to you, is so you would know "the riches of the glory of His inheritance" (Ephesians 1:18). So fasten your seat belts, and join us as we soar to new spiritual heights together.

Exploring God's Word can be as vast as a trip around the world, so we need a map to keep us on course. We've plotted the route by dividing each of the twelve lessons into five sections—one study for each weekday. Every day you will follow a pathway that leads you to deeper understanding and application of God's Word. Allow us to familiarize you with the steps you'll take:

Preparation is where each day's journey begins. Start with the prayer designed to lead you into the lesson, then read the relevant promise from Scripture. The story at the beginning of each day's study will help you begin to think about how the theme of the day's study expresses itself in our contemporary lives. Most of the stories in this book are written from Lenya's point of view; the stories that reflect Penny's life are indicated with a parenthetical note.

Exploration is the next stop. Here you will ask, *What are the facts?* These are the who-what-when-where-how questions that will help you explore the passage verse by verse. Unless otherwise indicated, the definitions have been adapated from *Nelson's Illustrated Bible Dictionary*. We have used the New King James Version in this study along with verses selected from the New Living Translation. Feel free to use other Bible translations as well.

Explanation sidebars will help you answer the question, *What does it mean?* Questions that have a related sidebar comment are marked with the symbol 🍃, and the sidebar insight with the same number will help you understand what the passage means through contemporary illustrations, biblical principles, and key definitions. We have gleaned insights from various Bible scholars and have relied on the *PC Study Bible* that contains many study resources (see bibliography).

Transformation exercises answer the question, *How should this change my life?* Here you will not only personally apply the lessons you have learned but also have the opportunity to reflect on what you've studied. The journal section of each lesson is an important place for you to open your heart and express your thoughts, goals, commitments, and prayers. It becomes a personal record of God's transforming work in your life. When you have completed all twelve lessons, you may want to take a few minutes to read through your journal responses, seeing how God has touched your heart and moved you to action during the weeks that you heard Him speak to you through Ephesians. The story at the end of each day's study will again help focus the day's theme.

Contemplation ends the day with inspiring quotes and encouraging insights from seasoned travelers who have learned much from their own life's journeys.

Before starting this study, read the How to Get the Most out of This Study section to find tips and checklists for individuals, groups, and group leaders.

Traveling to exotic places and experiencing new cultures may change your perspective, but exploring God's Word has the power to revolutionize your life. We pray that as you journey through Ephesians, you'll discover the vast treasures God has in store for you.

In His love,
Lenya Heitzig and Penny Pierce Rose

How to Get the Most out of This Study

*T*his book is ideal for discussion in a small-group setting as well as for individual study. The following suggestions will help you and your group get the most out of your study time.

PERSONAL CHECKLIST

——*Be determined.* Examine your daily schedule, then set aside a consistent time for this study.

——*Be prepared.* Gather the materials you'll need: the Bible, your Women's Bible Journal, and a pen.

——*Be inspired.* Begin each day with prayer, asking the Holy Spirit to be your teacher and to illuminate your mind.

——*Be complete.* Read the suggested Bible passage and finish the homework each day.

——*Be persistent.* Answer each question as fully as possible. If you're unable to answer a question, move forward to the next question or read the explanation, which may offer further insight.

——*Be consistent.* Don't get discouraged. If you miss a day, use the weekend to catch up.

——*Be honest.* When answering the transformation questions, allow the Lord to search your heart and transform your life. The journal questions will help you write out your thoughts, a form of reflection that has proved helpful to many fellow pilgrims. Take time to reflect honestly about your own feelings, experiences, sins, goals, and responses to God.

——*Be blessed.* Enjoy your daily study time with God as He speaks to you through His Word.

SMALL-GROUP CHECKLIST

——*Be prayerful.* Pray before you begin your time together.

——*Be biblical.* Keep all answers in line with God's Word; avoid personal opinion.

——*Be confidential.* Keep all sharing within your small group confidential.

——*Be respectful.* Listen without interrupting. Keep comments on track and to the point so that all can share.

——*Be discreet.* In some cases, you need not share more than absolutely necessary. Some things are between you and the Lord.

___*Be kind.* Reply to the comments of others lovingly and courteously.

___*Be mindful.* Remember your group members in prayer throughout the week.

SMALL-GROUP LEADER CHECKLIST

___*Be prayerful.* Pray that the Holy Spirit will "guide you into truth" so that your leadership will guide others.

___*Be faithful.* Prepare by reading the Bible passage and studying the lesson ahead of time, highlighting truths and applying them personally.

___*Be prompt.* Begin and end the study on time.

___*Be thorough.* For optimum benefit, allot one hour for small-group discussion. This should allow plenty of time to cover all of the questions and exercises for each lesson.

___*Be selective.* If you have less than an hour, you should carefully choose which questions you will address, and summarize the edited information for your group. In this way, you can focus on the more thought-provoking exploration questions. Be sure to grant enough time to address pertinent transformation exercises, as this is where you and the women will clearly see God at work in your lives.

___*Be sensitive.* Some of the transformation exercises are very personal and may not be appropriate to discuss in a small group. If you sense that this is the case, feel free to move to another question.

___*Be flexible.* If the questions in the Women's Bible Journal seem unclear, reword them for your group. Feel free to add your own questions to bring out the meaning of a verse.

___*Be inclusive.* Encourage each member to participate in the discussion. You may have to draw some out or tone some down so that all have the opportunity to participate.

___*Be honest.* Don't be afraid to admit that you don't have all the answers! When in doubt encourage ladies to take difficult questions to their church leadership for clarification.

___*Be focused.* Keep the discussion on tempo and on target. Learn to pace your small group so that you complete a lesson on time. Though participants may get sidetracked, you should redirect the discussion to the passage at hand.

___*Be patient.* Realize that not all people are at the same place spiritually or socially. Wait for the members of your group to answer the questions rather than jump in and answer them yourself.

Are You in the Will?

Have you dreamed about inheriting treasures from a long lost relative? To be "in the will" would change your life forever! Consider the rags to riches story of Jack Wurm. In 1949, Mr. Wurm was unemployed and bankrupt. As he strolled along a San Francisco beach, he found a bottle with a scroll inside. He discovered that this "message in a bottle" was the last will and testament of Daisy Singer Alexander, heiress to the Singer Sewing Company fortune.

The faded paper read: "To avoid confusion, I leave my entire estate to the lucky person who finds this bottle, and to my attorney, Barry Cohen; share and share alike." The courts discovered that she had written the note and thrown the bottle into the Thames River in London. It had drifted across the oceans to San Francisco and reached a penniless Jack Wurm. Jack inherited over $6 million in cash and Singer stock.

Similarly, God has sent us a "message in a Bible." Within this book you'll find the "last will and testament of our Lord" with a different kind of inheritance—spiritual treasures. How will you respond? Will you walk past it? Or, like Jack Wurm, will you step out in faith and take action? Failure to take God's promises seriously leads to spiritual poverty. Jack's inheritance can't begin to compare with the spiritual wealth God offers His heirs! The book of Ephesians reveals the magnitude of your heavenly treasures.

DAY 1
The Messenger

DAY 2
The Beneficiaries

DAY 3
The Benefactor

DAY 4
The Redeemer

DAY 5
The Guarantor

DAY 1 THE MESSENGER

preparation

Father, I confess that this world tugs at my heart to go in directions that are not Your will for me. Use this study to transform my mind and direct my heart to follow You. Amen.

GOD'S WILL

Don't copy the behavior and customs of this world, but let God transform you into a new person by changing the way you think. Then you will know what God wants you to do, and you will know how good and pleasing and perfect his will really is.
Romans 12:2, NLT

explanation

APOSTLE
In Greek, *apostle* literally means "a delegate"; one sent with a special message or commission *(New Unger's Bible Dictionary)*.

exploration

Meet Paul, the author of the letter to the Ephesians. Paul wrote this letter while imprisoned in Rome for preaching the gospel. Though on trial for his life, Paul was concerned with the spiritual well-being of the churches he established on his missionary journeys. It was his honor and duty to deliver the "last will and testament" of our Savior to the church in Ephesus. Let's spend some time getting to know Paul, the messenger. As you study, ask yourself, "Am *I* in God's will?"

Read Ephesians 1:1-23, then focus on verse 1.

> ***Paul, an apostle of Jesus Christ by the will of God, . . .***
> Ephesians 1:1

1. What did Paul call himself? . . . .

. . . .

2. How did he become an apostle of Jesus Christ? . . . .

. . . .

Read Acts 9:1-31 to discover how Saul the Pharisee became Paul the apostle.

3. According to Acts 9:1-2, what was Paul like before he became a Christian?

. . . .

4. Describe how Paul was converted to Christianity (Acts 9:3-6).

. . . .

5. According to verse 15, to whom did the Lord call Paul to go?

. . . .

6. Focus on verses 22-23. How did the Jews respond to Paul's conversion? Why?

. . . .

. . . .

7. According to verse 26, how did the disciples respond to Paul? Why?

. . . .

. . . .

transformation

8. We have seen that Paul knew God's will and purpose for his life. Write out what these verses teach you about God's will for your life.

SCRIPTURE	GOD'S WILL FOR YOU
1 Thess. 4:3	
1 Thess. 5:18	
1 Pet. 2:15	

3
TRANSFORMED
God took Saul, a murderous, vengeful man, and transformed him into Paul (see Acts 13:9), the apostle who faithfully spread the gospel. Take comfort—God can rescue you from your "Damascus road" and transform your life for His glory.

5
GENTILE
The Jews used the term *Gentile* to refer to all people who were not Jewish. In New Testament times this became a derogatory label filled with prejudice and disdain.

6
PREJUDICE
Prejudice is blinding. The Jewish leaders could not see that Jesus was their Messiah and crucified Him. They refused to acknowledge Saul's conversion and persecuted him. Don't let discrimination blind you—you may destroy something beautiful!

9

SANCTIFICATION
The process of God's grace by which the believer is separated from sin and becomes dedicated to God's righteousness. Accomplished by the Word of God and the Holy Spirit, sanctification results in holiness or purification from the guilt and power of sin.

11

DOING GOOD
To be a Christian is to become Christlike—to imitate our Savior. "God anointed Jesus of Nazareth with the Holy Spirit and with power. Then Jesus went around doing good" (Acts 10:38, NLT).

9. God's will includes our *sanctification.*

Journal about some of the areas in which God has helped you separate yourself from a sinful behavior.

. . . .

. . . .

. . . .

. . . .

. . . .

10. It is God's will for us to be thankful.

Journal a note of thanksgiving to God.

. . . .

. . . .

. . . .

. . . .

. . . .

11. It is God's will for His followers to be doers of good deeds. Which of the good deeds below will you perform *this week?*

_____ Phone an unbeliever
_____ Visit an elderly friend
_____ Baby-sit for a family
_____ Prepare meals for the needy
_____ Pray for a missionary
_____ Other _____

Saul of Tarsus thought he was in God's will when, in fact, he was in bondage to his strict religious observance of the law. When God interrupted his life, Paul was transported from religion to relationship. He became a new creation in Christ. Paul learned to breathe the air of freedom by living in God's will. Jesus said, "If the Son sets you free, you will indeed be free" (John 8:36, NLT).

Henrietta Mears, a beloved Bible teacher, taught the secret to true freedom. She explained, "A bird is free in the air. Place a bird in the water and he has lost his liberty. A fish is free in the water, but leave him on the sand and he perishes. He is out of his realm. So, the Christian is free when he does the will of God and is obedient to God's command. This is as natural a realm for God's child as the water is for the fish, or the air for the bird."

contemplation
All heaven is waiting to help those who will discover the will of God and do it.
J. Robert Ashcroft

DAY 2 THE BENEFICIARIES

A five-year-old named Justin heard the story of the monk Simon the Stylite, who attained sainthood by sitting on a lofty pillar for forty years. The boy was intrigued with literally climbing closer to God, so he decided to imitate Simon. Placing the kitchen stool on top of the table, he climbed his precarious perch and began his journey to sainthood. His mother saw him and cried, "Justin, get off that stool before you break something!" Justin jumped off his perch and marched out of the room saying, "You can't become a saint in your own home."

Paul called the Ephesians *saints*. It's easy to view some people as true saints—Mother Teresa or Billy Graham, for example. However, it's more difficult to comprehend that *all* believers (including you and me!) are saints in God's eyes. You don't have to stay perched on a lofty pillar to attain sainthood. A saint is simply a person who belongs to God and is set apart for Him. If Paul wrote a letter to you, a believer, he would call *you* a saint.

exploration

Yesterday we learned about Paul, the messenger of God's will. Today we turn our attention to the beneficiaries of his letter.

Review Ephesians 1, then focus on verses 1-2.

> *. . . to the saints who are in Ephesus, and faithful in Christ Jesus: . . .* Ephesians 1:1

1. How did Paul describe the Ephesians? . . . .

. . . .

2. What Christian attribute did the Ephesians display?

. . . .

3. Faithfulness is "making faith a living reality in one's life" (*Nelson's Quick Reference Topical Bible Index*). Look at the following verses, and write down what they teach about manifesting faithfulness in different areas of your life.

SCRIPTURE	FAITHFULNESS MANIFESTED
2 Chron. 34:10, 12	
Prov. 14:5	
Luke 16:10	
1 Cor. 4:1-2	
3 John 5	

Grace to you and peace from God our Father and the Lord Jesus Christ. Ephesians 1:2

4. In this benediction, what two things did Paul pray for the Ephesians to experience?

. . . .

5. Who gives this grace and peace? . . . .

. . . .

6. Note the titles given to God and to Jesus. What do these mean to you?

. . . .

explanation

2
FAITHFULNESS
Saving faith is ongoing and active. True faith goes beyond confession to implementation of God's Word. Faith must grow into faithfulness. "Just as the body is dead without a spirit, so also faith is dead without good deeds" (James 2:26, NLT).

4
GRACE AND PEACE
These blessings are known as the "Siamese twins of the New Testament"—you can't have one without the other. Peace will follow grace, and only by experiencing the grace of God will you know the peace of God.

8
PEACE
Jesus said His peace is unique—it's "out of this world!" "I am leaving you with a gift—peace of mind and heart. And the peace I give isn't like the peace the world gives. So don't be troubled or afraid" (John 14:27, NLT).

9
ANXIETY
To be anxious means to be pulled in different directions. The Spirit pulls us in one direction—toward hope and peace in the Lord. Fear, anxiety, and worry pull us in the opposite direction—away from the place of security and rest.

7. In Ephesians 1:2 we learned that saints experience grace and peace. Check the boxes below that indicate ways you have attempted to create peace in your life.

___ Listened to music
___ Called a psychic hotline
___ Ignored my problems
___ Used drugs or alcohol
___ Stayed busy
___ Other_____

Journal about whether or not these have been successful at giving you lasting peace. Why or why not?

. . . .

. . . .

. . . .

. . . .

. . . .

8. Jesus said, "I have told you all this so that you may have peace in me. Here on earth you will have many trials and sorrows. But take heart, because I have overcome the world" (John 16:33, NLT). Where (or with whom) can peace be found?

. . . .

9. Paul revealed the way to restore peace in an anxious heart: "Be anxious for nothing, but in everything by prayer and supplication, with thanksgiving, let your requests be made known to God; and the peace of God, which surpasses all understanding, will guard your hearts and minds through Christ Jesus" (Philippians 4:6-7). Using the space provided, journal through the three steps that lead to peace.

Step One: "Be anxious for nothing." Name your greatest fear, and then give that anxiety to the Lord.

. . . .

. . . .

. . . .

Step Two: "In everything by prayer . . . let your requests be made known to God." Write out a prayer about that fear or situation that causes stress.

. . . .

. . . .

. . . .

Step Three: "With thanksgiving." Write your own psalm of praise, thanking God for setting you free from this fear.

. . . .

. . . .

. . . .

We have discovered that saints are people who are faithful to the Lord Jesus Christ. We have learned that a faithful Christian life exhibits ongoing and active faith. Faith is tested by the tough stuff in life—when the chips are down and the heat is turned up. I read about an elderly woman, badly crippled by arthritis, who was asked, "Do you suffer much?" She pointed to her hand and responded, "Yes, but there is no nail here. He had the nails, I have the peace." She then pointed to her head saying, "There are no thorns here. He had the thorns, I have the peace." Finally, she touched her side and declared, "There is no spear here. He had the spear, I have the peace." This faithful woman was a modern-day saint. She understood the incredible gift of grace given to her by God, and she was filled with "God's peace, which is far more wonderful than the human mind can understand" (Philippians 4:7, NLT).

9

DAY 3 THE BENEFACTOR

preparation

Father, You have filled my life with immeasurable blessings. Instead of counting my woes, help me to number my blessings. With a grateful heart, let my lips bless You, Lord. Amen.

BLESSINGS
The blessing of the Lord makes a person rich, and he adds no sorrow with it. Proverbs 10:22, NLT

Have you ever gotten one of those "too good to be true" sweepstakes envelopes in the mail with Ed McMahon's face on it? What do you do with the envelope? If you're like me, you throw it in the trash even though it says you may have already won $10 million. I've figured out the scam—I've read the fine print and learned my chances of winning are slim to none.

Ephesians reminds us that God *has* given us (past tense in the Greek) *every* spiritual blessing, and there is no catch. The tragedy is that some of us merely underline, quote, or frame the promises in the Bible, treating the treasures of God the same way we would treat a sweepstakes letter. Are you throwing away God's blessings? Today learn how to make withdrawals from your benefactor's heavenly bank account. It's all there waiting for you!

exploration

We have met the messenger and the beneficiaries of this letter. Now we turn our attention to God the Benefactor, Christ the Redeemer, and the Holy Spirit the Guarantor. Today we concentrate on God the Father and the blessings He has for His children.

Review Ephesians 1, then focus on verses 3-6.

> **Blessed be the God and Father of our Lord Jesus Christ, who has blessed us with every spiritual blessing in the heavenly places in Christ, . . .** Ephesians 1:3

1. What things do you learn about God from this verse?

. . . .

2. Describe the kinds of blessings God has given to us.

. . . .

3. Where are these blessings?. . . . .

. . . .

> *. . . just as He chose us in Him before the foundation of the world, that we should be holy and without blame before Him in love, . . .* Ephesians 1:4

4. Ephesians 1:4 moves from telling us about God's blessings to the conditions for receiving them.

   a. When were we chosen in Christ?. . . . .

   . . . .

   b. Why has God chosen us? . . . .

   . . . .

   c. What should be our response to Him?. . . . .

   . . . .

> *. . . having predestined us to adoption as sons by Jesus Christ to Himself, according to the good pleasure of His will, . . .* Ephesians 1:5

5. Here we discover that God wants to bring us even closer to Him.

   a. How does God make us members of His family?

   . . . .

   b. Who has secured the right for our adoption as sons and daughters?

   . . . .

   c. Why has God adopted us?. . . . .

   . . . .

3

HEAVENLY PLACES
Why are your blessings stored in heaven? Jesus gave you the key to the storehouse when He said, "Wherever your treasure is, there your heart and thoughts will also be" (Matthew 6:21, NLT). He wants to make sure your heart is in the right place.

4

IN HIM
God is interested in the ins and outs of your life. Unless you are *in* Christ, in Him, and in the Beloved, then you are *out* of His will, out of His blessings, and outside of His family.

5

ADOPTION
Roman law required that the adopting parent be male and childless. The one to be adopted had to be an independent adult, able to agree to be adopted. In the eyes of the law, the adoptee became a new person and was regarded as being born again into the new family.

BLESSINGS

Out of God's richness, He bestows His blessings upon us. God's blessings to us are limitless—"every blessing" means *every* one! "No good thing will the Lord withhold from those who do what is right" (Psalm 84:11, NLT).

CHOICES

Life offers many choices, but God asks us to make the most important ones. "Today I have given you the choice between life and death, between blessings and curses. I call on heaven and earth to witness the choice you make. Oh, that you would choose life, . . . choose to love the Lord your God" (Deuteronomy 30:19-20, NLT).

. . . to the praise of the glory of His grace, by which He has made us accepted in the Beloved. Ephesians 1:6

6. In verse 6 God grants another incredible grace to His children.

   a. What more has God done for us?. . . . .

   . . . .

   b. In whom is our acceptance found? . . . .

   . . . .

   c. How should we respond to what God has done for us?

   . . . .

transformation

7. We have learned that God has given us every kind of spiritual blessing.

   Journal a list of some of the specific blessings God has placed in your life.

   . . . .

   . . . .

   . . . .

   . . . .

8. What a wonder that God chose us before the foundation of the world! Check the areas of your life where you have had the freedom to choose, thanks to our democratic society, which venerates freedom of choice.

   _____ Spouse   _____ Height

   _____ Talent   _____ Neighbors

   _____ Friends   _____ Hair color

   _____ Family   _____ Other_____

9. God wants you to become just like Him—a chip off the old block.

Since you became a Christian, in what ways have you chosen to become more like your Heavenly Father? Write out your thoughts.

· ·

· ·

· ·

What changes do you sense God wants you to make so you can become more like Him? Journal your thoughts.

· ·

· ·

· ·

A Sunday school teacher once had two new boys in class. When she asked their ages and birth dates for registration, the blond boy said, "We're both seven. My birthday is April 8, 1976, and my brother's is April 20, 1976." "That's impossible!" blurted the confused woman. The dark-haired boy piped in, "No it's not. One of us is adopted." Before she could stop herself, the teacher asked, "Which one?" The boys looked at each other and said, "We asked Dad a long time ago, but he just said he loved us both and couldn't remember which one was adopted."

God has only one begotten Son—the rest of us have been adopted. Your heavenly Father has not only adopted you but also completely accepted you in the Beloved. Your all-powerful, all-knowing heavenly Father has chosen to forget your past. He sees you just as He does His only begotten Son. You have become a coheir with Christ. You can now call the almighty God your Father. "You should behave instead like God's very own children, adopted into his family—calling him 'Father, dear Father' " (Romans 8:15, NLT).

CONFORMED
It is biologically impossible for people who are adopted to fully embody the attributes of their adoptive parents. However, as an adopted child of God, you are empowered by Him to become "conformed to the image of His Son" (Romans 8:29).

contemplation
Adoption is that act of God by which we who were alienated, and enemies, and disinherited, are made the sons of God, and heirs of his eternal glory.
R. Watson

DAY 4 THE REDEEMER

preparation

Jesus, before I met You, I was stuck in destructive patterns that enslaved me. Your blood has set me free to walk in newness of life. Amen.

REDEMPTION
I will shout for joy and sing your praises, for you have redeemed me.
Psalm 71:23, NLT

Potty training my son gave me insight into the meaning of redemption. When Nathan was a toddler, we were desperate to have him graduate from diapers to indoor plumbing. At first we bribed him with M&M's, but that didn't do the trick. Finally we discovered the ultimate motivator—a puppy. When the momentous dry-diaper day arrived, we headed to the Humane Society to set a puppy free. We chose Ginger, a bouncy cocker spaniel, paid the full price, and rescued her from captivity and death.

That's the essence of redemption: paying the price for another's freedom. That's what Jesus did for us. He redeemed us from bondage and death by paying the price for our sins with His blood.

exploration

Yesterday we focused on the blessings that God, our Benefactor, has given to His children. Today we turn our attention to the Beloved Son, our Redeemer.

Review Ephesians 1, then focus on verses 7-12.

> *In Him we have redemption through His blood, the forgiveness of sins, according to the riches of His grace which He made to abound toward us in all wisdom and prudence, . . .* Ephesians 1:7-8

1. "In Him" refers to Jesus—the Beloved Son—from verse 6. What do we as believers have in Him?

. . . .

2. By what means did Christ purchase our redemption?

. . . .

3. According to which of God's abundant attributes is redemption and forgiveness possible?

. . . .

> *. . . having made known to us the mystery of His will, according to His good pleasure which He purposed in Himself, that in the dispensation of the fullness of the times He might gather together in one all things in Christ, both which are in heaven and which are on earth—in Him.* Ephesians 1:9-10

4. Why has God made known the mystery of His will to us?

. . . .

5. What was the purpose of God's plan?

. . . .

> *. . . in whom also we have obtained an inheritance, being predestined according to the purpose of Him who works all things according to the counsel of His will, that we who first trusted in Christ should be to the praise of His glory.* Ephesians 1:11-12

6. What more have we obtained in Christ? . . . .

. . . .

7. What phrase confirms the idea that there are no accidents in a Christian's life?

. . . .

8. What is the end result of a life that trusts in Christ?

. . . .

explanation

2

DEBT PAID
Even the wealth of Bill Gates is insufficient to pay the debt your sin has incurred. Jesus owed no debt, yet He gladly paid the price for your sin—His blood. "The ransom he paid was not mere gold or silver. He paid for you with the precious life-blood of Christ" (1 Peter 1:18-19, NLT).

5

GATHERED TOGETHER
"The fullness of the times" (v. 10) refers to the great gathering together of all things in Christ. This will happen in the future during Christ's reign in the millennial kingdom. God has given believers special insight into His plans for a time yet to come.

7

PREDESTINATION
Predestination is God's sovereign determination of a person's eternal destiny working together with a person's right to freely choose or reject salvation. In His omnipotent wisdom, God chooses those who will choose Him.

9

FORGIVENESS
God is willing to forgive any sin if you accept Christ's sacrifice in repentance and faith. "No matter how deep the stain of your sins, I can remove it. I can make you as clean as freshly fallen snow" (Isaiah 1:18, NLT).

10

INHERITANCE
Inheritance is given only to those who have been qualified by Christ to be in God's will. "You are his heirs, and now all the promises God gave to him belong to you" (Galatians 3:29, NLT). With biblical inheritance, you're either a saint or you ain't in the will.

9. Sin has left its stain on all our lives. With this in mind, follow the steps below and journal your responses:

Step One: Write a list of some of the sins that have blackened your life.

. . . .

. . . .

Step Two: Write a prayer asking God to cleanse your sins with the blood of Christ. Thank Him that "the blood of Jesus, his Son, cleanses us from every sin" (1 John 1:7, NLT).

. . . .

. . . .

. . . .

Step Three: Now take a red pencil, crayon, or marker and cover over the list of sins you listed above, just as the blood of Jesus has covered over your sins.

10. We have discovered that Christ has blessed us with an inheritance. Fill in the following chart to learn some elements of that inheritance.

SCRIPTURE	INHERITANCE
Titus 3:7	
Heb. 1:14	
Heb. 11:7	
James 2:5	
1 Pet. 3:9	

11. God wants to reveal His mysteries—share His secrets—with His adopted children. As you journal today, include the following thoughts.

> Write down some things that you now understand about God (things you may not have understood earlier in your life).

· ·

· ·

> Write down some of the things you still don't understand or questions you still have.

· ·

· ·

> Now journal a prayer of praise, thanking God for revealing the mysteries (i.e., secrets) of His will to you and asking for wisdom to understand more.

· ·

· ·

· ·

11
MYSTERY
In the New Testament, *mystery* refers to a secret that is revealed by God to His servants through His Spirit. As such, it is an "open secret." Most of the occurrences of the word *mystery* are in the Pauline epistles and refer to the revelation of God's plan of salvation as that plan focuses in Christ.

I'm a mystery buff, and I'm crazy about Sherlock Holmes books, movies, and trivia. I guess the attraction lies in trying to detect all the clues Holmes considered so obvious. As he would say to his sidekick, "It's elementary, my dear Watson." Because I love mysteries, I'm intrigued by the clues God has given us about the great mystery of His will. I've become a detective in the Word of God, where I find solutions to the mysteries of the universe.

Today's lesson has unlocked some of the mysteries found in God's Word: God's plan for redemption through Christ, His mysterious timetable for the gathering of His people into one, and His rich spiritual inheritance to all believers. These are significant discoveries for all Christians. But the greatest mystery to ponder is not *what* Christ has done but *why*. Why would Jesus pay for the penalty of my sin with His precious blood? Because "Jesus loves me, this I know." It's elementary, my dear.

contemplation
The dying Jesus is the evidence of God's anger toward sin; but the living Jesus is the proof of God's love and forgiveness.
Lorenz Eifert

DAY 5 THE GUARANTOR

Do-it-yourself home-improvement projects are dangerous, especially if you're a novice like me. One day I decided to change the light fixtures in my bedroom. Without thinking, I grabbed the red and black wires at the same time. *Zap!* Not only did I get a free perm, but the breaker switch blew and I was left standing in the dark. Since then I've become savvy to the concept of electric currents. Next time I'll tap into electrical currents with a proper conductor instead of my own two hands.

I found out the hard way that electricity needs a conduit, a safe channel to transmit the currents. God has made His incredible, electrifying power available to us. However, if we attempt to tap into that source without a conduit, we might get burned out. We need the Holy Spirit, our heavenly conductor, to ensure safe access into God's power source. The Holy Spirit is mentioned many times in this letter because He is the one who guarantees that our riches are channeled to us from the Father through the Son.

exploration

As we complete this week's lesson, we turn our attention to the third person of the Trinity—the Holy Spirit, our guarantor of God's inheritance.

Review Ephesians 1, then focus on verses 13-14.

> *In Him you also trusted, after you heard the word of truth, the gospel of your salvation; in whom also, having believed, you were sealed with the Holy Spirit of promise, . . .* Ephesians 1:13

1. As expressed in this passage, what are the four steps in the process of salvation?

. . . .

. . . .

. . . .

2. Have you taken each of those steps in your faith journey? If not, and if you are ready, take the time now to walk through them with God in prayer.

. . . .

3. Paul revealed that we are sealed with the Holy Spirit. Fill in the chart to discover more of what this means.

SCRIPTURE	HOW YOU ARE SEALED
John 14:16-17	
. . . .	
Rom. 8:9	
. . . .	
1 Cor. 6:19-20	
. . . .	

. . . who is the guarantee of our inheritance until the redemption of the purchased possession, to the praise of His glory. Ephesians 1:14

4. What does the Holy Spirit guarantee for us? . . . .

. . . .

5. What is the purpose of redemption? . . . .

. . . .

6. How does Isaiah 43:21 confirm our purpose?

. . . .

1
TRUST
The biblical meaning of trusting God is that we have confidence and are fully persuaded in God. You may sometimes *feel* as if you're on shaky ground, but in fact, you stand on a firm foundation. "He alone is my rock and my salvation, my fortress where I will never be shaken" (Psalm 62:2, NLT).

3
SEALED
In the ancient East, a seal was an imprint pressed into wax. Like a brand, a seal indicated ownership and also was used to complete legal transactions. Being sealed with the Holy Spirit means that God has completed a transaction with us—He has placed His imprint upon us.

6
PRAISE
In a world that idolizes celebrities, it's easy to praise people who are unworthy of our devotion. Don't get caught up in a counterfeit religious experience—instead, praise God!

transformation

8

INDWELLING
To have the Holy Spirit dwelling in you is an honor. Before Jesus' birth the Holy Spirit visited only a few select people: prophets, priests, and kings. But Jesus opened the way for the Holy Spirit to dwell within all believers. "For He dwells with you and will be in you" (John 14:17).

9

TRUSTWORTHY
Put your trust only in someone who is trust-worthy. *Webster's Dictionary* says, "Trust is an assured reliance on the character, ability, strength, or truth of someone or some-thing." Human beings are corrupt; God is incorruptible. People are weak; God is omnipo-tent. The psalmist tells us, "It is better to trust the Lord than to put confidence in people" (Psalm 118:8, NLT).

7. Look up Revelation 4:10-11. We read that those who stand before God's throne in heaven will cast their crowns before him and worship.

> Why is God worthy of praise? Think about any good or praiseworthy things in your own life—your "crowns"—and journal a prayer, casting them down before God in worship.

. . . .

. . . .

. . . .

. . . .

. . . .

8. Today we learned that the Holy Spirit lives in—indwells—believers. In which of the following ways do the outside actions of your life reveal what has taken place on the inside?

___ Daily prayer   ___ Reach out to unbelievers
___ Regular church attendance   ___ Respond in love
___ Spend time in God's Word   ___ Changed lifestyle

9. We saw that to trust means to have full confidence in some-thing or someone. Name three people you trust, and tell why.

. . . .

. . . .

. . . .

. . . .

. . . .

Journal about a time when someone betrayed your trust. Did that misplaced trust in people damage or increase your trust in God? How?

. . . .

. . . .

. . . .

. . . .

What other areas in your life are causing you to doubt God today? Rewrite this prayer for your situation: "I do believe, but help me not to doubt!" (Mark 9:24, NLT).

. . . .

. . . .

. . . .

. . . .

Have people ever told you they loved you, but their actions betrayed their words? When I was in seventh grade, I thought a boy loved me. The notes he passed to me in math class said so. In reply, my notes were always "sealed with a kiss." But one day my boyfriend saw me being silly with my friends, got embarrassed, and dumped me! When I grew up I met Skip Heitzig. He also told me he loved me, but he showed me how much by sealing his love with a ring. That ring became my guarantee that Skip would do what he said. It represented the promise that one day Skip would take me as his bride.

Jesus loved you so much that when He made you His own, He put His "seal of approval" on your life. That seal is the Holy Spirit, who is your guarantee that God will do what He has promised you. He is completely trustworthy. Paul said that when you believed, "you were sealed with the Holy Spirit of promise." The Holy Spirit's indwelling in your life is your engagement ring. God intends to marry you, His bride, at the marriage supper of the Lamb. God's love letter, the Bible, is better than any romance novel, and He made certain it was "sealed with a kiss."

contemplation
Trustfulness is based on confidence in God, whose ways I do not understand. If I did, there would be no need for trust.
Oswald Chambers

21

Secret Treasure

DAY 1
Paul Prays

DAY 2
Prayer for Knowledge

DAY 3
Prayer for Hope

DAY 4
Prayer for Power

DAY 5
Prayer for Position

*G*rowing up, I was enthralled with the book *Treasure Island.* A poor boy named Jim Hawkins had no idea that the oilskin packet left by the dead pirate, Billy Bones, was indeed a map. But when Jim enlisted as cabin boy with Long John Silver on the *Hispaniola,* the eyes of his understanding were opened. He discovered that the oilskin map charted a path leading to secret treasure. On his adventure he would become rich beyond his wildest dreams.

As an adult, I read J. Wilbur Chapman's real-life story of another boy turned beneficiary. For over a year the young man was homeless, begging at the city train depot. One day he called out to a passerby, "Hey, mister, can you spare a dime?" When the person turned around, the young man was shocked to discover it was his own dad. "Father, do you recognize me?" Throwing his arms around his son, the father said, "At last I've found you! You want a dime? All I have is yours." A homeless son begged his father for spare change, when for years his dad had been looking to give him everything he had.

The apostle Paul wants Christians who are spiritually poor to know that their heavenly Father is searching for them to give them the key to His secret treasures. Too often believers lack knowledge of the riches God offers. What about you? Are you missing out on hidden treasure? God has left you a map that will chart a path to the adventure of a lifetime and open your eyes to "the riches of the glory of His inheritance."

DAY 1 PAUL PRAYS

FAITH
Daughter, your faith has made you well. Go in peace. You have been healed. Mark 5:34, NLT

explanation

REPUTATION
The Ephesians had a reputation; Paul had heard about them. Be careful how you live—people will hear about you, too.

exploration

This week we gain insight into Paul's prayer life by exploring the first of two prayers written for the believers in Ephesus. As you study, ask God to teach you how to be a person of prayer.

Read through Ephesians 1 to remember the tone, language, and content of the chapter, then focus on verses 15-16.

> *Therefore I also, after I heard of your faith in the Lord Jesus and your love for all the saints, . . .*
> Ephesians 1:15

1. What two things had Paul heard about the Ephesians?

. . . .

2. Who was the object of the Ephesians' faith? Of their love?

. . . .

3. What does this teach you about your responsibility as a believer?

. . . .

> *. . . [I] do not cease to give thanks for you, making mention of you in my prayers: . . .* Ephesians 1:16

4. What did Paul persistently do? . . . .

. . . .

5. We see in verse 16 that one requirement for an effective prayer life is giving thanks. Fill in the following chart to learn other keys to an effective prayer life.

SCRIPTURE	KEYS TO EFFECTIVE PRAYER
Ps. 66:18-19	
Matt. 21:22	. . . .
Mark 11:25	. . . .
John 14:13	. . . .
1 John 5:14	. . . .
Jude 20	. . . .

transformation

6. Today we learned that the Ephesians had a reputation of being faithful and loving. Lesson 1 taught us that before Saul was converted, he was vengeful and vindictive. After his conversion Paul became known for his love for the Lord. Using an acrostic format, fill in the blanks describing your reputation *before* and *after* you met Christ,

B (example: Bad temper) . . . . . A (example: Amiable) . . . . .

E . . . . F . . . .

F . . . . T . . . .

O . . . . E . . . .

R . . . . R . . . .

E . . . .

4

PERSISTENCE
To pray constantly does not mean we are to literally keep up an incessant verbal dialogue (they have places for people who do that, and the doors lock from the outside!). The idea here is persistent prayer rather than constant prayer—keep at it continually.

5

HEART PRAYERS
Many of us have the mistaken notion that if we ask God to do something, then He is obligated to respond. However, God listens to our hearts over the din of our words! A heart out of sync with God's Word speaks louder than the requests of a disobedient believer.

HINDERED PRAYER
God has selective hearing. He won't tune in to a prayer distorted by disobedience. "The Lord . . . is not becoming deaf. He can hear you when you call. But there is a problem— your sins have cut you off from God. Because of your sin, he . . . will not listen anymore" (Isaiah 59:1-2, NLT).

8
REPENTANCE
True repentance is a "godly sorrow" for sin, an act of turning around and going in the opposite direction. This type of repentance leads to a fundamental change in a person's relationship to God.

7. Today we discovered the keys to an effective prayer life. Which attitudes below have hindered your prayer life at times?

____ There's a sin I'm not willing to surrender to God.

____ I haven't believed God and taken Him at His word.

____ I have been praying "my will be done."

____ I haven't forgiven others for trespasses against me.

____ I trust too much in myself, not Christ.

____ Other _____.

8. It's not enough just to check a box—we must also check our hearts. Journal a prayer of repentance for these destructive patterns in your life based on the definition of repentance provided in the sidebar.

. . . .

. . . .

. . . .

. . . .

9. Paul prayed for the Ephesians. Now it's your turn. Write down the names of three Christians you want to pray for this week.

. . . .

. . . .

. . . .

As you give thanks to God for these people, write down the good things you know and have heard about them. Ask God to increase their faith.

. . . .

. . . .

. . . .

. . . .

A mother once asked her son after the first day of school, "Did you learn anything today?" "No," he replied in disgust. "I have to go back tomorrow." With prayer, as in life, don't be discouraged if God doesn't answer your prayers immediately or in the way you expect. Remember that Paul prayed without ceasing—he kept going back to God. Jesus also prayed persistently and consistently. In Matthew we learn that "he went back to pray a third time, saying the same things again" (Matthew 26:44, NLT). Prayer, like school, is a discipline that takes more than one day's attendance.

Keep praying, but be thankful that God's answers are wiser than your prayers!
William Culbertson

2 PRAYER FOR KNOWLEDGE

KNOWLEDGE
And this is the way to have eternal life—to know you, the only true God, and Jesus Christ, the one you sent to earth. John 17:3, NLT

explanation

🍀
1

THE SON
Although Jesus is equal with God, when He came to earth, "he made himself nothing; he took the humble position of a slave and appeared in human form" (Philippians 2:7, NLT). Throughout His earthly life Jesus gladly submitted Himself to God the Father.

Knowledge is fleeting and is constantly changing. It has been estimated that the accumulated knowledge from the beginning of recorded history to the year 1845 could be represented by one inch, further accumulated knowledge from 1845 until 1945 would amount to three inches, and what we have learned from 1945 until 1975 would represent the height of the Washington Monument. Since 1975, that total knowledge has doubled! Who can keep up with such rapidly growing knowledge?

However, when it comes to biblical knowledge, it's not *what* you know but *Who* you know. Unlike the wisdom of the world, the knowledge of the Holy One never changes. He is the same yesterday, today, and forever. The knowledge of God is the only source of true wisdom: "The fear of the Lord is the beginning of wisdom, and the knowledge of the Holy One is understanding" (Proverbs 9:10).

exploration

We've seen that Paul was a man of prayer who prayed for the believers in Ephesus. Today let's examine Paul's prayer for believers to discover the kind of knowledge God wants us to have.

Review Ephesians 1, then focus on verses 17-18.

> *. . . that the God of our Lord Jesus Christ, the Father of glory, may give to you the spirit of wisdom and revelation in the knowledge of Him, . . .* Ephesians 1:17

1. What does the phrase "the God of our Lord Jesus Christ" teach you about the relationship between Father and Son?

. . . .

2. What more do we learn of God's character in verse 17?

. . . .

3. What is the first thing Paul prayed for God to give believers?

. . . .

4. What is the second thing he prayed for? . . . .

. . . .

5. Describe the specific type of knowledge Paul prayed the Ephesians would receive.

. . . .

> *... the eyes of your understanding being enlightened; ...* Ephesians 1:18

6. What did Paul pray for believers? . . . .

. . . .

7. Fill in the chart to discover the sources of true spiritual enlightenment.

SCRIPTURE	SOURCE OF SPIRITUAL ENLIGHTENMENT
Ps. 18:28	
Ps. 119:105	
Prov. 6:23	
Matt. 5:16	
John 8:12	
John 16:13-14	

3

WISDOM
Wisdom is the ability to judge rightly and follow the best course of action based on knowledge and understanding. There is a difference between wisdom and knowledge. Wisdom is what you do with what you know.

5

KNOWLEDGE
Knowledge is the truth or facts that a person gains through experience or thought. The greatest truth that a person can possess is truth about God. God doesn't want us to merely know about Him in our heads. He wants us to know Him personally in our hearts.

7

THE SPIRIT
Without the present illumination of the Holy Spirit, the Word of God must remain a dead letter to every man. . . . It is just as essential for the Holy Spirit to reveal the truth of Scripture to the reader today as it was necessary for him to inspire the writers of it in their day.
William Law

transformation

8. Read Matthew 5:16. Once we have received God's light, what is our responsibility toward others?

   Journal about ways you are letting your light shine before others.

   . . . .

   . . . .

   . . . .

9. Jesus told His disciples not to hide the lamp of their faith under a basket but to let it shine for all to see. In the appropriate columns place the following items that help your faith burn bright or can cause your faith to burn out: Bible study, watching TV, witnessing, shopping, prayer, humility, arguments, powerful teaching, busy schedule, fellowship, seeking God's kingdom, envy, self-pity, sacrifice, pride, love, lust, anger.

BURN BRIGHT	BURN OUT

10. List some people who need the light of God's love and power. Commit to pray for these people.

    . . . .

    Journal a prayer asking God to say to their hearts, "Let there be light" (Genesis 1:3).

    . . . .

    . . . .

    . . . .

11. We have learned that God desires us to have knowledge, wisdom, and revelation that will lead to a personal relationship with Him. With this in mind, work through the steps below:

Step One—Knowledge: Describe the things you knew about God in your head before you asked Him into your heart.

. . . .

Step Two—Wisdom: Once God came to live in your heart, describe how He gave you the wisdom to live your life differently.

. . . .

. . . .

Step Three—Revelation: Describe what God has revealed to you recently that you never understood about Him before.

. . . .

. . . .

REVELATION
Revelation is God's communication to people concerning Himself, His moral standards, and His plan of salvation. People, on their own, can never create truth about God. God has graciously unveiled and manifested Himself to humanity.

We've seen that when it comes to spiritual knowledge, it's not *what* you know but *Who* you know. I experienced the value of knowledge that is up close and personal during the 1996 World Series between the Atlanta Braves and the New York Yankees. The cleanup pitcher for the Yankees, John Wetteland, is a close friend and gave my son and me tickets to attend a game in Atlanta. Because we knew John, his name was the key to untold opportunity wherever we went. It unlocked a hotel room in a city that was overbooked. It gained us entrance to the Yankee locker room. It even provided seats on the team bus right next to Reggie Jackson! My son, Nathan, and I kept pinching ourselves to make sure the whole experience wasn't a dream. But it was—a dream come true.

What personally knowing John Wetteland did for us in Atlanta, intimately knowing God does for a Christian in this life—it opens the entrance to eternity; it reserves a seat in heaven; and it unlocks the treasure house of God's wisdom.

contemplation
Wisdom is the combination of honesty and knowledge applied through experience.
Denis Waitley

31

DAY 3 PRAYER FOR HOPE

preparation

Lord, help me to realize that my hope is in You and is therefore unshakable. Send Your Spirit to fill my heart with hope like this. Amen.

HOPE
I pray that God, who gives you hope, will keep you happy and full of peace as you believe in him. May you overflow with hope through the power of the Holy Spirit. Romans 15:13, NLT

Life seemed hopeless in 1986. I (Penny) was a young wife and mother whose life was bleak. My husband's work was his mistress, my daughter was colicky, and we were mired in an ugly lawsuit. My plans to live the American Dream seemed like a nightmare. One day my mother came to my house, told me to get dressed, and drove me to a women's Bible study. She said, "You need this."

Mother knew best. My backslidden soul was thirsty for God. I soon rededicated my life to Jesus. For the first time in years I had hope. My circumstances didn't change, but my heart did. I clung to God's promise, "I know the plans I have for you . . . plans to give you hope and a future" (Jeremiah 29:11, NIV). I developed a confident expectancy that things would work out God's way. I learned to trust His way as the best way. Things didn't turn out as I planned, but they worked out better than I hoped or dreamed. Though we lost the lawsuit, God used it to bring my husband into His kingdom and to turn us into a family of faith. Hope springs from the Eternal One.

exploration

This week we have examined the reasons Paul prayed for his friends and one of the requests he made—that by knowing God they would become spiritually enlightened. In today's lesson, we explore two more aspects of Paul's prayer.

Review Ephesians 1, then focus on the second part of verse 18.

> *. . . that you may know what is the hope of His calling, what are the riches of the glory of His inheritance in the saints, . . .* Ephesians 1:18

1. What is the first thing Paul prays the Ephesians will know?

. . . .

2. In verse 18, Paul links hope with the concept of God's "calling." In other words, he is praying for people to respond to God's call. Let's examine this concept. According to Matthew 9:13,

   a. Whom does Jesus call?. . . . .

   . . . .

   b. To what does He call them?. . . . .

   . . . .

3. Name the second request Paul prays for the believers in verse 18.

   . . . .

4. In whom is this glorious inheritance found? . . . .

   . . . .

5. Read Matthew 6:19-21.

   a. What two types of treasure does Jesus describe in this passage?

   . . . .

   b. What happens to the treasure in each of these places?

   . . . .

   c. Summarize in your own words the message of Matthew 6:21.

   . . . .

   . . . .

transformation

6. Fill in the chart to discover the different ways Christ called His disciples.

---

explanation

1
HOPE
Hope is confident expectancy. In the Bible, *hope* stands for both the act of hoping and the thing hoped for. Hope does not arise from the individual's desires or wishes but from God, who is Himself the believer's hope. "My only hope is in you" (Psalm 39:7, NLT).

4
ETERNAL RICHES
God offers riches untold to those who believe. Yet often we think He is speaking of earthly treasures that will rust, rot, or be stolen. God's spiritual treasures can never be taken away from you. God promises eternal riches—make certain you don't settle for money.

6
RESPONSE
The call of God involves two important elements: (1) God calling us to follow him; (2) our response. Many people hear Jesus calling but don't answer affirmatively. Sadly, they will discover that saying no means they're not one of His chosen few.

THE COST

To follow Jesus you must count the cost. For Simon and Andrew, it cost their careers. For the rich young ruler the cost was his cash, but his riches weighed him down. For Zacchaeus the cost was his business conduct. Jesus said, "No one can become my disciple without giving up everything for me" (Luke 14:33, NLT).

Matt. 4:18-20. . . . .

Mark 10:17-22. . . . .

Luke 19:1-8 . . . .

7. Examine your heart. Have you heard Jesus' call to follow Him and answered it? If you have not, take some time to pray and listen for it now in your heart.

Journal a prayer in answer to the Lord's call.

. . . .

. . . .

. . . .

8. People who live without Christ often place their hope in things that will ultimately leave them hopeless. Some people live in lust but end up lonely. Some hope in wealth but find themselves weeping.

Journal about some of the things you placed your hope in before you became a follower of Christ. How did those things leave you hopeless?

. . . .

. . . .

Rewrite the following verse into a personal prayer of hope in God: "I pray that God, who gives you hope, will keep you happy and full of peace as you believe in him. May you overflow with hope through the power of the Holy Spirit" (Romans 15:13, NLT).

. . . .

. . . .

. . . .

9. Today's lesson has helped us discover the spiritual treasures God offers. Have you personally experienced these riches? Check the boxes that indicate the riches you currently enjoy.

____ Riches of His grace (Ephesians 1:7)

____ Riches of His goodness (Romans 2:4)

____ Riches of the wisdom and knowledge of God (Romans 11:33)

____ All my needs according to His riches in glory (Philippians 4:19)

If you have not received the riches that God so freely gives, journal a prayer of acceptance to receive your spiritual inheritance from God.

. . . .

. . . .

. . . .

. . . .

. . . .

Did you know that Jesus is a treasure seeker? He said, "The kingdom of heaven is like a merchant seeking beautiful pearls, who, when he had found one pearl of great price, went and sold all that he had and bought it" (Matthew 13:45-46). The church of Christ, you and I and all the saints, is the precious pearl for whom Christ gave His all—we are His inheritance (Ephesians 1:18).

Pearls are the product of pain; an oyster that hasn't been hurt does not grow a pearl. When the shell of an oyster is pierced, a foreign substance—usually sand—gets inside. When this happens, the oyster's cells cover the grain of sand with layer after layer of nacre in order to protect the soft body of the oyster. The result is a beautiful pearl.

Not only is Jesus a treasure seeker, but He is also a treasure maker! He wants to transform our pain into pearls. When the grains of sand invade your life, let the soothing nacre of Christ's riches—His wisdom, His goodness, His grace, and His mercy—turn your troubles into treasures.

contemplation
Hope means expectancy when things are otherwise hopeless.
G. K. Chesterton

DAY 4 PRAYER FOR POWER

Think about the greatest manifestation of power you could witness. Perhaps a hurricane or tornado came to mind, maybe an earthquake or an atomic bomb. I read about something more powerful than any of these. On May 18, 1980, there was an incredible explosion, estimated at 500 times the force of the atomic bomb that destroyed Hiroshima. The blast ripped 1,200 feet off the top of a 9,700-foot volcano named Mount Saint Helens. Within one minute a cloud of ash blocked out the sun. *Sports Illustrated* reported that the "heat, blast and ash destroyed 26 lakes, 154 miles of resident trout streams and 195 square acres of wildlife habitat."

That display of raw power is impressive. However, the Bible tells us that the presence of our God could make not only Mount Saint Helens crumble but also all the mountains known on earth. The psalmist wrote, "The mountains melt like wax before the Lord, before the Lord of all the earth" (Psalm 97:5, NLT). God is an awesome and *powerful* God, Creator of both heaven and earth. Ephesians teaches us that the greatest manifestation of God's power was not for destruction but for the resurrection of Christ from the dead!

exploration

We have seen how Paul prayed for believers to experience spiritual enlightenment, hope, and spiritual riches. Now we examine another element of his prayer about knowing God.

Review Ephesians 1, then focus on verses 19-20.

. . . and what is the exceeding greatness of His power toward us who believe, according to the working of His mighty power which He worked in Christ when He raised Him from the dead . . . Ephesians 1:19-20

1. Continuing his prayer, what more did Paul pray the Ephesians would come to know?

. . . .

. . . .

2. Who is given "the exceeding greatness of His power"?

. . . .

3. What word does Paul use to describe God's power?

. . . .

4. What visible evidence of God's power did Paul point out?

. . . .

5. Read John 11:43-44. How did Jesus manifest this divine power during His earthly ministry?

. . . .

. . . .

6. Read John 11:25-26, then answer the following questions:

   a. How does Jesus describe Himself?

. . . .

. . . .

   b. What does He promise those who believe in Him?

. . . .

. . . .

explanation

GOD'S POWER
It is important to remember that it is God's power that is given and not your own. There is danger in trusting in the power of "self." On the contrary, God told Paul, "My power works best in your weakness" (2 Corinthians 12:9, NLT).

POWER EQUIPS
God's power equips you to use God's wealth. It is impossible to tap into God's riches without His power enabling us. Peter linked knowledge and power, saying, "His divine power has given to us all things that pertain to life and godliness, through the knowledge of Him" (2 Peter 1:3).

JESUS IS LIFE
There is no life apart from the Son of God. A saying goes: "No Jesus? No resurrection. Know Jesus? Know resurrection." Come to know Jesus, and let real life begin! "Life itself was in him, and this life gives light to everyone" (John 1:4, NLT).

PHYSICAL RESURRECTION
Before resurrection there must be a death. Jesus died literally and was resurrected. All Christians live in the hope of a literal resurrection, too. "Since we believe that Jesus died and was raised to life again, we also believe that when Jesus comes, God will bring back with Jesus all the Christians who have died" (1 Thessalonians 4:14, NLT).

7. The hope of mankind is the resurrection of Jesus from the dead. He conquered death and gives resurrection life to all who believe in Him. Therefore, Paul told the Corinthians, "O death, where is your victory? O death, where is your sting?" (1 Corinthians 15:55, NLT).

Journal about the loss of a Christian you have known. From what you've learned today, was death defeat or victory for your loved one?

. . . .

. . . .

. . . .

When you die (or Christ returns), you will be reunited with those you love. How does this knowledge give you hope?

. . . .

. . . .

. . . .

8. Believers can experience death and resurrection spiritually. Baptism represents death of the old nature and resurrection to a new spiritual life. "You were buried with Christ when you were baptized. And with him you were raised to a new life because you trusted the mighty power of God, who raised Christ from the dead" (Colossians 2:12, NLT). Which areas of your old life have you kept out of the water?

____ My will, wanting my own way.

____ My heart, seeking its own passions rather than God's.

____ My eyes, viewing things that are not edifying.

____ My hands, touching things I shouldn't.

____ My mouth, uttering words that displease God.

____ My thoughts, letting my mind wander.

9. This week, plan a funeral service for your old life. Write down a list of the things that you want to put to death, and then bury the list in your backyard. Don't be tempted to go back later and dig in the dirt!

10. According to Romans 8:11, how can you experience the resurrection power of God in this present life?

. . . .

. . . .

Celebrate new life in the Spirit by writing out a psalm or prayer of praise to the Lord.

. . . .

. . . .

. . . .

. . . .

The natives of the Fiji Islands have a hopeless custom known as "calling to the dead." The one who has suffered the death of a loved one climbs to a high tree or cliff. He mentions the name of the deceased, then cries out desperately, "Come back! Come back!" The eerie echo of grief fills the air. Those who have suffered the loss of their soul mate, companion, or beloved child can sympathize deeply.

The Christian does not need to climb to the top of a cliff, because Jesus climbed the hill of Calvary. You don't have to cry out, "Come back!" from a high tree, because Jesus cried out, "Father, forgive them," from a wooden cross. The resurrection power of Christ over death and hell brings a Christian hope in this life and the life to come.

10
NEW CLOTHES
Now that you've buried the old nature, it's time to take off your grave-clothes and put on the garment of praise. God wants to update your wardrobe: "He will give beauty for ashes, joy instead of mourning, praise instead of despair" (Isaiah 61:3, NLT).

contemplation
Death to the Christian is the funeral of all his sorrows and evils, and the resurrection of all his joys.
Aughey

DAY 5 PRAYER FOR POSITION

There have been some powerful people throughout history: Napoleon, Alexander the Great, Caesar Augustus. But Jesus' power and dominion exceeds them *all*. God has seated Him "far above . . . every name that is named, not only in this age but also in that which is to come" (Ephesians 1:21).

Even one of the most powerful rulers in the nineteenth century understood Christ's sovereignty. The story is told that during Queen Victoria's reign in England, she once attended a performance of Handel's *Messiah*. Traditionally during the singing of the "Hallelujah Chorus," the audience would stand. However, Queen Victoria had been instructed not to behave like a commoner and to remain seated. As the choir reached the refrain, "Hallelujah! For the Lord God omnipotent reigneth," she could barely keep her seat. When the song reached its pinnacle, proclaiming Jesus as King of kings, she rose to her feet despite protocol and humbly lowered her head in reverence to the One above every other name . . . including her own!

exploration

Paul prayed for believers to experience the many blessings of Christ in their lives. He ends his prayer focusing on the One who is in the position to provide these treasures—Jesus Christ.

Review Ephesians 1, then focus on verses 20-23.

> *. . . and seated Him at His right hand in the heavenly places, far above all principality and power and might and dominion, and every name that is named, not only in this age but also in that which is to come.* Ephesians 1:20-21

1. Where is Jesus seated now? . . . .

. . . .

2. Over what is Christ exalted? . . . .

. . . .

3. How long will Christ reign supreme?. . . . .

. . . .

> *And He put all things under His feet, and gave Him to be head over all things to the church, which is His body, the fullness of Him who fills all in all.*
> Ephesians 1:22-23

4. What is under Jesus' feet? . . . .

. . . .

5. Over what is Jesus the head? . . . .

. . . .

6. What word picture does Paul use to describe the church?

. . . .

7. Read further about the body of Christ in 1 Corinthians 12:12-27.

   a. How did the church become one body (v. 13)?

   . . . .

   b. Who ordains how each part of the body is to serve (v. 18)?

   . . . .

   c. How should the members of Christ's body treat one another (vv. 25-26)?

   . . . .

8. What final image of Jesus are we given in verse 27?

. . . .

explanation

2

OVER ALL
Principalities, powers, and *dominions* are terms used to describe the ranking of fallen angels. The power of Christ in the believer's life can't be defeated because it's greater than the hosts of Satan. "Greater is he that is in you, than he that is in the world" (1 John 4:4, KJV).

5

HEAD
The word *head* denotes a position of ultimate authority. It is a lovely thing to willingly pour out your life in submission to your loving head, Jesus. "A woman came in with a beautiful jar of expensive perfume. She broke the seal and poured the perfume over his head" (Mark 14:3, NLT).

8

ALL IN ALL
Jesus is the truth, the whole truth, and nothing but the truth! John tells us that Jesus was full of the truth. When you're completely filled with something, there's no room for anything else. "The Word became flesh and dwelt among us, . . . full of grace and truth" (John 1:14).

9

SERVING

transformation

9. Throughout the New Testament we are encouraged to care for one another because we are all members of one body. Which things below are you doing for other members of Christ's body, the church?

___ "Be kindly affectionate to one another" (Romans 12:10).

___ "Be of the same mind toward one another" (Romans 12:16).

___ "Through love serve one another" (Galatians 5:13).

___ "Forgiv[e] one another" (Ephesians 4:32).

___ "Submit to one another in the fear of God" (Ephesians 5:21).

___ "Comfort one another" (1 Thessalonians 4:18).

___ "Be hospitable to one another" (1 Peter 4:9).

___ "Above all things have fervent love for one another" (1 Peter 4:8).

10. Name a Christian whom you can serve with your gifts. Write down a "one another" action or attitude from the list above that you will perform for that person this week.

. . . .

. . . .

Journal a prayer asking Jesus to make you a servant by rewriting the following verse into a personal prayer. "Whoever wants to be a leader among you must be your servant, and whoever wants to be first must become your slave. For even I, the Son of Man, came here not to be served but to serve others, and to give my life as a ransom for many" (Matthew 20:26-28, NLT).

. . . .

. . . .

. . . .

. . . .

11. Draw a picture of a person in the space provided below. (Stick men, cartoon characters, or works of art are all appropriate.) Label the parts of the body from head to toe. Beside each body part write the name of a church member who fulfills that role. (Example: Jesus is the head, your pastor is the mouth, etc.)

Perhaps you don't know yet how God has called you to serve in His body, the church. Journal a prayer asking Him to reveal this to you.

. . . .

. . . .

. . . .

Inspector Clouseau, the bumbling detective of the *Pink Panther* movies, was a master of disguise. At different times he transformed himself into the Hunchback of Notre Dame with an inflatable hump, a salty sea dog with a wooden peg leg, and a mafioso godfather with cotton balls stuffed in his cheeks.

When impersonating a godfather, someone asked Clouseau, "Hey! Where's your bodyguard?" He mumbled, "I don't need a bodyguard. I take care of my body, my body takes care of me." Funny words, but good advice for the members of the body of Christ. A dysfunctional body becomes lopsided when one member takes more than its fair share, selfishly pursuing "What's in it for me?" All parts of a healthy body work together, sharing the load, asking, "What can I do for you?" You don't have to be a detective to figure it out: Take care of Christ's body, the church, and His body will take care of you.

The Greatest Gift

Divorce shattered my family when I was eight years old. The first Christmas without my father being home to string up the lights was dark. We hung our stockings and left out sugar cookies as usual for Santa's late-night arrival. But on the night before Christmas all through my house, the only creature I longed to see stirring was my dad, not a mouse.

The next day we went to my uncle's home for Christmas dinner with all the trimmings. We arrived dressed up in our Sunday best, toting the toys we'd found under our tree. During dinner we heard a knock at the door, and in walked the skinniest Santa I'd ever seen. He said, "Sit on my lap and tell me what you want for Christmas." I thought, *Santa can't give what I really want—my father's presence*. As I climbed onto Santa's lap, his eyes twinkled as he pulled off his white beard. Underneath the disguise I discovered the loving face of my dad! My father's presence was the best present he's ever given me.

In this week's lesson, Paul describes how God gave the world the gift of His presence—in a baby wrapped in swaddling cloths and laid in a manger. God understood how empty and alone we were, so He visited our dark world, lighting our lives with His presence. He gave us the greatest possible gift—Himself!

DAY 1 THE LIVING DEAD

preparation

Heavenly Father, thank You for Your good gifts. They make Your love real to my heart. Thank You for Your greatest gift—Jesus. His presence fills my empty world. Amen.

GOD'S GIFT

For the wages of sin is death, but the free gift of God is eternal life through Christ Jesus our Lord. Romans 6:23, NLT

explanation

DEAD

Paul did not describe unbelievers as "sick," "searching," or "misguided." Instead, he says they are *dead.* Life without God is a death sentence, not only in the afterlife but also in this earthly life.

exploration

Paul now discusses our lives before we came to know Christ. It is good to remember where we have come from so we can truly appreciate God's marvelous gift of grace.

Read Ephesians 2 several times to get a feel for the tone, language, and content of this chapter, then focus on verses 1-3.

> *And you He made alive, who were dead in trespasses and sins, . . .* Ephesians 2:1

1. What words does Paul use to describe the unbeliever's spiritual condition?

. . . .

2. What was the cause of this spiritual death? . . . .

. . . .

> *. . . in which you once walked according to the course of this world, according to the prince of the power of the air, the spirit who now works in the sons of disobedience, . . .* Ephesians 2:2

3. Name the two influences under which believers once walked.

. . . .

. . . .

4. Where is the prince of the power of the air at work?

. . . .

> *. . . among whom also we all once conducted ourselves in the lusts of our flesh, fulfilling the desires of the flesh and of the mind, and were by nature children of wrath, just as the others.* Ephesians 2:3

5. In what ways did we all once conduct our lives, and what desires were we enticed to fulfill?

. . . .

6. What, by nature, are we all? . . . .

. . . .

transformation

7. We've been warned not to walk according to this world. Fill in the chart to discover how to avoid the world's pitfalls.

SCRIPTURE	LESSON ABOUT THE WORLD
Rom. 12:2	
Gal. 6:14	
James 1:27	
1 John 2:15-17	

Choosing one of the Scripture passages from the chart above, journal a prayer asking God to give you victory over the influence of the world.

. . . .

. . . .

4

SATAN'S POWER
Our children are taught to be environmentally conscious—beware of air pollution. In a spiritual sense Satan, the prince of the power of the air, has influenced our culture and media for evil—beware of mind pollution.

5

SINFUL FLESH
Paul said that in his flesh there was "nothing good." Too often society tries to rehabilitate the sinful flesh with self-help programs. That's about as effective as giving a pig a bath. In Scripture, there is one edict for the flesh—death! Only then can new life begin.

7

THE WORLD
This term denotes "the fleeting character of life's riches and pleasures and the folly of making them of central importance in life. 'And how do you benefit if you gain the whole world but lose your own soul in the process? Is anything worth more than your soul?'" (Matthew 16:26, NLT).

8. This passage in Ephesians has made us aware of an enemy who works in the sons of disobedience. Fill in the chart to find out ways to avoid the devil's path of destruction.

SCRIPTURE	LESSON ABOUT THE DEVIL
Eph. 4:26-27	
James 4:7	
1 Pet. 5:8	
Jude 9	

Choosing one of the passages from the chart above, journal a prayer to God asking Him to give you victory over the influence of the devil.

....

....

....

....

9. The devil takes advantage of an area of weakness in all of us— our flesh. Fill in the chart below to discover how to gain victory in this area.

SCRIPTURE	LESSON ABOUT THE FLESH
Matt. 26:41	
Rom. 8:5	
Rom. 13:14	
Gal. 5:16	

Choosing one of the passages from the chart above, journal a prayer to God asking Him to give you victory over the influence of the flesh.

. . . .

. . . .

. . . .

. . . .

. . . .

. . . .

When I was in grade school, my friend Julie and I walked to the neighborhood market to peek at the candy aisle. Our pockets were empty but our eyes were filled with the enticing confections on the shelves. Out of nowhere came this devious thought, *I can slip that piece of candy into my pocket. No one will ever know.* My fingers began to twitch. My flesh wanted that candy. My mind had figured out a way to get it. But my heart knew it was wrong. Mom had told me that stealing was wrong. The decisive moment came when Julie dared me to take a piece. I grabbed the candy and bolted from the store, followed closely behind by the sales clerk. Busted! I learned my lesson the hard way.

I wish I could say that I have outgrown the temptation to do things that are wrong, but I can't. The world and my flesh still dare me to follow a voice that is not my heavenly Father's. As a believer, you are not immune to evil influences either. The world, your flesh, and the wicked one will constantly seek to entice you. But praise God, the allure of sin that made us "children of wrath" can be overcome by the power of God. Because of Christ's sacrificial death, "he allows us to be called his children, and we really are!" (1 John 3:1, NLT).

contemplation
God clothed himself in vile man's flesh so he might be weak enough to suffer.
John Donne

DAY 2 THE DEAD WHO LIVE

preparation

Jesus, before I met You, my existence was lifeless and without meaning. Since You've come into my heart, I'm alive! I give You my life to live for Your kingdom and glory. Amen.

ABUNDANT LIFE
My purpose is to give life in all its fullness.
John 10:10, NLT

The city dump caught the attention of a young black woman named Mary McLeod Bethune in 1904. Mary didn't see just a dump, she saw a way to fulfill her dream that, with God's help, she could teach illiterate black women to read and write. She shared her dream, and others came alongside her to help build a shack on that desolate place. They built desks from wooden crates and used blackberry juice for ink.

If you wander among the tall buildings, classrooms, and dormitories of Bethune-Cookman College, you will find a headstone that commemorates where Mrs. Bethune's body was laid to rest at the age of seventy-nine. The inscription on the stone tells her story: "She has given her best so that others might live a more abundant life."

It takes a unique personality to see ruins and dream of restoration. Paul reminds us that God saw our desolate lives and was delighted to send our deliverer to restore our souls. He gave His Son so that we, who were dead, might live.

exploration

One phrase in today's passage has made an eternal difference in the lives of many: "But God." With these two words Paul turns our attention away from sinful man and toward our powerful God.

Review Ephesians 2, then focus on verses 4-5.

> **But God, who is rich in mercy, because of His great love with which He loved us,** . . . Ephesians 2:4

1. What is the first attribute of God described in this verse?

. . . .

2. How much mercy is in God's bank account? . . . .

. . . .

3. How is God's love described? . . . .

. . . .

> *. . . even when we were dead in trespasses, made us alive together with Christ (by grace you have been saved), . . .* Ephesians 2:5

4. When did God show His rich mercy and great love to us?

. . . .

5. What did God do for us "even when we were dead in trespasses"?

. . . .

6. Can dead things live again? Only God can bring life out of death and hope out of despair. Fill in the chart below to discover situations where God brought new life and hope.

SCRIPTURE	NEW LIFE
1 Kings 17:17-24	. . . .
Matt. 8:14-15	. . . .
John 11:41-44	. . . .
Acts 3:2-8	. . . .

explanation

2
MERCY
Mercy *is the outward manifestation of pity; it assumes need on the part of the one who receives it and resources adequate to meet the need on the part of the one who shows it. It is used of God, who is rich in mercy, and who has provided salvation for all men*
Vine's Expository Dictionary

3
LOVE
We read in 1 John 4:8 that God is love. If you looked up the word *love* in a dictionary, a picture of God should be there as a full defini-tion. Because God is love, His love for us is picture perfect.

5
RESCUE
Jesus is our life preserver! When we were drowning in a sea of sin and shame, God planned a rescue operation. He threw out a lifeline—Jesus! "Reach down from heaven and rescue me; deliver me from deep waters, from the power of my enemies" (Psalm 144:7, NLT).

transformation

NEW LIFE
Nature reveals some of God's hidden qualities. His faithfulness is seen in each new dawn. His ability to resurrect life from death is seen every spring. "From the time the world was created, people have seen the earth and sky and all that God made. They can clearly see his invisible qualities—his eternal power and divine nature" (Romans 1:20, NLT).

RECEIVING MERCY
This means not getting what we deserve, not paying the consequences for our actions. When we slip up, we deserve to fall. When we fall down, God's mercy makes sure we are never down and out. "If I say, 'My foot slips,' Your mercy, O Lord, will hold me up" (Psalm 94:18).

7. Jesus can bring life from death. Draw lines from items in one column to the corresponding item in the other column to indicate how we see life emerge from death in the world God created.

Sunset	Spring
Barren trees	Butterflies
Caterpillar	Frog
Tadpole	Crops
Seeds	Sunrise
Winter	Budding trees

8. Our God is rich in mercy, which means he has pity or compassion on those in need. Keeping this attribute in mind, prayerfully do these exercises:

a. Write down the name of someone who is in need of God's mercy. (Example: a loved one who has made unwise financial decisions and is suffering)

. . . .

b. Consider the present circumstances this person is in and write down the consequences that may occur. (Example: poor financial decisions could result in bankruptcy.)

. . . .

Journal a prayer of mercy on the person's behalf, asking God to withhold the consequence and to show mercy instead.

. . . .

. . . .

. . . .

9. God wants you to be merciful also. Jesus said, "Blessed are the merciful, for they shall obtain mercy" (Matthew 5:7). Sometimes you get exactly what you give. Which will you give, mercy or judgment? Prayerfully do the following exercises:

a. Have you been harboring bitterness or resentment toward someone who has wronged you? If yes, then write down that person's name.

. . . .

Take the time now to ask God to cleanse you from your sin of unforgiveness. Jesus said, "Forgive us our debts, as we forgive our debtors" (Matthew 6:12). Write out a prayer asking God to give you a heart of mercy toward that person—not giving them what they deserve.

. . . .

. . . .

. . . .

. . . .

b. Decide now to call, write, or visit that person and offer him or her the mercy God has so freely given you.

While studying this lesson, I drove to meet a friend for lunch. I was meditating on the truth of God's mercy and wondering who I knew that might need this. As I entered the parking lot, I eyed a space right up front. *What a blessing,* I thought. I waited patiently while my blinker kept time to the praise music on my radio. Then, out of nowhere, a woman in a Mercedes pulled up and stole my spot. "Ughhhhh!" My first thought was, *I'll roll down my window and give her a piece of my mind.* Next, I imagined myself bumping into her shiny, silver Benz, my way of saying, "Thanks for nothing!" Then that still, small voice of the Holy Spirit said, "What have you been studying about, Lenya?" I answered, "Uh . . . Your mercy, Lord, not giving others what they deserve."

Why does God make things so personal? He always holds me accountable to live out the things I learn. Words are cheap when they are not followed by actions. How about you? Do you practice what you preach? When you leave the quiet place of study today, make sure you take the lesson of God's mercy with you. I'm certain He'll provide the opportunity for you to share His mercy with someone who needs it. "Remember, it is a message to obey, not just to listen to. If you don't obey, you are only fooling yourself" (James 1:22, NLT).

contemplation
Among the attributes of God, although they are all equal, mercy shines with even more brilliancy than justice.
Miguel de Cervantes

THE GOD WHO GIVES

preparation

Heavenly Father, Your kindness has touched my life and softened my heart. It is that kindness that leads me to repentance. May I reflect Your kindness to the world around me. Amen.

KINDNESS
When she speaks, her words are wise, and kindness is the rule when she gives instructions. Proverbs 31:26, NLT

Long ago, Persia was ruled by a kind shah who concealed his identity and visited the public baths as a beggar. Seeking the lowest place and worker, the shah went to the cellar where a man stoked the furnace. The shah befriended him, and the man shared his simple food and conversation. Over time the worker grew attached to this stranger who visited him. When the ruler finally revealed his true identity, he expected the worker to ask for a gift. Instead, the furnace tender said, "You left your palace and your glory to sit with me in this dark place, to eat my coarse food, and to care about what happens to me. On others you may bestow rich gifts, but to me you have given yourself."

What an illustration of what Jesus did for us. He left His throne of glory and came to our place of labor and loneliness to befriend us. That's amazing enough, but it gets even better. Jesus has invited us to sit together with him in "the heavenly places." As you sit by His side, you will discover He is the God who gives.

exploration

The gift of God is new life in Christ—we have been saved by grace! Today we discover that there are marvelous benefits for those in Christ.

Review Ephesians 2, then focus on verses 6-7.

> *. . . and raised us up together, and made us sit together in the heavenly places in Christ Jesus, . . .*
> Ephesians 2:6

1. What phrase does Paul use to describe the "life out of death" experience?

. . . .

2. What position do believers occupy?. . . . .

. . . .

3. What is the significance of the repeated words in verse 6?

. . . .

> *. . . that in the ages to come He might show the exceeding riches of His grace in His kindness toward us in Christ Jesus.* Ephesians 2:7

4. Why has God raised us up together in Christ?. . . . .

. . . .

5. How is God's grace described?. . . . .

. . . .

6. What more do you learn here about what it means to be "in Christ"?

. . . .

transformation

7. Today we learned that Jesus has raised us up from the dead. New life begins here on earth and continues in His kingdom to come. Have you found yourself downcast in heart instead of looking up? Check the boxes that describe circumstances that get you down.

___ Financial struggles   ___ Physical illness

___ Difficult relationships   ___ Unrealistic expectations

___ Busy schedule   ___ Unfulfilled dreams

explanation

2

HEAVENLY PLACES
Some people think of heaven as a future place, "the sweet by and by." The verbs in this passage, "raised" and "made us sit," are in the past tense because they're already a reality. For the Christian, heaven is for the present as well as the future—it's a done deal!

4

AMAZING GRACE
What's so amazing about grace? We don't deserve it! We're all sinners under a death sentence. But our gracious Savior pardoned us at the cross. "For all have sinned; all fall short of God's glorious standard. Yet now God in his gracious kindness declares us not guilty . . . through Christ Jesus, who has freed us by taking away our sins" (Romans 3:23-24, NLT).

6

IN CHRIST
One aspect of being *in* Christ means that we are *intimate* with Him. Jesus came to earth to obtain a bride for eternity—His church. What a concept! Jesus wants to spend all of His time "together" with us.

8. David wrestled with a downcast soul and found three ways to lift his spirits: "Why are you cast down, O my soul? . . . Hope in God, for I shall yet praise Him for the help of His countenance" (Psalm 42:5). With this passage in mind, follow the steps below:

Step One—Hope in God! In Lesson 2 we learned that hope is a confident expectancy. Our hope is not based on wishful thinking but in God. Journal a prayer of hope in the space provided regarding that circumstance in life that gets you down.

. . . .

. . . .

. . . .

. . . .

Step Two—Praise God! Take time now to journal your words of worship, praising God for His mercy, love, grace, and kindness.

. . . .

. . . .

. . . .

. . . .

Step Three—Look to His countenance! Now look to God and away from your circumstance. Journal about one of God's attributes that gives you hope.

. . . .

. . . .

. . . .

. . . .

9. Since we are seated in heavenly places with Christ Jesus and our true citizenship is in heaven, we are to "seek those things which are above" (Colossians 3:1). Place the following items into the appropriate column either of things that keep you tied to earth or of things that turn your heart toward heaven: Bible study, financial investments, prayer, fashion magazines, church attendance, TV, fellowship, shopping malls, hospital visitation, hobbies, teaching Sunday school, sports, giving to missions, home remodeling, sharing the gospel, illness, volunteer work.

TOWARD HEAVEN	TIED TO EARTH
. . . .	
. . . .	
. . . .	
. . . .	
. . . .	

HEAVENLY MINDED
Some people are "so heavenly minded that they're no earthly good." Jesus debunks that idea. He had heaven on His mind when He came to earth to rescue us. When heaven is on your mind, you'll be conscious of your duty to do good deeds on earth, too.

My friend Louise is a stargazer. She loves to drive far from the city lights to marvel at the heavens and worship the Creator. When the Hale-Bop comet streaked across the sky, she would faithfully follow its course. One day my friend asked me if I had seen the comet yet. I glibly answered, "I've got too much to do here on the earth to be gawking at the heavens." As I said it, I realized my priorities were out of orbit. It had been a dark time in my life; illness and disappointment had eclipsed the glory of heaven. I had become so "earthly minded" that I was no "heavenly good."

About this time, another stargazer helped turn my eyes upward. My stepfather, Richard, named a star "Lenya" to brighten my life. I received a certificate from the Star Registry with a detailed map showing the exact location of *my* star. If you look out into the night sky, you'll see me, seated in a "heavenly place." Now my eyes sparkle when I gaze at the stars, reminded that God is faithful and my true home is in heaven.

You don't need a star named after you to remind you of your heavenly home—you have the bright and morning star, Jesus Christ, to point the way. "I, Jesus, have sent my angel to give you this message for the churches. . . . I am the bright morning star" (Revelation 22:16, NLT).

DAY 4 THE GREATEST GIFT

A headline in the *Grand Rapids Press* read, "Conversion to Hindu Faith Is Tortuous." The article stated that a German businessman had completed his conversion to the Hindu faith by piercing himself through the cheeks with a ¼-inch-thick steel rod and pulling a chariot for two miles by ropes attached to his back and chest by steel hooks. Other converts had walked through long pits of fire, donned shoes with soles made of nails, or hung in the air spread-eagle from hooks embedded in their backs.

Aren't you glad that conversion to Christianity is not accomplished by self-inflicted torture? In contrast, Jesus Christ was afflicted with one of the cruelest forms of torture ancient Rome could devise so that He could freely give you the gift of salvation. Jesus paid the price for your conversion so that you could not and would not have to do a thing to earn it. The only requirement is for you to receive the greatest gift God gave.

exploration

Two key components make salvation available to all: God's grace and our faith.

Review Ephesians 2, then focus on verses 8-9.

> *For by grace you have been saved through faith, and that not of yourselves; it is the gift of God, . . .* Ephesians 2:8

1. What is the "gift of God" given to you? . . . .

. . . .

2. By what means have you been saved? . . . .

. . . .

3. What response is necessary on your part? . . . .

. . . .

4. Read Romans 10:9, then answer the following questions.

   a. What are two important components in expressing a saving
      faith?

   . . . .

   . . . .

   b. What is the result of your confession and belief?

   . . . .

   c. If you have not taken these steps of faith, take the time
      now to do so. "Behold, now is the day of salvation"
      (2 Corinthians 6:2).

   > *For by grace you have been saved through faith, and that
   > not of yourselves; it is the gift of God, not of works, lest
   > anyone should boast.* Ephesians 2:8-9

5. What two phrases in these verses tell what you are *not* saved by?

   . . . .

6. Why is salvation a gift rather than the result of merit or effort?

   . . . .

   . . . .

7. According to 1 Corinthians 1:31, what should believers boast
   or glory in?

   . . . .

   . . . .

explanation

2

GRACE
Grace is favor or kindness shown without regard to the worth or merit of the one who receives it and in spite of what that same person deserves. Grace is one of the key attributes of God.

3

FAITH
To have faith is to have a firm persuasion, a conviction based on hearing. It is used in the New Testament always of faith in God or Christ, or things spiritual *(Vine's Expository Dictionary)*. Theologian John Stott defines faith as "a reasoning trust, a trust which reckons thoughtfully and confidently upon the trustworthiness of God."

7

GOD'S DOING
A woodpecker was tapping away on a tree when the tree was struck by lightning and split in two. The proud bird boasted to his friends, "Look what I did!" Are you like the woodpecker, failing to give credit where credit is due? Salvation is God's work—He gets the glory.

8

WORKS

Why do you do what you do? Works done to gain salvation are empty: "By the works of the law no flesh shall be justified" (Galatians 2:16). Works performed to display your love to God are eternal: "By works faith was made perfect" (James 2:22). Works don't open heaven's doors, but they do bless the Father's heart.

RECEIVING

Gifts require two parties, a giver and a receiver. The right motivation of a giver is love—no strings attached. The right attitude of the receiver is gratitude—no hoops to jump through.

transformation

8. We've seen that being good enough or working hard enough does not achieve salvation. Using the letters from the acronym WORKS, write about the ways you have mistakenly tried to earn your salvation.

W (Went to church religiously). . . . .

. . . .

O (Offered money as a way of buying my way to heaven)

. . . .

R (Repeated rituals I'd seen others perform) . . . .

. . . .

K (Kept strict rules and regulations) . . . .

. . . .

S (Said prayers I didn't mean) . . . .

. . . .

9. As you think about God's gracious gift of salvation, journal your thoughts below.

Describe the best gift someone has ever given you. Did you *do* anything to earn the gift?

. . . .

. . . .

How might the giver feel if you offered to reimburse him or her for the gift through work or money?

. . . .

. . . .

Journal a prayer of thanks to God for His "indescribable gift" of salvation (2 Corinthians 9:15).

. . . .

. . . .

. . . .

10. Salvation comes through faith in Jesus Christ. Faith is key in the life of every Christian. Fill in the chart below to discover ways to strengthen your faith.

SCRIPTURE	WAYS TO STRENGTHEN FAITH
Rom. 4:20	
Rom. 10:17	
1 Cor. 2:5	
1 Cor. 16:13	

We live in New Mexico near the city of Roswell, where aliens are said to have crash-landed back in the 1940s. Recently I looked up "Roswell" on the Internet. I was astounded to find thousands of sites that reported the story about the aliens as if it were true. Literally millions of people believe "the truth is out there—we're not alone." They actually put their faith in UFO conspiracies.

One site explained the Roswell incident, which is supposed to have happened in July 1947. According to reports, a UFO crashed and four dead aliens of the so-called gray variety were found near the ship. Mac Brazel found portions of the ship on his ranch and reported it to the local sheriff, who contacted the local nuclear air base in Roswell. Several officers from the base investigated the site and sent out a press release. But the next day the United States Air Force contradicted the report.

Over five decades later, this incredible myth lives on, fueled by books, television, and movies. If so many otherwise intelligent and responsible adults can put their faith in "little gray men" based on inconclusive evidence, why can't you put your complete trust in the "God man," who unquestionably came to earth and changed the course of history? "Have faith in God" (Mark 11:22, NLT).

contemplation

Salvation is worth working for. It is worth a man's going round the world on his hands and knees, climbing its mountains, crossing its valleys, swimming its rivers, going through all manner of hardship in order to attain it. But we do not get it in that way. It is to him who believes.
Dwight Lyman Moody

DAY 5 THE GIFT THAT KEEPS ON GIVING

explanation

WORKMANSHIP
The word *workmanship* comes from the Greek word *poiema*, from which we get the English word *poem*. God views your life as poetry in motion.

While on a trip to Paris, I visited the Louvre Museum. I stood speechless in the presence of so many priceless paintings. I saw the Mona Lisa, up close and personal. My mother and I stood in awe, whispering in hushed tones, "Can you believe we're looking at her? She's the real thing, not a cheap imitation!" Leonardo da Vinci had no idea when he painted the portrait that it would be a gift to the entire world—a gift that inspires generation after generation.

God is *the* Master artist; all of creation declares His handiwork. Each sunset is a stroke of the Master's brush. And *you* are His living masterpiece. Mona Lisa can't hold a candle to you. As God's work of art, you are not intended to hang on a wall in a museum, gathering dust. He created you with a purpose—His purpose—to do good works that reflect His artistry.

exploration

Yesterday Paul reminded us of the indescribable gift of new life in Christ. Today we discover that we must not be selfish with this gift.

Review Ephesians 2, then focus on verse 10.

> *For we are His workmanship, created in Christ Jesus for good works, which God prepared beforehand that we should walk in them.* Ephesians 2:10

1. How are believers described here? . . . .

. . . .

2. In Revelation 4:11 the apostle John records words that shed more light on God's workmanship: "You are worthy, O Lord our God, to receive glory and honor and power. For you created everything, and it is for your pleasure that they exist and were created" (NLT).

    a. Who is the Master Creator, and what has He created?

    . . . .

    b. Why did the Lord create all things? . . . .

    . . . .

    c. How should we respond? . . . .

    . . . .

3. We (the church) are God's corporate workmanship created in Christ Jesus. According to Ephesians 2:10, what purpose does God have for His workmanship?

    . . . .

4. Fill in the chart below to discover some examples of good works God has for us to accomplish.

SCRIPTURE	GOOD WORKS
Acts 9:36, 39	
1 Tim. 5:10	
Heb. 10:24-25	
James 2:14-17	

5. When did God prepare the good works for us to accomplish?

    . . . .

GOOD WORKS
A Christian should always remember that the value of his good works is not based on their number and excellence, but on the love of God, which prompts him to do these things.
St. John of the Cross

GOD'S WORK
It's all God! God planned *your* good works before you were born. He guarantees that *His* work in you will be completed. Praise God, who goes before and behind you! "I am sure that God, who began the good work within you, will continue his work until it is finally finished" (Philippians 1:6, NLT).

BEAUTIFUL
Beauty is in the eye of the beholder. If you don't see yourself as beautiful, perhaps you should look at yourself through God's eyes. Your not-so-secret admirer has something to tell you: "Listen, O daughter, consider and incline your ear; . . . the King will greatly desire your beauty; because He is your Lord, worship Him" (Psalm 45:10-11).

7

WILLINGNESS
People don't do good works for one of two reasons: either they *can't* (no ability) or they *won't* (no desire). Since we all have gifts or talents, we are all equipped to do something. You are able, but are you willing?

transformation

6. As God's workmanship, you are His masterpiece. Do you really believe that? The psalmist said that God made you "wonderfully complex" and "marvelous" (Psalm 139:13-14, NLT). Journal about your perception of yourself and God's perception of you.

Step One: Describe your physical appearance. What is your stature, shape, hair and eye color, features, etc.?

. . . .

. . . .

. . . .

Step Two: Evaluate your physical appearance. What are your assets and deficits? What do you like? dislike?

. . . .

. . . .

Step Three: God designed and created *you* exactly the way you are because it brings Him joy. *You*—His masterpiece—are perfect just the way you are. Journal a psalm of praise, thanking God for each aspect of your physical appearance—the good, the bad, but beautiful to Him!

. . . .

. . . .

. . . .

. . . .

7. God planned your good works before time began. He designed them to suit you perfectly. God told the prophet Jeremiah, "I knew you before I formed you in your mother's womb. Before you were born I set you apart and appointed you as my spokesman to the world" (Jeremiah 1:5, NLT). Check the talents and gifts that God has created within you:

___ Good sense of humor	___ Great singing voice
___ Aptitude in mathematics	___ Writing ability
___ Heart of compassion	___ Sewing ability
___ Cooking skills	___ Athletic skills
___ Patience with children	___ Love for books
___ Multitasking abilities	___ Organizational skills
___ Green thumb	___ Other_____

Journal some ideas of ways to bless God by blessing someone else with one of your talents this week.

. . . .

. . . .

Rewrite this verse into a personal prayer: "For God is working in you, giving you the desire to obey him and the power to do what pleases him" (Philippians 2:13, NLT).

. . . .

. . . .

. . . .

What do a disabled woman and peanut butter and jelly sandwiches have in common? God used them both to reach hundreds of kids. In the summer of 1990, Bea Salazar didn't consider her life a work of art. She was unemployed with five kids, no money, and little hope. Then she found a crying boy digging for food in a Dumpster. She took the boy home and made him a peanut butter and jelly sandwich. Good news about the peanut-butter lady spread through the neighborhood, and more kids showed up on her doorstep. Today, she influences hundreds of kids through her organization, Bea's Kids, which offers tutoring, clothes, medical assistance, food, and counseling. Bea Salazar has received numerous awards for her good deeds. When Oprah gave Bea the Use Your Life Award, Bea said, "It gives me a purpose to live, it gives me life. . . . There is no greater joy."

There is no greater joy than doing good works for others in the name of the Lord. Won't you give the gift that keeps on giving, the gift of yourself, for God's honor and glory?

contemplation
To me it seems when God conceived the world, that was poetry; he formed it, and that was sculpture; he colored it, and that was painting; he peopled it with living beings, and that was the grand, divine, eternal drama.
Emma Stebbins

65

Share the Wealth

When Mahatma Gandhi was a student, he became intrigued with the Bible. Reading the Gospels touched his heart, so he considered becoming a convert. Christianity seemed to offer real solutions to the caste system that divided India's population. One Sunday he attended a church to seek the way of salvation. An usher refused him a seat and said, "Go and worship with your own people." Tragically, he left and never came back. Gandhi said, "If Christians have caste differences also, I might as well remain a Hindu."

Ancient Israel suffered from a similar form of prejudice, a caste system of its own. Religious Jews treated the Gentiles with scorn. Gentiles were regarded as unclean—diseased. Any association with a Gentile was unlawful for a Jew. Israel mistakenly believed that Gentiles would not be included in God's family or inherit any of God's blessings.

Jesus changed all that! He broke down the social barriers that separated Jews and Gentiles, and His life removed the great divide. God invites both Jew and Gentile into His house to worship together as one family. This week's study reveals that these two groups (and all believers) must learn how to share the wealth of God's great treasures.

DAY 1 THE GREAT DIVIDE

TOGETHERNESS

I am convinced that nothing can ever separate us from his love. Death can't, and life can't. The angels can't, and the demons can't. Our fears for today, our worries about tomorrow, and even the powers of hell can't keep God's love away. . . . Nothing in all creation will ever be able to separate us from the love of God that is revealed in Christ Jesus our Lord. Romans 8:38-39, NLT

explanation

THEREFORE

A good rule of thumb in Bible study is that when you see a "therefore," find out what it's there for. *Therefore* is a connecting word; it joins what has been said with what is about to be said.

exploration

In lesson 3, Paul reminded us that we were once spiritually dead, but now we have received new lives through Christ. Now Paul looks more closely at the contrast between then and now.

Read through Ephesians 2 several times to review the tone, language, and content of this chapter. Then focus on verses 11-12.

> *Therefore remember that you, once Gentiles in the flesh—who are called Uncircumcision by what is called the Circumcision made in the flesh by hands—* . . .
> Ephesians 2:11

1. Paul begins by saying "therefore" and "remember." In other words, remember what phrases he used before from Ephesians 2:8-10: "by grace you have been saved; not of yourself; through faith; that no one should boast; gift of God; not of works." Now write these phrases in the appropriate columns below.

SAVED BY	NOT SAVED BY
. . . .	. . . .
. . . .	. . . .
. . . .	. . . .
. . . .	. . . .

2. According to Ephesians 2:11 what were the Gentiles once called? By whom?

. . . .

3. By what means was the circumcision accomplished?

. . . .

4. Read Romans 2:28-29.

   a. What type of circumcision does God desire? . . . .

. . . .

   b. How is this accomplished? . . . .

. . . .

   c. What is the result of a circumcised heart? . . . .

. . . .

> *. . . that at that time you were without Christ, being*
> *aliens from the commonwealth of Israel and strangers*
> *from the covenants of promise, having no hope and*
> *without God in the world.* Ephesians 2:12

5. Paul uses five terms to describe the unbeliever's spiritual condition. What are they?

. . . .

. . . .

. . . .

transformation

6. God is more concerned with the spiritual condition of your heart than the physical condition of your body. Look up the following verses to discover ways to develop a circumcised heart.

3

CIRCUMCISED FLESH
The physical sign of God's covenant with the Jews was circumcision "in the flesh," by removing the male foreskin. Since Gentiles didn't have the physical mark of circumcision to set them apart as God's people, many Jews considered them to be inferior and of no concern to God.

5

ALIEN AND STRANGER
An alien is a person of another family, race, or nation; a foreign-born resident who has not been naturalized; a person different in nature or character; a stranger. Aliens don't come from another planet, just a different place. Just because they're strangers doesn't mean they're strange.

6

CIRCUMCISED HEART
Circumcision was intended to be an outward sign of an inward change. Cutting away your flesh without changing your heart is self-mutilation. There are those in our society who are caught up in tattooing and body piercing to change their looks. But changing your appearance won't change your heart and life.

STRANGER
This means a foreigner or alien; what we might today call an immigrant. America, like Israel, is a land of foreigners. God says, "Neither mistreat a stranger nor oppress him, for you were strangers" (Exodus 22:21). Treat strangers kindly, and they'll become friends.

Deut. 30:6

. . . .

1 Cor. 7:19

. . . .

Gal. 5:6

. . . .

7. Which of the following need to be circumcised—cut away— from your heart?

Pride   Self-focus
Lack of love   Bitterness
Envy   Materialism
Stubbornness   Criticism
Ingratitude   Other _____

Rewrite Ezekiel 36:26-27 into a personal prayer: "I will give you a new heart with new and right desires, and I will put a new spirit in you. I will take out your stony heart of sin and give you a new, obedient heart. And I will put my Spirit in you so you will obey my laws and do whatever I command" (NLT).

. . . .

. . . .

. . . .

. . . .

. . . .

8. God told the Israelites, "If a stranger dwells with you in your land, you shall not mistreat him. . . . You shall love him as yourself; for you were strangers" (Leviticus 19:33-34). With this in mind, follow these steps.

Step One: Journal about a time when you felt like a stranger. (Example: first day of school or moving to a new neighborhood)

. . . .

. . . .

. . . .

. . . .

Step Two: Think about strangers "who dwell among you." Journal about how you will make them feel at home in a strange place.

. . . .

. . . .

. . . .

. . . .

When I was younger, I spent some time as a missionary on Oahu, where I worked in a coffeehouse ministry that reached out to prostitutes, drug addicts, and the homeless. Working the midnight shift meant the streets would literally be buzzing. One night someone shouted at me, "Hey, Haole, you go home!" It sounded as if he said "Howlie," and I would have been insulted if I'd known what a Haole was. A local friend explained, "That's what we call 'whitey' here on the islands." For once in my life, I was the outsider, and I didn't like it a bit!

The Gentiles were the "Haoles" in Israel, and the Jews wanted them to go home! But God is not prejudiced. Jews and Gentiles can all find a home in God's kingdom. Jesus Christ can bring all factioning parties together into one big, happy family. "There is no longer Jew or Gentile, slave or free, male or female. For you are all Christians—you are one in Christ Jesus" (Galatians 3:28, NLT).

contemplation
To the frightened, God is friendly; to the poor in spirit, he is forgiving; to the ignorant, considerate; to the weak, gentle; to the stranger, hospitable.
A. W. Tozer

DAY 2   THE TIE THAT BINDS

FRIENDSHIP
This includes you who were once so far away from God. You were his enemies, separated from him by your evil thoughts and actions, yet now he has brought you back as his friends.
Colossians 1:21-22, NLT

In 1936 a radio broadcast was transmitted to America from England. Just before King Edward VIII was to be on the air, someone stumbled over a wire in the New York radio control room and snapped the only line of communication between the two great countries. The engineers were frantic. Then, with only a few moments remaining before airtime, a quick-thinking apprentice grasped the two broken ends of the wire, one in each hand, and bridged the gap. Seconds later the king addressed the nation. In a real sense, his words were being transmitted literally through the body of that man!

In Paul's day, an ocean of rules and regulations separated the Jews and Gentiles. No matter how frantically they tried, the Gentiles could not make the connection with God and His people. On the cross, Jesus—the God/Man—stretched out one hand to the Jews and the other to the Gentiles, uniting them with His own body. He became the tie that binds.

exploration

We've seen the hostility that separated the Jew from the Gentile, as well as those things that separate unbelievers from God. Now we are introduced to a new state of affairs based on God's intervention.

Review Ephesians 2, then focus on verse 13.

> **But now in Christ Jesus you who once were far off have been brought near by the blood of Christ.**
> Ephesians 2:13

1. What two key words transport us from the past to the present?

. . . .

2. Who can change our focus from the past to the present?

. . . .

3. How does Paul describe where we once were without Christ?

. . . .

4. How are sinners brought near to God?

. . . .

5. Fill in the following chart to learn how and why we can draw near to God through Christ's blood.

SCRIPTURE	CHRIST'S BLOOD AND SACRIFICE
Matt. 26:28	
Heb. 9:12-14	
1 Pet. 1:18-19	
1 John 1:7-9	

6. Three of the Scriptures in the chart above refer to the remission of our sins at salvation. Which of the verses offer cleansing of the sins a Christian commits *after* salvation?

. . . .

7. According to James 4:8, how can you close the distance between yourself and God?

. . . .

explanation

1

THEN AND NOW
The past can rob you of the present and hinder your future. Paul believed in "forgetting the past and looking forward to what lies ahead" (Philippians 3:13, NLT). Christ frees you to live in the now.

3

FAR OFF
Is any place too far off for God to find you? Timbuktu? Kalamazoo? Katmandu? No! On the contrary, the psalmist said, "If I ride the wings of the morning, if I dwell by the farthest oceans, even there your hand will guide me" (Psalm 139:9-10, NLT).

7

DRAWING NEAR
God wants to be closer to you; not just to your body but close to your heart and soul as well. Judas drew near to Christ with his lips— the kiss of betrayal. But his heart was drawn away for thirty pieces of silver. Jesus said, "These people honor me with their lips, but their hearts are far away" (Matthew 15:8, NLT). Kisses from a hard heart are "lip service," not love.

8 FRIENDS

Solomon said, "A man who has friends must himself be friendly" (Proverbs 18:24). In other words, friendships don't just happen; you make them happen by being friendly. God wants you to be a near and dear friend. Have you extended the hand of friendship to Him?

9 FRIEND OR FOE?

Unhealthy friendships pull us away from stable ones. James warns us how our friendship with God can be jeopardized. "Don't you realize that friendship with this world makes you an enemy of God? I say it again, that if your aim is to enjoy this world, you can't be a friend of God" (James 4:4, NLT).

10 LUST

A strong desire for something that is forbidden or an obsessive sexual craving. Lust yearns for things that are contrary to the will of God. Christians can resist lust through the power of the Spirit. The flesh and its lusts are to be crucified. "Those who are Christ's have crucified the flesh with its passions and desires" (Galatians 5:24).

8. Our promise today was friendship with God. Pick an activity to do this week from the list below that will strengthen your friendship with Him.

Tell Him a secret.   Visit His house.
Take Him on a walk.   Give Him a gift.
Invite Him to dinner.   Call Him for advice.
Write Him a letter.   Show Him your photo album.
Make friends with His friends.

9. Just as there are things that strengthen friendships, there are things that will tear them down.

Journal about a time when a friendship failed or ended. What contributed to the breakdown? How did it make you feel?

. . . .

. . . .

. . . .

. . . .

. . . .

. . . .

. . . .

10. We've seen that friendship with the world can distract us from our relationship with God. John divided friendship with the world into three categories, "For all that is in the world—the lust of the flesh, the lust of the eyes, and the pride of life—is not of the Father but is of the world" (1 John 2:16). With this Scripture in mind, journal about a specific way you have made "friends" with the world by participating in some aspect of each catagory.

Lust of the flesh: Something that feels good.

. . . .

. . . .

. . . .

. . . .

Lust of the eyes: Something that looks good.

. . . .

. . . .

. . . .

. . . .

Pride of life: Something to impress others

. . . .

. . . .

. . . .

. . . .

I love the story of a little girl named Ruth, who was sent on an errand by her mother. She was gone for such a long time that her mother became frantic with worry. When Ruth finally returned, her mother hugged her tightly, asking, "Where have you been? What took you so long?"

Ruth replied, "On my way home I saw Sally sitting in front of her house. She was crying because her doll was broken."

"So," said the mother, "you stopped to help her fix her doll?"

"Oh no!" replied Ruth. "I stopped to help her cry."

Jesus said, "The greatest love is shown when people lay down their lives for their friends" (John 15:13, NLT). He saw that our sins caused great sorrow, so He stopped and shed not tears, but His blood, for our sins.

contemplation
You cannot say that
you are friendless
when Christ has said,
"Henceforth I call
you not servants . . .
but I have called
you friends."
Billy Graham

DAY 3 LET THE WALLS FALL DOWN

The politics of division separated Germany on August 13, 1961, when the residents of Berlin woke to a barbed-wire barrier between the communist East and the noncommunist West. The Cold War had begun. Soldiers quickly fortified the barrier, creating a concrete wall twelve feet high and over a hundred miles long. Loved ones were torn apart, and more than two million people attempted to escape East Germany by climbing, vaulting, tunneling, or crashing through checkpoints. Unsuccessful attempts resulted in more than four hundred deaths. In 1989, restrictions between the two Berlins were lifted. The Berlin Wall came down, announcing the end of the Cold War. Celebrations around the world culminated with Germany's reunification as one country on October 3, 1990. Though now free, a city and a nation had been divided by disagreement, laws, and treaties, culminating in a literal wall of separation. Laws lead to walls.

In the same way, laws and legalism kept the nation of Israel and other nations divided by a wall of prejudice. But two thousand years ago, a babe in a manger heralded the end of the Cold War between the Jews and Gentiles. Jesus tore down the spiritual wall of separation. Let the walls fall down!

exploration

The blood of Christ is able to bring near to God all who are far off. Now let's see what Christ's role is in tearing down walls between us and God.

Review Ephesians 2, then focus on verses 14-17.

For He Himself is our peace, who has made both one,
and has broken down the middle wall of separation, . . .
Ephesians 2:14

1. How is Jesus described here? . . . .

. . . .

2. What has Jesus done? . . . .

. . . .

3. How has Jesus made both Jew and Gentile one?

. . . .

. . . having abolished in His flesh the enmity, that is,
the law of commandments contained in ordinances, so
as to create in Himself one new man from the two, thus
making peace, . . . Ephesians 2:15

4. What did Christ abolish? . . . .

. . . .

5. What was the result? . . . .

. . . .

. . . and that He might reconcile them both to God in
one body through the cross, thereby putting to death the
enmity. Ephesians 2:16

6. How were they reconciled? . . . .

. . . .

7. What was the result of reconciliation? . . . .

. . . .

He came and preached peace to you who were afar off
and to those who were near. Ephesians 2:17

---

explanation

1

PRINCE OF PEACE
Some kings rule with
a rod of iron. The king-
dom of Christ is ruled
by peace. Jesus is the
King of hearts. If you
don't have peace in
your heart, then who's
sitting on the throne?
"Let the peace that
comes from Christ
rule in your hearts"
(Colossians 3:15, NLT).

4

ENMITY
Enmity is deep-seated
animosity or hatred.
The apostle Paul
declared that the
human mind in its natu-
ral state has a natural
"enmity against God."
This enmity can be
changed only through
the redemptive power
of Christ.

6

RECONCILIATION
Reconciliation is the
process by which God
and humanity are
brought together
again. The Bible
teaches that we are
alienated from God
because of God's holi-
ness and our sinfulness.
Through the sacrifice
of Christ, our sin is
atoned and God's
wrath is appeased.

8. Who were the recipients of Christ's message of peace?

. . . .

transformation

9. Until you've surrendered your sinful nature, you remain at war with God. Circle any words from the passage below that describe sinful areas that reveal hostility toward God: "When you follow the desires of your sinful nature, your lives will produce these evil results: sexual immorality, impure thoughts, eagerness for lustful pleasure, idolatry, participation in demonic activities, hostility, quarreling, jealousy, outbursts of anger, selfish ambition, divisions, the feeling that everyone is wrong except those in your own little group, envy, drunkenness, wild parties, and other kinds of sin" (Galatians 5:19-21, NLT).

Journal a prayer of surrender to God. Ask Him to forgive you for engaging in the sinful desires of your flesh. Ask Him to help you to crucify the flesh so that you no longer act on its cravings. Pray to be filled with His Spirit to walk in newness of life.

. . . .

. . . .

. . . .

. . . .

10. Today we learned that God wants you to be reconciled to other members of His family. Identify a person to whom you need to be reconciled and the cause of the division between you.

Journal a prayer of reconciliation, creating a "bridge" to that person's heart.

. . . .

. . . .

. . . .

Reconciliation builds bridges. The cross of Christ constructed a wooden bridge reuniting God with His creation. Forgiveness builds bridges between people who are separated. Jesus said, "If you . . . remember that your brother has something against you, . . . go your way. First be reconciled to your brother, and then come and offer your gift [to God]" (Matthew 5:23-24).

11. Jesus is the great reconciler! And He asks us to fulfill the same role, serving as His ambassadors of reconciliation. "Now all things are of God, who has reconciled us to Himself through Jesus Christ, and has given us the ministry of reconciliation" (2 Corinthians 5:18).

Identify two divided people who need reconciliation. (Example: Your brother refuses to speak to your parents.) Journal about how you can bridge the gap between these people, helping them to be reconciled. Ask God how you can serve as His ambassador of peace.

. . . .

. . . .

. . . .

. . . .

The Hatfield-McCoy feud began in 1863, when the Hatfields fought with the McCoys on the Kentucky–West Virginia border. Historians disagree on the reasons for the feud; some say it began over a pig theft, others say it was because of a secret romance. Whatever the reason, the feud caused the death of more than one hundred men, women, and children. More than a century later, in May 1976, Jim McCoy and Willis Hatfield, the last two survivors of the original families, shook hands. The survivors came together to build a monument memorializing the victims of the feud. Jim McCoy died in 1984, at the age of ninety-nine. He bore no grudges, and the Hatfield Funeral Home handled his burial.

We know the reason for the feud between God and man— sin. But God was willing to meet us at a monument on the hill of Calvary. He was willing to bury His grudge in a tomb sealed with a stone. What about you? Are you still feuding with God? Perhaps it's time to accept the invitation to meet Jesus at the cross and bury your grudges along with your past.

FORGIVE
Former U.S. Senate chaplain Peter Marshall said, "If you hug to yourself any resentment against anybody else, you destroy the bridge by which God would come to you." Jesus said, "If you forgive those who sin against you, your heavenly Father will forgive you. But if you refuse to forgive others, your Father will not forgive your sins" (Matthew 6:14-15, NLT).

contemplation
Like the father of the Prodigal Son, God can see repentance coming a great way off and is there to meet it. The repentance is the reconciliation.
Dorothy L. Sayers

DAY 4 EQUAL ACCESS

EQUALITY

There is no longer Jew or Gentile, slave or free, male or female. For you are all Christians—you are one in Christ Jesus.
Galatians 3:28, NLT

explanation

THREE IN ONE
The members of the Trinity are separate yet equal. Think of an egg that has three separate parts: yolk, white, and shell. Each has a different function yet remains part of the whole. God the Father, Jesus the Son, and the Holy Spirit are one unit, each with a separate purpose.

Over a century ago, the Supreme Court of the United States ruled that blacks and whites should be considered "separate but equal." However, white America focused on being separate, not equal. Black citizens were required to drink from separate water fountains, to eat at separate lunch counters, to sit in separate sections of schools, churches, and courthouses. This legislation stood unchallenged until 1955. One black woman in Alabama, a seamstress named Rosa Parks, refused to be treated separately and by her actions insisted on being treated with equality. Her refusal to give up her seat on a bus to a white person sparked a cultural revolution culminating in a federal court order for desegregation.

Over two thousand years ago, the Sanhedrin in Israel insisted that Gentiles were not only separate from the Jews, they were unequal as well. One Jewish man from Nazareth, a carpenter named Jesus, refused to treat Jews and Gentiles unequally. He reminded the world that in God's eyes, all people are created equal.

exploration

This week we have been reminded what life was like apart from God. Today we will examine our new position as believers in God's kingdom.

Review Ephesians 2, then focus on verses 18-19.

> **For through Him we both have access by one Spirit to the Father.** Ephesians 2:18

1. Identify the three members of the Trinity named here.

. . . .

2. Examine the process by which we have access to the Father by filling in the blanks provided: "For _____ we both have access _____ to _____."

3. Who is included in the phrase "we both"? (See Ephesians 2:11-12.)

. . . .

> *Now, therefore, you are no longer strangers and foreigners, but fellow citizens with the saints and members of the household of God, . . .* Ephesians 2:19

4. What are we no longer known as? . . . .

. . . .

5. Instead of being outsiders, this verse reveals two new positions we possess. What are they?

. . . .

6. To whose household does Paul say we now belong? . . . .

. . . .

7. Verse 19 begins with a reference of time. When do we receive our new positions?

. . . .

transformation

8. What special rights or privileges did you enjoy as a member of your household? (Examples: food and clothing)

. . . .

Journal a prayer thanking God for them.

. . . .

. . . .

3
TOGETHER
God included both Jews and Gentiles in His nation and His family. But during Paul's day, God's children did not reflect His heart. Instead, God's kids had a bad case of sibling rivalry. Jesus was God's messenger telling His kids to "kiss and make up."

5
FELLOW CITIZENS
"Can't we all just get along?" Read the news and the answer is, "Apparently not!" Look at a penny, and you'll find the solution: "In God We Trust." Only when citizens look to God's plan instead of their own agendas will there be true unity.

6
OPEN HOUSE
Jews believed that Gentiles should be excluded from God's house—the Temple. God made it clear in both the Old and New Testaments that His house was open to all nations: "Is it not written, 'My house shall be called a house of prayer for all nations'?" (Mark 11:17). God doesn't want anyone to be homeless.

God's house is full of glory, holiness, and goodness. Isn't that the kind of house you'd like to live in? Jesus said He was going to prepare a place for you in His house. Until then, Jesus has come to take up residence in *you*—His home away from home.

9. God invites you to reside in His household of faith. Fill in the chart below to discover the privileges and joys you'll find in God's household.

SCRIPTURE	IN GOD'S HOUSE
Ps. 26:8	
Ps. 65:4	
Ps. 93:5	
John 14:2	

Journal a prayer of thanksgiving to your heavenly Father who has prepared a place for you in His household filled with good things.

. . . .

. . . .

. . . .

. . . .

. . . .

. . . .

10. Using the chart, list the members of your current household, along with a description of their outlook on life. (For example, are they timid, outgoing, optimistic, negative?) Then put a smiling face by the people with a healthy outlook and a frowning face next to the people who need a new outlook. Finally, in the prayer box, write a prayer of thanks for the people who make you smile and a prayer of healing for the people who make you sad.

PERSON   ☺☹   PRAYER

. . . .

. . . .

. . . .

. . . .

. . . .

11. If your home is unbearable, maybe you're the bear. Look in the mirror.

> Journal about the kind of attitude you display to others at home. Would you get a smiley face or a frown?

. . . .

. . . .

. . . .

In a Peanuts cartoon created by Charles Schulz, Lucy demands that Linus change TV channels and then threatens him with her fist if he doesn't.

"What makes you think you can walk right in here and take over?" asks Linus.

"These five fingers," says Lucy. "Individually they're nothing, but when I curl them together like this into a single unit, they form a weapon that is terrible to behold."

"Which channel do you want?" asks Linus.

Linus looks at his fingers and says, "Why can't you guys get organized like that?"

Weak things united become strong. Jesus took two weak and warring peoples, the Jews and the Gentiles, and brought them together to create a holy nation, the church, whose holy creed is love. Because of this unity based on love, Christianity became a powerful force in the ancient world and changed the course of history.

SMILE
Smile and the world smiles with you? But even if you frown, God will smile back at you. God told Aaron to offer this blessing over His family, "May the Lord bless you and protect you. May the Lord smile on you and be gracious to you. May the Lord show you his favor and give you his peace" (Numbers 6:24-26, NLT).

contemplation
If your father and mother, your sister and brother, if the very cat and dog in the house, are not happier for your being Christian, it is a question whether you really are.
Hudson Taylor

DAY 5 COMMON GROUND

Back in 1957 the First Brethren Church of Sarasota, Florida, had a groundbreaking ceremony. Instead of using a silver shovel for VIPs to dig up the first clump of dirt, they brought a one-horse plow. Two strong ushers were harnessed to the yoke to break up the fallow ground. But the plow didn't budge an inch. Next, Sunday school officers and teachers were strapped in, but still the plow was immovable. Finally, all the church members present took hold of the rope, tugging with all their might. With every member pulling together, the plow moved forward, the ground was broken, and the church was built.

Our Savior was born in a barn, not Buckingham Palace. He was a blue-collar carpenter, not a blue-blooded aristocrat. His friends were commoners: fishermen, farmers, and homemakers. Jesus broke new ground in ancient Israel by using common people to build an uncommon community, His church. He is our firm foundation. We are all on common ground as members of His church.

exploration

We learned that Paul typified believers as "fellow citizens with the saints and members of the household of God" (Ephesians 2:19). Today we discover a different metaphor for the body of believers.
Review Ephesians 2, then focus on verses 20-22.

> *. . . having been built on the foundation of the apostles and prophets, Jesus Christ Himself being the chief cornerstone, . . .* Ephesians 2:20

1. What do you learn about the foundation and chief cornerstone of the household of God?

. . . .

. . . .

> *. . . in whom the whole building, being joined together, grows into a holy temple in the Lord, . . ."* Ephesians 2:21

2. How much of the building is dependent upon the chief cornerstone?

. . . .

3. Once this building is joined together, what does it become?

. . . .

4. From beginning to end, upon whom is this growth dependent?

. . . .

> *. . . in whom you also are being built together for a dwelling place of God in the Spirit.* Ephesians 2:22

5. Who else is being built together into the Lord's temple?

. . . .

6. Why are we being built together? . . . .

. . . .

7. How will God dwell in His holy temple, the church?

. . . .

explanation

1

CORNERSTONE
Christ is called the "cornerstone" in reference to His being the foundation of the Christian faith (Ephesians 2:20), and the conspicuousness of the place He occupies *(New Unger's Bible Dictionary).*

6

DWELLING PLACE
God is infinite; human beings are finite. Can the uncontainable be contained? Solomon said, "Will God really live on earth? Why, even the highest heavens cannot contain you. How much less this Temple I have built!" (1 Kings 8:27, NLT). Yet God has made *you* His dwelling place—filling the finite with the infinite through His Spirit.

7

IN SPIRIT
God created us as a trilogy—spirit, soul, and body. Your body and soul are made for earth, to communicate with other people. Your spirit is equipped for eternity to worship God. "God is Spirit, so those who worship him must worship in spirit and in truth" (John 4:24, NLT).

transformation

8. Read 1 Peter 2:5. What does this verse reveal about your role in God's holy temple? What should you offer in this temple?

. . . .

. . . .

9. Fill in the chart below to discover what spiritual sacrifices God desires.

SCRIPTURE	SPIRITUAL SACRIFICES
Ps. 51:17, 19	
Ps. 141:2	
Rom. 12:1	
Heb. 13:15	

10. Remember in the movie *The Sound of Music*, when Maria taught the von Trapp children to sing, "These are a few of my favorite things"?

Make a top ten list of some of your favorite things.

. . . .

. . . .

. . . .

. . . .

. . . .

. . . .

8

LIVING TEMPLE
God doesn't inhabit buildings of brick and mortar but bodies of flesh and blood. Your church building is dead until you fill it with the presence of God living in you. "Don't you know that your body is the temple of the Holy Spirit, who lives in you and was given to you by God?" (1 Corinthians 6:19, NLT).

10

LIVING SACRIFICES
We have seen that God desires unique sacrifices. The dictionary defines *sacrifice* as "an act of offering something precious to deity." God doesn't want your hand-me-downs but your heart's delight! He loved you so much He gave His favorite thing—His Son.

Write a prayer offering a sacrifice of praise to God for creating and providing one of these delightful things.

. . . .

. . . .

. . . .

. . . .

Journal about how, this week, you can offer to God one of your favorite things as an act of sacrificing your very best for Him. (Example: Instead of reading the latest novel, I'll take time to read God's Word. Be creative!)

. . . .

. . . .

. . . .

. . . .

"There's no place like home" were the words Dorothy uttered as she clicked the heels of her ruby-red slippers. Her journey began in Kansas with ordinary folks like Uncle Henry and Auntie Em. But Dorothy was not content with her common existence on a pig farm and pictured herself "somewhere over the rainbow." An adversary on a bicycle, a carpetbagger in a wagon, and a journey through a tornado blew Dorothy into the Land of Oz. At last she was living her dream: unusual sights, uncommon personalities, and unique encounters. But on the other side of the rainbow, all Dorothy could think about was the comfort of home sweet home.

"Father, forgive them" were the words Jesus uttered as His feet were nailed to the cross. His journey began in heaven with extraordinary company, the Father of lights. But Jesus was not content with *our* common existence on this clump of dirt and longed to bring all of us over the rainbow to our true home— seated with him "in the heavenly places." His uncommon kindness opened the doors of eternity to all humanity, not just those who lived in the land of Israel. There's *no place* like His home!

contemplation

"Where is the church at 11:25 on Monday morning?" The church then is in the dentist's office, in the automobile salesroom and repair shop. . . . It is in the hospital, in the classroom, and in the home. It is in the offices. . . . That is where the church is, wherever God's people are. . . . They are honoring God, not just while they worship in a building, but out there.
Arthur H. DeKruyter

Trustee of God's Will

Before his conversion to Christianity, Paul had an impressive résumé: "For I was circumcised when I was eight days old, having been born into a pure-blooded Jewish family that is a branch of the tribe of Benjamin. So I am a real Jew if there ever was one! What's more, I was a member of the Pharisees, who demand the strictest obedience to the Jewish law. And zealous? Yes, in fact, I harshly persecuted the church. And I obeyed the Jewish law so carefully that I was never accused of any fault" (Philippians 3:5-6, NLT). Impressed? Paul wasn't. He learned that God is more concerned with what Christ had done for him than with what he had accomplished himself. He threw his résumé away, knowing it was "worthless because of what Christ has done" (Philippians 3:7, NLT).

After Paul had been on the job for God a few years, his résumé looked something like this: "I'm over fifty years old. I've never held down a pulpit position for more than three years. I had to leave some towns because I caused civil disturbances or riots. I have served time in jail at least three or four times, but I was innocent. My health isn't good either. I don't have letters of recommendation since I don't get along with most religious leaders. In fact, some have threatened me and attacked me physically." Based on this résumé, would your church hire Paul? Maybe not—but God did! This week, let's examine Paul's credentials and discover his qualifications as trustee of God's will.

DAY 1 PAUL THE PRISONER

explanation

1

PRISONER
Paul was imprisoned because he believed in uniting Jews and Gentiles in the church. Paul did the right thing, but he was treated wrongly. Jesus will right the wrongs. "God blesses those who are persecuted because they live for God, for the Kingdom of Heaven is theirs" (Matthew 5:10, NLT).

exploration

Last week we learned that God desires unity and reconciliation rather than discord and division. In this lesson, we gain more insight into Paul himself—how he viewed himself, his circumstances, and his role in the kingdom of God.

Read through Ephesians 3 several times to get a feel for the tone, language, and content of this chapter, then focus on verses 1 and 13.

> *For this reason I, Paul, the prisoner of Christ Jesus for you Gentiles—* . . . Ephesians 3:1

1. How does Paul describe himself? . . . .

   . . . .

2. Knowing that Paul was a prisoner in a Roman jail, why do you think he described himself as a "prisoner of Christ Jesus" instead of a "prisoner of Caesar"?

   . . . .

   . . . .

3. Paul reveals that he was a prisoner for the Gentiles. Read Acts 24:5-6 to understand better the charges against Paul.

   a. He was the creator of . . . .

   . . . .

b. He was the ringleader of . . . .

. . . .

c. He tried to . . . .

. . . .

4. According to Acts 24:12-13, how did Paul respond to the charges?

. . . .

> *Therefore I ask that you do not lose heart at my tribulations for you, which is your glory.*
> Ephesians 3:13

5. Paul asks them to not lose heart. What could cause them to lose heart?

. . . .

6. Whom did Paul say his tribulations were for? . . . .

. . . .

7. What was the ultimate result of Paul's tribulations?

. . . .

transformation

8. Paul considered himself a prisoner of Christ Jesus. In which of the following ways have you been "taken captive" by Christ?

Guarded my thoughts
Protected my heart
Gave up rights to self
Protected my emotions
Restrained sinful actions
Other _____

4
INTOLERANCE
It's odd how the "tolerant" can be so intolerant. The Roman government tolerated many pagan practices but would not tolerate true religious freedom. Thus, to preserve the *pax Romana* (Roman peace), they imprisoned Paul and sent him to Rome to stand trial before Caesar.

5
TRIBULATION
Tribulation means great adversity and anguish; intense oppression or persecution. Tribulation is linked to God's process for making the world right again. His Son underwent great suffering, just as His people undergo a great deal of tribulation from the world.

8
LOOK UP
"Two men looked out prison bars; one saw mud, the other saw the stars." The difference? One looked down while the other gazed upward. When you're taken captive by Christ you have every reason to look up! The captivity of the world will only make you hang your head.

10
FREE INDEED

Paul was a prisoner physically, but his knowledge of God's freedom liberated his heart and soul. You may feel trapped by your circumstances, but like Paul, you can experience spiritual freedom in Jesus. "If the Son makes you free, you shall be free indeed" (John 8:36).

9. Behaviors such as gossip hold us captive. Activities like worship set us free. In the chart below, list behaviors that hold you captive (i.e., bad habits) and those that set you free.

HOLDS YOU CAPTIVE   SETS YOU FREE

. . . .

. . . .

. . . .

. . . .

. . . .

10. Because of his relationship with Christ, Paul was able to find contentment and see God's purpose in his tribulations.

Journal about a tribulation you are now experiencing.

. . . .

. . . .

. . . .

. . . .

. . . .

Write a prayer asking God for His perfect will to be done—either to remove the troubles or to strengthen you through them. Pray that however He responds to your prayer, He will be glorified.

. . . .

. . . .

. . . .

. . . .

Experience is the best teacher. Paul learned through experience that tough times could teach him even more than tranquil times. Suffering in prison made him a better man, and he wanted to make certain that his pain was for the gain of others. Jerry McAuley was another example of such an individual. A thief and a counterfeiter, he ended up spending seven years in Sing Sing Prison. After his conversion there, he began witnessing to other men who were imprisoned by sin. Later he started America's first rescue mission in New York City, where he befriended the worst sorts of criminals and street people.

Just before his death he said to his wife, "I know that soon tuberculosis will take my life, but I want to die on my knees, praying for the lost. I'd rather have some poor soul that I led to the Lord put one small rose on my grave than to have the wealth of a millionaire." His wish was granted, for at his funeral an aged, shabbily dressed man appeared and placed a few flowers on the coffin, saying, "I hope Jerry, who was my friend, will know that they came from old Joe Chappy." Mrs. McAuley preserved that little bouquet for a long time in remembrance of the fact that her husband had been a true friend of sinners.

contemplation
Jesus' guilt is our innocence; as his captivity is our freedom, and his death our life.
Malcolm Muggeridge

DAY 2 PAUL THE APOSTLE

When I hear the word *apostle* or *prophet,* my mind conjures up visions of men in flowing white robes, sandal-clad feet, long matted hair, and eyes blazing with zeal. I imagine Charlton Heston playing Moses in *The Ten Commandments* as the Red Sea divided. Or I envision Anthony Hopkins as he portrayed Paul the apostle in the movie *Peter and Paul.*

So what does the genuine article look like? History tells us that Paul the apostle was probably a short, bow-legged man with a big hook nose and runny eyes. The Bible describes David, both king and prophet, as "ruddy and handsome, with pleasant eyes" (1 Samuel 16:12, NLT). Obviously, you can't judge a book by its cover or God's messengers by their looks. They come in all shapes and sizes.

What makes an ordinary person become an apostle or a prophet? God's call on their lives! A prophet was God's chosen messenger who courageously communicated His words to His chosen people—Israel. An apostle was a chosen messenger of Christ, specially sent out as an ambassador of the gospel.

Judging from his appearance, Paul was an unlikely candidate to be God's messenger. But Paul had everything he needed to be an apostle—Christ's call upon his life!

exploration

Yesterday we looked into Paul's role as a prisoner. Today we discover that he was also an apostle.

Review Ephesians 3:1-14, then focus on verses 2-6.

. . . if indeed you have heard of the dispensation of the grace of God which was given to me for you, . . .
Ephesians 3:2

1. What dispensation was given to Paul for others? . . . .

. . . .

2. Who gave this special dispensation to Paul? . . . .

. . . .

. . . how that by revelation He made known to me the mystery (as I have briefly written already, by which, when you read, you may understand my knowledge in the mystery of Christ), . . . Ephesians 3:3-4

3. What word here indicates that Paul was given supernatural enlightenment?

. . . .

4. What was Paul given supernatural knowledge of? . . . .

. . . .

. . . which in other ages was not made known to the sons of men, as it has now been revealed by the Spirit to His holy apostles and prophets: . . . Ephesians 3:5

5. Who else was given this revelation, and how did they receive it?

. . . .

. . . that the Gentiles should be fellow heirs, of the same body, and partakers of His promise in Christ through the gospel, . . . Ephesians 3:6

6. What details of the "mystery of Christ" were revealed to Paul?

. . . .

7. Of what are the Gentiles partakers?

. . . .

explanation

1

DISPENSATION
A *dispensation* is a formal authorization or an act of dispensing (*Webster's*). As an apostle, Paul was formally authorized by God to dispense the grace of God to the Ephesians— to Gentiles. Paul was like a vending machine; if you pushed his buttons, out came grace!

4

MYSTERY
Mystery means a secret untold; a hidden truth. God revealed a mystery to Paul: He was the Gentiles' secret admirer. Once the secret was told, the truth could come out. There is room in God's heart and His church for everyone.

5

GOOD NEWS
Once the apostles and prophets heard the Good News of reconciliation through Christ, they got busy telling others. "So they began their circuit of the villages, preaching the Good News" (Luke 9:6, NLT). Are you busy telling others the Good News, or are you goin' nowhere fast?

MESSENGER

How do you know if a messenger is from God? It's not by their looks but by what comes from their lips. Messengers may come in many shapes and sizes, but the message reveals the authenticity of the messenger. "This is the message he has given us to announce to you: God is light and there is no darkness in him at all" (1 John 1:5, NLT).

transformation

8. Paul was a dispenser of God's grace—when you pushed his buttons, out came grace. Use your imagination to complete the exercise below:

Assess yourself honestly: If you were a vending machine, what would you be stocked with? (Example: Stress, because your life's too busy? Fun, because life's a blast?)

. . . .

. . . .

. . . .

. . . .

We all have buttons: people, places, or positions that turn us off, ring our bells, or hit the jackpot. Journal about the things that really push your buttons.

. . . .

. . . .

. . . .

. . . .

9. We saw that Paul was God's messenger, faithfully conveying His words to His people. Keep this in mind as you journal through these exercises.

Journal about some messengers who have inspired you to follow Christ and how. Why were they effective?

. . . .

. . . .

. . . .

. . . .

Write a prayer of thanks to God for placing them in your life. Ask Him to bless them in their ministries.

. . . .

. . . .

. . . .

. . . .

10. God used the prophetic Scriptures to reveal the mysteries of the church to the apostle Paul. Draw a line connecting the Old Testament prophecies to their corresponding New Testament fulfillment.

PROPHECY	FULFILLMENT
Gen. 12:3	Acts 10:44-48
Isa. 49:6	Gal. 3:8
Joel 2:28-29	Acts 13:46-47

Scientists at the Goddard Space Flight Center report that one of the largest stars in our galaxy is about to self-destruct. Eta Carinae, which has a mass 100 times greater than that of our sun, is giving signs that its life is almost over. Researchers say that it could become a supernova—a blazing, exploding star—within the next 10,000 years. What was especially interesting about the Science 82 report was the statement that since light from the star could take 9,000 years to reach the earth, the actual explosion could have already taken place.

This phenomenon reminds me of the nature of biblical prophecy. For example, the predictions found in the Bible are often written in the past tense. This was done because even though the prophet was writing of a future event, he had already "seen" it. In the mind of God it's as if the event had already happened. God knows it all and has seen it all—past, present, and future. When God reveals future events to a prophet, though the event may have taken place in time (eternity past), it may take light-years until we can see the results here on Earth (eternity present).

10
PROPHECY
Predictions about the future and the end time; special messages from God, often uttered through human spokesmen, which indicate the divine will for humanity.

contemplation
In God there is no was or will be, but a continuous and unbroken is. In him history and prophecy are one and the same.
A. W. Tozer

DAY 3 PAUL'S POWER SOURCE

Abraham Lincoln had his share of setbacks on his way to success. He lost his position as captain in his short time of military service. His little country store "winked out," as he said, making him a failure at business. As a lawyer he was too impractical and unpolished to be very successful. And in politics he was defeated several times in bids for the legislature, Congress, and the vice presidency. At last, in 1861 he was elected president of the United States.

Lincoln viewed all of his frustrations and victories through the eyes of eternity, observing, "That the Almighty directly intervenes in human affairs is one of the plainest statements in the Bible. I have had so many evidences of His direction, so many instances when I have been controlled by some other power than my own will that I have no doubt that this power comes from above."

Paul also experienced a long list of catastrophes on the road to a power-filled life: "Five different times the Jews gave me thirty-nine lashes. Three times I was beaten with rods. Once I was stoned. Three times I was shipwrecked. . . . I have faced danger in the cities, in the deserts, and on the stormy seas. . . . I have lived with weariness and pain and sleepless nights. Often I have been hungry and thirsty and have gone without food" (2 Corinthians 11:24-27, NLT). In spite of these setbacks Paul could say that God had given to him "the effective working of His power."

exploration

We have gained new insight into Paul as a prisoner and an apostle. Today we examine another aspect of Paul, the trustee of God's will, and discover that he was a power-filled man.

Review Ephesians 3:1-14, then focus on verses 7-8a.

. . . of which I became a minister according to the gift of the grace of God given to me by the effective working of His power. Ephesians 3:7

1. How did Paul describe himself here? . . . .

. . . .

2. What gift did Paul receive that enabled him to be God's minister?

. . . .

3. How was that gift given to him? . . . .

. . . .

To me, who am less than the least of all the saints, this grace was given, . . . Ephesians 3:8

4. Three phrases here reveal the humble way Paul viewed himself. Fill in the blanks below to discover his descending path:

"To me, who am _____".

"To me, who am less _____"

"To me, who am less than the least _____"

5. Looking back at verses 2, 7, and 8, what key word is repeated in reference to Paul's ministry?

. . . .

transformation

6. Paul was truly a minister—a servant—of the people. Look ahead to Ephesians 4:12. Who else is equipped for the ministry? Why?

. . . .

. . . .

explanation

1

MINISTER
This is a distinctive biblical idea that means "to serve" or "to be a servant." Men and women who join the ministry shouldn't be trying to get ahead, but to stand behind.

3

POWER
Power is the ability or strength to perform a task. Power is sometimes linked to authority. Power suggests physical strength; authority suggests a moral right. One can have power to perform a task but not authority to do it. Jesus Christ had both, and He bestowed these upon His followers. God gives His power to do His work.

4

THE LEAST
God's kingdom runs contrary to our human ideas of power. He tells us the last will be first, the meek will inherit, and the humble will be exalted. God's philosophy of success? The way down is the way up. To prosper with God, ask yourself, *How low can I go?*

SERVING

You are most like Christ when you serve. "Even I, the Son of Man, came here not to be served but to serve others" (Mark 10:45, NLT). Serving Jesus has its benefits—intimacy with him. "My servants must be where I am. And if they follow me, the Father will honor them" (John 12:26, NLT).

SUPPLIES

When people join the army, they don't have to purchase their own gear or gun. They are fully equipped by Uncle Sam with all the supplies necessary. God's soldiers are also equipped with supplies for the task at hand. "My God shall supply all your need according to His riches in glory by Christ Jesus" (Philippians 4:19).

Journal a prayer to God by rewriting the following Scripture: "I have become a servant of everyone so that I can bring them to Christ" (1 Corinthians 9:19, NLT).

. . . .

. . . .

. . . .

. . . .

. . . .

. . . .

7. To which of the following people have you been a servant this week?

____ Husband	____ Children
____ The homeless	____ Parents
____ Neighbors	____ The sick
____ Siblings	____ Coworkers
____ Friends	____ The elderly
____ Other _____	

8. You are called and equipped to be God's minister by His grace.

Journal about your experience in serving the person(s) you marked above. How did God empower and equip you for service?

. . . .

. . . .

. . . .

. . . .

. . . .

. . . .

Shortly after I (Penny) rededicated my life to Christ, I developed a burning desire to serve the Lord but didn't know what He wanted me to do. I thought, *Maybe I should teach a Sunday school class.* But I really didn't feel qualified to teach—I was still learning. I thought about making meals for the homebound, but I could barely get meals on the table for my own family. Then one Sunday I read in the church bulletin: "Toy Washers Needed in the Children's Ministry." Immediately I thought, *I could do that.* So I volunteered to go in once a week to wash the toys in the nursery. I would take my kids and let them play as I washed buckets of toys week after week for two years. The service wasn't glamorous, but it was gratifying. As I stood at the sink, I had time to listen to praise music or think about the pastor's message. My time at the washbasin brought me closer to Jesus.

Teddy Roosevelt said, "Do what you can, with what you have, where you are." What could *I* do? I could use my hands. What did I have? I had a heart for service. Where was I? I was at home with my kids. And God used my limited resources to work for Him. Do you think you're not equipped to serve God? Then think again. He will take the smallest act of service and transform it into something sacred.

DAY 4 PAUL THE PREACHER

Unfortunately, preachers have gotten a bad name in recent history because some have behaved poorly. The PTL Network and ministry fell as the result of the indiscretions of Jim and Tammy Faye Bakker. Fast on the heels of the PTL collapse, the Jimmy Swaggart scandal rocked the evangelical world. Larry King wrote about Rev. Swaggart: "I would buy all of the sadness and tears and recriminations if, and this is a big if, Jimmy had come forward with his problem before somebody had pictures proving it. Anybody can be repentant when caught. Also, if he really wanted true forgiveness, he could donate his estate and all that property to some worthy charity. Give up all his earthly goods."

If you don't live what you've learned, then you are a liar. "Be doers of the word, and not hearers only, deceiving yourselves" (James 1:22). This week we have learned that Paul practiced what he preached. He was able to say with confidence, "You should follow my example, just as I follow Christ's" (1 Corinthians 11:1, NLT). Being a preacher involves both doing what you say and saying words of truth. Since we already know some of what Paul did, let's look at what Paul the preacher had to say.

exploration

Today we examine yet another position this amazing man assumed in his ministry to the Gentiles: preacher of God's Word.

Review Ephesians 3:1-14, then focus on verses 8-11.

> *. . . that I should preach among the Gentiles the unsearchable riches of Christ, . . .* Ephesians 3:8

1. Paul was given grace for what purpose? . . . .

. . . .

2. What was Paul to preach to the Gentiles? . . . .

. . . .

> *. . . and to make all people see what is the fellowship of the mystery, which from the beginning of the ages has been hidden in God who created all things through Jesus Christ; . . .* Ephesians 3:9

3. What did Paul want all to see through his preaching? . . . .

. . . .

4. How long had this mystery been hidden? Where was this mystery hidden?

. . . .

> *. . . to the intent that now the manifold wisdom of God might be made known by the church to the principalities and powers in the heavenly places, . . .* Ephesians 3:10

5. By whom was the manifold wisdom of God made known?

. . . .

6. To whom? . . . .

. . . .

> *. . . according to the eternal purpose which He accomplished in Christ Jesus our Lord, . . .* Ephesians 3:11

7. What phrase lets you know that the mystery of the church was not an afterthought?

. . . .

8. Who accomplished this eternal purpose?

. . . .

---

explanation

2

ENDLESS RICHES
Searching for buried treasure? You don't need a pirate's map; you need the Word of God. It holds the key to the unsearchable riches of Christ. "Oh, the depth of the riches both of the wisdom and knowledge of God!" (Romans 11:33).

5

MANIFOLD WISDOM
In his book *Be Rich*, Warren Wiersbe says, "This word carries the idea of 'variegated' or 'many-colored.' This suggests the beauty and variety of God's wisdom in His great plan of salvation."

6

PRINCIPALITIES
This refers to angelic beings. People believe that angels know everything, but they don't. Here we see something the angels were curious about—God's plan of salvation for the Gentiles—"things which angels desire to look into" (1 Peter 1:12).

10

GOD SEES
My mother had eyes in the back of her head. If I misbehaved, she always found out. God has the eyes of eternity. Nothing escapes His view. If you misbehave, He'll always see. "For the eyes of the Lord run to and fro throughout the whole earth" (2 Chronicles 16:9).

11

GREAT COMMISSION
Some get the great commission backward. Instead of a "go into all the world" mentality, they develop a "come to our church service" mindset. Christians are salt to a tasteless world. Pour the salt of your testimony out of the saltshaker and into your world. "Go into all the world and preach the Good News to everyone, everywhere" (Mark 16:15, NLT).

9. Paul was a man who practiced what he preached. You may not be a preacher in the pulpit, but God expects your life to speak volumes.

> Journal about a way your actions can speak God's love language this week. (Example: Give your time to a lonely neighbor.)

. . . .

. . . .

. . . .

10. Sometimes your actions, public or private, can distort the message of God's grace to the world around you. List any behaviors in your life that are contradictory. (Example: I'm unethical in my business dealings, making promises I don't intend to keep.)

. . . .

. . . .

. . . .

> Write a prayer confessing this conduct as sin. Ask God to empower you to turn away from it. Pray for a life that proclaims the goodness of God to those people you come in contact with.

. . . .

. . . .

. . . .

11. Maybe your actions have made an impression on unbelievers, but they don't know about your faith. You've shown them the gospel, now it's time to tell them. Name someone who needs to hear the Good News of God's love.

Write a prayer asking God to give you the boldness and opportunity to witness to the person you named.

. . . .

. . . .

. . . .

. . . .

Billy Graham has been called "America's Preacher." *Time* magazine included him in their list of "Heroes of the 20th Century," saying that Billy Graham exemplifies "courage, selflessness, exuberance, superhuman ability and amazing grace." He's a hero admired not just for his achievements but, more important, for his character.

Billy Graham has remained faithful while so many others have faltered because he determined that integrity would be the hallmark of his life and ministry. The foundation to that commitment came early in his organization when his team developed the "Modesto Manifesto" while at a crusade in California. In his autobiography, *Just As I Am,* Billy Graham shared the four commitments included in the manifesto:

Financial Accountability: "We determined to do all we could to avoid financial abuses and to downplay the offering and depend as much as possible on the money raised by the local committees in advance."

Sexual Purity: "We pledged among ourselves to avoid any situation that would have even the appearance of compromise or suspicion. From that day on, I did not travel, meet, or eat alone with a woman other than my wife."

Church Cooperation: "We were determined to cooperate with all who would cooperate with us in the public proclamation of the Gospel, and to avoid an antichurch or anticlergy attitude."

Publicity Integrity: "The tendency among some evangelists was to exaggerate their successes or to claim higher attendance numbers than they really had. This likewise discredited evangelism and brought the whole enterprise under suspicion. . . . In Modesto we committed ourselves to integrity in our publicity and our reporting."

Like the apostle Paul, Billy Graham has been committed to practicing what he preaches. What about you? If you haven't been doing what you've been saying, maybe it's time to make a manifesto of your own.

contemplation
There are many who agree with God in principle but not in practice.
Richard Owen Roberts

105

DAY 5 PAUL'S APPROACH

HIS NAME

There is salvation in no one else! There is no other name in all of heaven for people to call on to save them.
Acts 4:12, NLT

"You kids are going to have to follow me down to the station," the police officer said as I dropped my head and shuffled my feet in the sand. At that moment I knew our little prank had gone too far. It was the middle of a long, hot summer, and we were bored. So a pack of my high school friends decided to take a midnight excursion to the wooded area known as the "twilight zone," where a crazy hermit lived in a dilapidated shack. We were young, stupid, and cocky enough to harass this mythical creature with toilet paper, rock throwing, and name-calling.

It all seemed perfectly innocent until the flashing lights and roaring siren rushed down the dirt road. We ran screaming into the bushes for shelter. The diligent officer of the Ludington Police Department found us anyway. I learned then that it's good to have friends in high places. When I told him my mother was married to Eugene Christman, the city attorney, he immediately changed his tone. Approaching him in my own name only made him scowl. Coming to him in the name of a man more powerful and influential than I was changed everything. Instead of taking us to jail, he sent us home with a stern lecture and a warning to keep out of trouble.

Paul knew the value of friends in high places, too. He knew the only way to approach almighty God was in the name of His Son, turning judgment into justification.

exploration

This week we have gained valuable insight into the life of Paul and have been challenged to a higher standard because of his example. Today we look at the manner in which Paul approached God.

Review Ephesians 3:1-13, then focus on verses 11-12.

. . . in Christ Jesus our Lord, in whom we have boldness and access with confidence through faith in Him.
Ephesians 3:11-12

1. In whom do we have confident access to God? . . . .

. . . .

2. What two titles did Paul give Jesus? . . . .

. . . .

3. What words describe how we can approach God? . . . .

. . . .

4. What gives us access to God? . . . .

. . . .

5. What four things motivated Paul to approach God?

B_____

A_____

C_____

F_____

6. According to Hebrews 4:15-16, to what do we have access?

. . . .

7. Paul used the preposition *in* three times to describe his approach to God. Fill in the blanks to discover who opened the door of access.

In _____

In _____

In _____

explanation

2
CHRIST
Christ is sometimes translated "Messiah." It is a name that showed that Jesus was the long-awaited king and deliverer. Jesus was clearly identified as the Messiah, "You are the Christ, the Son of the living God" (Matthew 16:16).

3
BOLDNESS
A courageous or daring spirit in the face of danger. Boldness is the courage to do something despite fear. Peter feared the storm but got out of the boat anyway, boldly going where only God had gone before.

5
CONFIDENCE
Paul's confident access to God was not the result of his bravery but of his belief. In the Old Testament only the high priest could enter God's presence once a year. Jesus changed that—now anyone can boldly approach God. "We can boldly enter heaven's Most Holy Place because of the blood of Jesus" (Hebrews 10:19, NLT).

transformation

8
LORD
The word *lord* denotes ownership, implying absolute control. It applies to owners over slaves and kings over subjects. . . . It is applied to God as owner and ruler of the earth. *Lord* is also applied to Jesus since by His death He acquired a special ownership of mankind (*New Unger's Bible Dictionary*).

9
LORD OF LIFE
Jesus taught his disciples that responding to His lordship is not just verbal, it's active. He doesn't want to be just the Lord of your lips, but the Lord of your life. "Not all people who sound religious are really godly. They may refer to me as 'Lord,' but they still won't enter the Kingdom of Heaven. The decisive issue is whether they obey my Father in heaven" (Matthew 7:21, NLT).

8. Paul used two titles to describe Jesus: Christ and Lord. Jesus wants to be much more than the Savior from your sins. He wants to be the Lord of your life. Fill in the chart below to discover ways to surrender to your Lord Jesus Christ.

SCRIPTURE	LESSON ON LORDSHIP
Matt. 9:36-38.	
Mark 2:27-28.	
Rom. 14:8-9.	
1 Cor. 6:13-14; 19-20	
Col. 3:17-21; 23-24.	

9. God owns you. He is the Lord of your life and death, physical appetites, and relationships. The one thing you should never say is, "No, Lord." Lordship demands obedience.

Journal about an area from the chart above where you have not surrendered to your Lord. What ways have you "just said no" to Him?

. . . .

. . . .

. . . .

. . . .

Journal a prayer of repentance asking the Lord to forgive you for disobedience. Ask Him to help you "just say *yes*"!

. . . .

. . . .

. . . .

. . . .

10. We discovered that the role of subjects in relationship to their lord is obedience. The role of a lord in relationship to His subjects is provision. Our Lord is a good shepherd who provides all our needs.

Read Psalm 23, then circle the good things He has provided: "The Lord is my shepherd; I have everything I need. He lets me rest in green meadows; he leads me beside peaceful streams. He renews my strength. He guides me along right paths, bringing honor to his name. Even when I walk through the dark valley of death, I will not be afraid, for you are close beside me. Your rod and your staff protect and comfort me. You prepare a feast for me in the presence of my enemies. You welcome me as a guest, anointing my head with oil. My cup overflows with blessings. Surely your goodness and unfailing love will pursue me all the days of my life, and I will live in the house of the Lord forever" (NLT).

After applying for a marriage license in Detroit, a bachelor didn't return to the county clerk's office until eleven years later to pick up the important piece of paper. When the clerk asked why he and his bride had waited so long to get married, he admitted, "We had a few disagreements about the details." How tragic that this couple let years pass by because they were too stubborn to yield on minor details!

Christians have the same problem. Some waste years refusing to let the Lord Jesus arrange and govern the details of their agreement. A 1991 Gallup poll revealed that 78 percent of Americans expect to go to heaven. However, many of them hardly ever pray, read the Bible, or attend church. They admit that they live to please themselves instead of God. Today we learned that if He's not Lord of all, He's not Lord at all! To be your Savior, He must also be your Lord. When you surrender all to Him, you will experience the confidence and boldness to approach His throne in faith. You will discover that your Lord wants to be your provider and husband, too. Are you ready to sign on the dotted line?

Exceedingly Abundantly More

$\mathcal{D}$anny Sampson used a hand-me-down Colt .45 to rob a bank in Canada, getting away with $6,000. When the Mounties caught up with him, they confiscated the gun and sent it to their laboratory, where it was recognized as a collector's item. Danny discovered that he didn't have to rob a bank; his gun was worth $100,000!

As Christians, we are exhorted to have knowledge of all that we possess in Christ. Danny Sampson didn't realize the value of what was already his, so he did something foolish. When we don't take advantage of our resources in God's promises, we are tempted to fulfill our needs through fleshly means. It's human nature to look for power, love, and knowledge to make our lives rich. Through the "path of flesh," some find power in politics, love through lust, knowledge at a university, and fullness from a bottle. But these attempts to fulfill our needs are as futile as Danny's attempt to get rich by stealing. Paul says you don't have to rob a bank to get rich; you simply need to ask your heavenly Father.

This week we come to Paul's second prayer in the book of Ephesians. His first prayer was for believers to receive illumination—to *see* what treasures God has for us. Now Paul asks for inspiration—to *utilize* the wealth that is exceedingly, abundantly more than we can conceive.

DAY 1
Bowing Down—Looking Up

DAY 2
Glorious Riches

DAY 3
Mansion Maker

DAY 4
Hidden Treasure

DAY 5
There's More?

DAY **1** BOWING DOWN—
LOOKING UP

preparation

Father, I bow down to You because You alone are worthy of praise. I look up to You because You are the source of all that is good. Please inspire me to use all that You have for me. Amen.

INSPIRATION

All Scripture is inspired by God and is useful to teach us what is true and to make us realize what is wrong in our lives. It straightens us out and teaches us to do what is right.
2 Timothy 3:16, NLT

explanation

2

BOWING
The practice of bowing was intended to convey an attitude of reverence, respect, humility, and homage toward others. A bent knee reveals a surrendered heart. "'As surely as I live,' says the Lord, 'every knee will bow to me and every tongue will confess allegiance to God'" (Romans 14:11, NLT).

exploration

Paul gives us clues here about his view of the God to whom he prayed. As you study today, ask God to reveal Himself to you in a new and powerful way.

Read through Ephesians 3 to get a feel for the tone, language, and content of this chapter, then focus on verses 14-15.

> *For this reason I bow my knees to the Father of our Lord Jesus Christ, . . .* Ephesians 3:14

1. "For this reason" is a transitional phrase encouraging the reader to look back before looking forward. Looking back at last week's lesson, what are the reasons for Paul's prayer?

. . . .

2. What was Paul's physical posture as he prayed? . . . .

. . . .

3. To whom did Paul bow? . . . .

. . . .

> *. . . from whom the whole family in heaven and earth is named, . . .* Ephesians 3:15

4. Who is named after the Father? . . . .

. . . .

5. What two locations are given for God's family? . . . .

. . . .

6. According to John 1:12-13,

   a. Who makes up the family of God? . . . .

   . . . .

   b. Based on these verses, how do you know that you are
      a member of God's family?

   . . . .

transformation

7. Paul's prayers were so passionate they brought him to his knees.
   How would you describe your prayer life?

   Journal how you see your prayer life now and how you
   would like to see it be strengthened.

   . . . .

   . . . .

   . . . .

   . . . .

   . . . .

   . . . .

   . . . .

   . . . .

4
BORN OF GOD
Biblical adoption
cannot be rescinded—
you are God's child now
and forever. "You
received the Spirit of
adoption by whom we
cry out, 'Abba, Father.'
. . . We are children of
God" (Romans 8:15-16).

5
EXTENDED FAMILY
"Family in heaven and
earth" speaks of saints
from every age—those
presently in heaven and
those who remain on
earth. God is the Father
of the living and the
dead. The moment
Christian loved ones
leave your side they
will find themselves by
His side. "To be absent
from the body and to
be present with the
Lord." (2 Corinthians
5:8).

7
RED-HOT PRAYER
What's the temperature
of your prayers? Luke-
warm prayers are inef-
fective. James tells us
to pray red-hot prayers:
"The effective, fervent
prayer of a righteous
man avails much"
(James 5:16). The word
fervent means "to be
hot or to boil." Is your
prayer closet chilly?
Then turn up the heat!

POSTURE
Don't be an imposter in your posture. You could have your knees bent with a stiff neck praying, "My will be done," instead of, "Thy will be done." Your posture is more than a physical position; it's a spiritual condition.

Think about a person who is a vital, confident prayer warrior. What qualities of that person's prayer life attract you?

. . . .

. . . .

. . . .

. . . .

. . . .

. . . .

. . . .

8. Paul bowed down while he prayed. Fill in the chart to discover what other postures for prayer are recorded in Scripture.

SCRIPTURE	PERSON	POSTURE
Exod. 34:8		
1 Kings 8:22		
1 Chron. 17:16		
Matt. 26:39		

9. How's your prayer posture? Which of the postures from the chart above have you practiced in your prayer life? Pick one that you've never experienced before, and try it now by reciting the Lord's Prayer: "Our Father in heaven, hallowed be Your name. Your kingdom come. Your will be done on earth as it is in heaven. Give us this day our daily bread. And forgive us our debts, as we forgive our debtors. And do not lead us into temptation, but deliver us from the evil one. For Yours is the kingdom and the power and the glory forever. Amen" (Matthew 6:9-13).

Emperor worship began in the first century B.C. after the Roman senate voted to deify Julius Caesar. In his honor a temple was erected as a place of worship. Under Augustus Caesar, emperor worship flourished and was incorporated into local religions. Under Emperor Trajan, Christians who would not renounce their allegiance to Christ and bow down to worship the emperor were often executed.

The penalties early Christians suffered were terrible beyond description. Christians were flung to the lions or burned at the stake. Caesar Nero drenched Christians in pitch and set them on fire, using them as living torches to light his gardens. They were tortured on the rack or scraped with pincers; molten lead was poured upon them; red-hot brass plates were affixed to the tenderest parts of their bodies; their eyes were torn out.

There's a time to bow down and a time to stand tall. Christians have one true allegiance—to God. Jesus demonstrated the delicate balance between God and country when He said, "Render to Caesar the things that are Caesar's, and to God the things that are God's" (Mark 12:17). We may be called to honor king and country, but we, like Paul, must never bow down and worship anyone else but God.

DAY 2 GLORIOUS RICHES

ABUNDANCE
God will generously provide all you need. Then you will always have everything you need and plenty left over to share with others. 2 Corinthians 9:8, NLT

At a church meeting a very wealthy man rose to tell those present about his Christian faith. "I'm a millionaire," he said, "and I attribute it all to the rich blessings of God in my life. I remember that turning point in my faith. I had just earned my first dollar, and I went to a church meeting that night. The speaker was a missionary who told about his work. I knew that I only had a dollar bill and had to either give it all to God's work or nothing at all. So at that moment I decided to give my whole dollar to God. I believe that God blessed that decision, and that is why I am a rich man today."

There was an awed silence at his testimony. As he sat down, a little old lady sitting in the same pew whispered, "I dare you to do it again."

It's easier to give all that you have when you don't have very much. This man gave when the stakes were small. But would he be willing to give big when the stakes were raised? God is an extravagant giver—His riches and resources are limitless. He's got it all and He's willing to share it all with His children, "according to the riches of His glory."

exploration

Yesterday we learned of Paul's posture in prayer. Today we will examine the first petition in Paul's prayer for believers.

Review Ephesians 3, then focus on verse 16.

> *. . . that He would grant you, according to the riches of His glory, to be strengthened with might through His Spirit in the inner man, . . . Ephesians 3:16*

1. What did Paul ask God to grant the Ephesians?. . . . .

. . . .

2. According to what resources does God grant prayer requests?

. . . .

3. The riches of God's glory are a powerful resource. How can they help us, according to verse 16?

. . . .

4. Through what means does God strengthen believers? . . . .

. . . .

5. Where does God strengthen believers? . . . .

. . . .

6. In 2 Corinthians 4:16-18 Paul contrasts differences between the "inward" and the "outward" person. Read the passage, then place the following key phrases under the heading that indicates where these things happen: perishing, renewed, light affliction, eternal glory, seen, not seen, temporary, eternal.

INWARD PERSON	OUTWARD PERSON

. . . .

. . . .

. . . .

. . . .

transformation

7. We all need to be strengthened inwardly through God's Spirit. Mark an *s* by the items that *strengthen* you spiritually (i.e., inwardly) and mark with a *w* those activities that *weaken* you spiritually.

---

explanation

2

GOD'S RICHES
This term is used in a figurative sense to represent the gifts and graces of God's Holy Spirit, as in, "Do you despise the riches of His goodness, forbearance, and longsuffering, not knowing that the goodness of God leads you to repentance?" (Romans 2:4).

4

THE SPIRIT
This is power in a Person—the Holy Spirit. This is power with a purpose—"When the Holy Spirit has come upon you, you will receive power and will tell people about me everywhere" (Acts 1:8, NLT). With the Holy Spirit's power we will tell the world about Jesus!

7

SPIRITUALLY STRONG
Gold's Gym or God's Gym—where do you work out? Society is obsessed with the beautiful body; God is concerned with the strong soul. "Physical exercise has some value, but spiritual exercise is much more important, for it promises a reward in both this life and the next" (1 Timothy 4:8, NLT).

9

INNER TURMOIL

The inner person is made up of two entities: the spirit and the flesh. There is a constant battle between them. The one you surrender to is the one that will grow stronger and win the war. "Watch and pray, lest you enter into temptation. The spirit indeed is willing, but the flesh is weak" (Mark 14:38).

10

INNER STRENGTH

If you discovered a genie in a bottle and were granted three wishes, would "strength" make it to the top of your list? Probably not. But more than fame or fortune, God knows that supernatural strength is one of our greatest needs— "we are weak but He is strong."

____ Reading the Bible   ____ Surrender

____ Prayer   ____ Entertainment

____ Worry   ____ Life-dominating habits

____ Godly counsel   ____ Seeking pleasure

____ Fellowship with others   ____ Jealousy

____ Adversity   ____ Other_____

8. Which of the above activities (or others) do you need to incorporate more into your life?

. . . .

. . . .

9. Which of the above activities (or others) do you need to eliminate from your life through God's strength?

. . . .

. . . .

Journal your thoughts about what keeps you from doing things that will strengthen you spiritually. How can you begin to make these changes in your life through the glorious riches of God?

. . . .

. . . .

. . . .

. . . .

. . . .

. . . .

10. Paul showed that it is God's will for us "to be strengthened with might through His Spirit in the inner man" (Ephesians 3:16).

Rewording Ephesians 3:16, journal a personal and specific prayer asking God to help you overcome the flesh through the power of His Spirit.

. . . .

. . . .

. . . .

. . . .

. . . .

. . . .

. . . .

Iris Bammert walked slower than most to the podium. Her face reflected a quiet confidence that no matter how long it took, she would reach her goal. At last, she reached the microphone and spoke with gentle strength. "God has let me know that in this life we have tribulation, but be of good cheer. I have overcome the world."

Iris had suffered a debilitating stroke in the prime of her life. Her whole world changed in a moment—from self-sufficiency to complete dependency. She can't drive a car anymore; instead, she's driven to her knees in prayer, seeking a strength that is not her own. She can barely speak, but God enabled her to remind the women in our Bible study, "This life is not so important. Don't forget the Lord is the One who does everything in and through us."

God does not ask you to walk in your own strength—He knows that is impossible. However, He does promise to give you the strength you need to walk in a way that is pleasing to Him. Philippians 4:13 reminds us, "I can do everything with the help of Christ who gives me the strength I need" (NLT).

DAY 3 MANSION MAKER

It was a vintage home nestled among the tall trees near the University of New Mexico. Perhaps it was old-fashioned with its hardwood floors instead of carpet, but it suited our young family perfectly. The old furnace was noisy and inefficient, but that didn't matter. Our hearts were warmed by the love we felt toward one another. At least that's what I thought, until the day Skip called to say, "Would it be okay if I bring Franklin Graham home for dinner?"

"Franklin Graham!" I said. "Son of Ruth and Billy Graham? The president of Samaritan's Purse International?" As I switched into high gear tidying up the place and putting dinner in the oven, the walls began to close in around me. I thought, *We don't have enough dining-room chairs for everyone. If that furnace acts up tonight, I'll be so embarrassed. Why did we buy an old worn-down house with only one bathroom?* When our guest arrived, he disarmed us with his genteel southern charm and grateful spirit. He insisted on sitting on the floor with Skip while they ate. Franklin made me feel like our little house was more than an old home; it felt like a mansion.

Guess who's coming to have dinner with you? Jesus. He said, "If you hear me calling and open the door, I will come in, and we will share a meal as friends" (Revelation 3:20, NLT). You may not have the latest fashion to wear, and perhaps you've got problems with the plumbing. Yet, your humble Savior will come in, sit down, and make Himself at home. Your heart can become a mansion for the Maker of heaven and earth!

exploration

We know that we need to be strengthened inwardly by God's power. Paul's second petition is for Christ to dwell in us.

Review Ephesians 3, then focus on verse 17.

. . . that Christ may dwell in your hearts through faith;
that you, being rooted and grounded in love, . . .
Ephesians 3:17

1. Summarize the two requests Paul made here. . . . .

. . . .

IN YOUR HEART
God promises to take up residence in your heart. The God who can measure the universe with His hand is at home in your heart. "If anyone loves Me, he will keep My word; and My Father will love him, and We will come to him and make Our home with him" (John 14:23).

2. Where did he pray for Christ to dwell? How? . . . .

. . . .

3. Read John 14:17. What other member of the Trinity takes up residence in the heart of the believer?

. . . .

ROOTED
This is an agricultural metaphor referring to the underground roots of a plant. To be grounded is an architectural term that speaks of a building's foundation. These two word pictures show that God's love toward a believer is both deep and strong.

4. What two words in Ephesians 3:17 describe stability in the life of a believer?

. . . .

5. What are Christians to be rooted and grounded in?. . . . .

. . . .

6. According to Matthew 22:37-39, who are believers commanded to love?

. . . .

THE OWNER
God is more than a houseguest. He is the rightful owner of your heart/home. You're not leasing the place to God—He holds the title deed. "For you were bought at a price; therefore glorify God in your body and in your spirit, which are God's" (1 Corinthians 6:20).

transformation

7. We've seen that the Trinity of God dwells within a believer's heart. Check the areas below that are evidence that your heart is God's home.

___ I believe Jesus is Messiah.

___ I believe Jesus died for my sins.

___ I have repented of my sins.

___ I asked Jesus to be Lord and Savior.

___ He has a place at our table.

___ We've cleaned out the closets.

___ He's rearranged the furniture.

Bible scholar Leon
Morris said, "If Christ
dwells in our hearts he
is at the very center of
our being and exercises
his influence over all
that we do and are."
That may mean it's time
for spring-cleaning. Are
there areas in your life
that need to be washed,
painted, or repaired?"

8. Since your heart is Christ's home, journal through the exercise below:

Ask God to reveal any closet space or dark corners that are not under His influence. (Perhaps you've been keeping a bad habit neatly tucked away—He sees it.)

. . . .

. . . .

. . . .

. . . .

. . . .

Acknowledge what other things have cluttered your heart and distracted your focus. (A good thing can become a bad thing if it keeps you from the best thing—Jesus!)

. . . .

. . . .

. . . .

. . . .

. . . .

Write a prayer and purposefully open each "room" in your heart to the fresh work of Christ. (Spring-cleaning includes airing out the place—let His Spirit blow through.)

. . . .

. . . .

. . . .

. . . .

. . . .

9. A heart full of God's love needs to reach out. Jesus commanded us to love our neighbors as ourselves. Who are the people in your neighborhood? In the chart, name some of your neighbors, then list a way you will demonstrate God's love to them.

NEIGHBOR	HOW I WILL DEMONSTRATE GOD'S LOVE
. . . .	
. . . .	
. . . .	
. . . .	
. . . .	
. . . .	

IN LOVE
The Greek word used for *love* is *agape*—love that is a matter of the will, not of the emotions. Thus, we choose to love whether we feel like it or not. "Love your enemies! . . . In that way, you will be acting as true children of your Father in heaven" (Matthew 5:44-45, NLT).

James Hewett tells the story of a sailor shipwrecked on a South Sea Island. He was seized by the natives, carried to the village, and set on a crude throne. He soon learned that it was their custom each year to make one man a king—for a year. He liked this, until he discovered that every year each king was banished to an island where he starved to death. The sailor didn't like that, but he was smart and he *was* king. So he put his carpenters to work making boats, his farmers to work transplanting fruit trees and crops, and his masons to work building houses. When his reign was over, he was banished, not to a barren island, but to an island of abundance. This sailor was wise. He learned to live for the future, not merely the present.

Foolishly, some people are so busy taking care of their earthly homes they neglect their heavenly dwelling place. Paul taught that while the deeds we perform now don't purchase a place in heaven, they do supply spiritual "building materials" for our heavenly homes. What will your mansion look like? "For no one can lay any other foundation than the one we already have—Jesus Christ. Now anyone who builds on that foundation may use gold, silver, jewels, wood, hay, or straw. But there is going to come a time of testing at the judgment day to see what kind of work each builder has done. Everyone's work will be put through the fire to see whether or not it keeps its value" (1 Corinthians 3:11-13, NLT).

contemplation
Father! replenish
  with thy grace
this longing heart
  of mine;
Make it thy quiet
  dwelling place,
thy sacred inmost
  shrine!
Angelus Silesius

DAY 4 — HIDDEN TREASURE

There was a man in Wales who sought to win the affection of a certain lady for forty-two years before she finally said yes. The couple, both seventy-four, recently became man and wife. For more than forty years the persistent, rather shy man slipped a weekly love letter under his neighbor's door. But she continually refused to speak to him and mend the spat that had parted them many years before.

After writing 2,184 love letters without ever getting a spoken or written answer, the single-hearted old man eventually summoned up enough courage to present himself in person. He knocked on the door of the reluctant lady and asked for her hand. To his delight and surprise, she accepted.

Like these two senior citizens, we discover that the greatest treasure in life is true love. Gold loses its luster. Money sprouts wings and is gone. Eventually, we all concede, things don't really matter, relationships do!

Paul understood the value of a relationship with God. So he prayed that Christians would know the unknowable and discover His hidden treasure. God's letters of love were delivered over centuries by prophets and apostles to the hearts of His people. But when God did not get the desired response from His loved ones, He sent His Son. That was God's way of revealing to us the height, depth, width, and length of His love. Open the door of your heart and say "I do" to your persistent God.

exploration

God's love is a firm foundation. In Paul's third petition, we discover just how great that love is.

Review Ephesians 3, then focus on verses 18-19.

... [that you] may be able to comprehend with all the saints what is the width and length and depth and height—... Ephesians 3:18

 1. What more did Paul want for the Ephesians?

. . . .

2. Who else will be able to comprehend this knowledge?

. . . .

3. Paul offers some insight into Christ's love. What are the four dimensions Paul uses to describe the love of Christ?

. . . .

. . . .

4. Connect the dots from width to length, then separately from height to depth.

height
●

● width   ● length

● depth

a. How do these four dimensions illustrate Christ's love?

. . . .

. . . .

b. Now draw an arrow pointing outward from each of these dimensions. Label the arrows like a compass. What insight do you gain about Christ's love from this picture?

. . . .

. . . .

---

explanation

COMPREHEND
To comprehend is "to lay hold of so as to possess as one's own, to appropriate; to seize upon, take possession of" *(Vine's Expository Dictionary).* Paul is praying for saints to grasp and possess the incredible love of Christ. This is the kind of love you can take to the bank!

 4a

CROSS OF LOVE
On a highway in Louisiana there's a billboard high above the city as you reach the Mississippi River bridge. On it is a picture of Jesus hanging on the cross, head bowed. The caption says, "It's Your Move!" If you reach up as far as you can, God will reach all the way down.

 4b

REACHING OUT
The love of Christ reaches out in every direction, extending beyond the horizon. No matter which way you turn you'll find God's love. "Your unfailing love is higher than the heavens. Your faithfulness reaches to the clouds" (Psalm 108:4, NLT).

UNKNOWABLE
Knowing the unknow-able is possible only through the inspiration of the Holy Spirit. The Spirit of God is the best teacher to have. "The Helper, the Holy Spirit, whom the Father will send in My name, He will teach you all things" (John 14:26).

. . . to know the love of Christ which passes knowledge;
. . . Ephesians 3:19

5. What did Paul pray believers will know?

. . . .

6. What phrase leads you to believe this knowledge is beyond human comprehension?

. . . .

7. Why do you think Paul made this seemingly contradictory request?

. . . .

transformation

8. What is the most profound or creative way you have ever demonstrated your love for another person?

. . . .

. . . .

. . . .

TRUE LOVE
The evidence of true love is not in whispering sweet nothings but in showing sincere actions. Words of adoration that never lead to acts of devotion are empty. "This is My command-ment, that you love one another as I have loved you. Greater love has no one than this, than to lay down one's life for his friends" (John 15:12-13).

9. What is one of the best ways someone else has revealed their love toward you?

. . . .

. . . .

Journal about how that action made you feel and what it meant to you.

. . . .

. . . .

. . . .

. . . .

10. Name those who desperately need to truly comprehend—grab hold of—God's boundless love.

. . . .

. . . .

Journal a prayer that God will go knocking on the door of their hearts. Pray for your opportunity to go knocking on the door of their house and show God's love to them.

. . . .

. . . .

. . . .

. . . .

10
LOVE'S JOURNEY
To comprehend God's love requires a trip of eighteen inches from the head to the heart. It's not enough to know God's love intellectually; we must feel it experientially and demonstrate it practically. "If we love each other, God lives in us, and his love has been brought to full expression through us" (1 John 4:12, NLT).

God's love knows no limits; He has gone to great lengths to express His boundless love to us. It reminds me of the story Richard Seltzer tells in his book *Mortal Lessons,* a story of a deep and wide kind of love.

"I stand by the bed where a young woman lies, her face postoperative, her mouth twisted. A tiny twig of the facial nerve, the one to the muscles of her mouth, has been severed. The surgeon had followed with religious fervor the curve of her flesh; I promise you that. Yet, to remove the tumor in her cheek, he had cut the little nerve. Her young husband is in the room. He stands on the opposite side of the bed, and together they seem to dwell in the evening lamplight, isolated from me, private. They touch each other so generously, greedily.

"The woman speaks: 'Will my mouth always be like this?'

"I respond: 'Yes, it will. It is because the nerve was cut.'

"She nods, and is silent. But the young man smiles.

"'I like it,' he says. 'It is kind of cute.'

"At once I know who he is, and I lower my gaze. One is not bold in an encounter with God. Unmindful, he bends to kiss her crooked mouth, and I am so close I can see how he twists his own lips to accommodate to hers, to show her that their kiss still works."

contemplation
If we have got the true love of God shed abroad in our hearts, we will show it in our lives. We will not have to go up and down the earth proclaiming it. We will show it in everything we say or do.
Dwight Lyman Moody

DAY 5 — THERE'S MORE?

When my husband and I were new to the ministry, our first dinner invitation came from Paul and Millie Ciaccio, an affectionate couple who had been raised in New York by old-world Italian parents. We arrived at their mountain home with big appetites. Paul ushered us into the kitchen as Millie set out chips and salsa. "Hope you're hungry," she said. A bountiful salad and crusty Italian bread was the first course, and Millie beamed with pride as she served one of her mother's famous pasta dishes. "Do you want seconds?" she asked, heaping a mountain-sized portion on my plate. My eyes bulged and my waistband was getting tight, but I thought, *I'd better eat what's put before me; dinner is almost over.* At that moment Paul came in with the main course.

In disbelief I said, "There's more?" Oh yes, there was more—exceedingly, abundantly more: pot roast with potatoes and vegetables, followed by homemade peach pie à la mode along with fresh fruit and coffee. I learned that old-world Italians express their love by filling you with food, and the Ciaccio's love was so great I was ready to pop!

God loves to fill His children full of goodness, too! God has sent His Spirit to fill our inner being, Jesus to fill our hearts, and still there's more—exceedingly, abundantly more. Paul prays that we will be filled with all the fullness of God—what more could you possibly want?

exploration

We have learned so much from this beautiful passage. Today we examine the fourth and last element of Paul's prayer for believers.

Review Ephesians 3, then focus on verses 19-21.

. . . that you may be filled with all the fullness of God.
Ephesians 3:19

1. Paul prayed for believers to be filled with what? . . . .

. . . .

Now to Him who is able to do exceedingly abundantly above all that we ask or think, according to the power that works in us, . . . Ephesians 3:20

2. Now we come to the conclusion of Paul's prayer, in which he shares the reasons he believes God can and will answer his prayer. How does Paul first describe God?

. . . .

3. What words describe God's amazing ability to act? . . . .

. . . .

4. Above what does God's power exceed? . . . .

. . . .

5. Where is God's exceptional power at work? . . . .

. . . .

. . . to Him be glory in the church by Christ Jesus to all generations, forever and ever. Amen.
Ephesians 3:21

6. Who receives glory?. . . . .

. . . .

7. To whom is it revealed and for how long? . . . .

. . . .

explanation

1

FILLED UP
When you're full of something, there's no room for anything else. A person filled with hostility has no room for peace; a person filled with love has no room for hate. To be filled with *all* the fullness of God means there's no room for self. All of God, none of me.

5

POWER AT WORK
We often desire power to control others—"a power trip." God gives us power so we can control ourselves. The transition from having power to using power wisely is a trip worth taking. "God has not given us a spirit of fear and timidity, but of power, love, and self-discipline" (2 Timothy 1:7, NLT).

7

TO HIM BE GLORY
Candles melt away, lightbulbs burn out, sunsets fade, but in the heavenly city God's glory will shine brightly forever and ever. "And the city has no need of sun or moon, for the glory of God illuminates the city, and the Lamb is its light" (Revelation 21:23, NLT).

DAILY INVESTMENT
What would you do
if you were given
$86,400? Would you fill
your checkbook or your
closet? You have been
given 86,400 seconds
in every day. Are you
spending them wisely
or squandering them?
"Teach us to number
our days, that we may
gain a heart of wisdom"
(Psalm 90:12).

9

POSSIBILITIES
How big is your God?
Can He heal a cold as
easily as cancer? Is He
able to repair relation-
ships as well as resurrect
the dead? "Humanly
speaking, it is impossi-
ble. But not with God.
Everything is possible
with God" (Mark 10:27,
NLT). Don't put limits on
a limitless God! What-
ever box you've put
Him in—it's too small.

transformation

8. What are your days full of? On a sheet of lined paper, make
a grid: In a column on the left, list the hours of the day from
6:00 A.M. to 10:00 P.M.; In a row across the top, list the days of
the week. Then fill in your activities and routines. If there's no
room for God in your daily schedule, perhaps it's time to do
some holy editing. Place an *E* by the activities that are essential,
that cannot be removed (work, meals, church worship, etc.);
place an *O* by the items that are optional (TV viewing, hobbies,
phone calls, etc.).

Journal about the ways you can empty your schedule
of distractions and fill it with devotion to God.

. . . .

. . . .

. . . .

. . . .

9. Paul concluded his prayer with an amazing declaration of God's
overwhelming ability to answer our requests. God is "able to do
exceedingly abundantly above all that we ask or think." With
this in mind work through the steps below.

Step One: Journal about the most difficult situation you
are aware of.

. . . .

. . . .

. . . .

. . . .

. . . .

Step Two: Use your spiritual imagination to dream of the best possible solution to that situation. Journal about the solution you came up with.

. . . .

. . . .

. . . .

. . . .

. . . .

Step Three: Now journal a prayer asking God to do something bigger and better than your wildest dreams. Ask Him to put His unlimited resources to work.

. . . .

. . . .

. . . .

. . . .

. . . .

Is there such a thing as an "impossible dream"? One small-minded man living in the nineteenth century believed so. When asked if he thought it would be possible for men to fly in the air like birds, he responded skeptically, "Flight is strictly reserved for the angels, and I beg you not to repeat your suggestion lest you be guilty of blasphemy!" Ironically, the man was Milton Wright, father of Orville and Wilbur—two men who dreamed big dreams. Only thirty years later near Kitty Hawk, North Carolina, they made their first flight in a heavier-than-air machine, the prototype for modern airplanes. They proved that impossible dreams can come true.

The apostle Paul wanted Christians to believe that the impossible is possible with God. He wanted them to understand that impossible prayers can come true through the ability of a God who can do exceedingly abundantly above all that you ask or think. Go ahead, dream big dreams; then pray impossible prayers. God can make them soar!

contemplation
God calls us to live a life we cannot live, so that we must depend on him for supernatural ability. We are called to do the impossible, to live beyond our natural ability.
Erwin W. Lutzer

Coming of Age

When a mother eagle builds a nest, she begins with broken branches, sharp rocks, and a number of other items that seem unsuitable for the project. Then she lines this prickly foundation with a thick layer of feathers, wool, or fur from animals she has killed, making a soft place to lay her eggs. When the baby birds reach flying age, this comfortable nest and the free meals the mother brings make them a bit reluctant to leave. That's when the mother eagle begins "stirring up the nest." She pulls away the soft layers, exposing the sharp rocks and branches. Eventually, this and other promptings force the young eagles to leave their once-comfortable home and move on to maturity.

Coming of age isn't easy for eagles or human beings; there are dues to be paid all along the way. Like a mother eagle, God knows when you are fully equipped, ready to leave the nest and fly into adventures untold. This week in Ephesians, Paul urges you to grow up in Christ, because you "should no longer be children, tossed to and fro, . . . but, . . . [growing] up in all things into Him who is the head—Christ" (Ephesians 4:14-15).

DAY 1
The Father's Business

DAY 2
All in the Family

DAY 3
Dues Paid

DAY 4
Fully Equipped

DAY 5
All Grown Up

DAY 1 THE FATHER'S BUSINESS

preparation

Dear Father, the work that You've given me to do has given purpose to my life. Thank You for including me in Your family's business. Please give me the time and energy to get the job done. Amen.

GOD'S WORK

All of us must quickly carry out the tasks assigned us by the one who sent me, because there is little time left before the night falls and all work comes to an end. John 9:4, NLT

explanation

WORTHY CALLING

Worthy means "to weigh as much," like the balancing of scales. For a believer to walk worthy of his calling, his daily life must weigh as much as his high position as a member of God's family.

exploration

In the first three chapters of Ephesians, Paul taught Christians what to *believe*. Beginning with Ephesians 4 and continuing through the end of the book, Paul taught Christians how to *behave* in light of their faith.

Read through Ephesians 4 to get a feel for the tone, language, and content of this chapter, then focus on verses 1-3.

> *I, therefore, the prisoner of the Lord, beseech you to walk worthy of the calling with which you were called,* . . . Ephesians 4:1

1. What is Paul asking believers to do? . . . .

. . . .

2. Of what should believers walk worthy? . . . .

. . . .

3. Fill in the chart to discover more about our worthy calling.

SCRIPTURE	DESCRIPTION OF CALLING
Rom. 11:29	
1 Cor. 1:26-27	
Phil. 3:14	

2 Tim. 1:9 . . . .

Heb. 3:1 . . . .

> *. . . with all lowliness and gentleness, with longsuffering, bearing with one another in love, . . .* Ephesians 4:2

4. We must learn *how* to walk worthy of this high call. What four virtues characterize a worthy walk?

. . . .

. . . .

5. What do these attributes help a believer do? . . . .

. . . .

> *. . . endeavoring to keep the unity of the Spirit in the bond of peace.* Ephesians 4:3

6. What kind of unity is described? . . . .

. . . .

7. How is this unity achieved? . . . .

. . . .

8. What phrase lets us know that keeping unity requires effort?

. . . .

transformation

9. Today we discovered there are godly virtues that help believers to "bear with one another." Jesus is the perfect example of forbearance because He exhibits all of these virtues in bearing with us. Fill in the chart below to discover His character traits.

5
BEAR WITH LOVE
To bear with love is to display endurance or tolerance toward another's faults or frailties. Although our sin deserves punishment, God in His forbearance is patient, allowing us the opportunity for repentance. "Don't you realize how . . . tolerant . . . God is with you? . . . Can't you see how kind he has been in giving you time to turn from your sin?" (Romans 2:4, NLT).

6
UNITY
Unity means oneness, harmony, agreement. Unity was apparent on the Day of Pentecost when the believers "were all with one accord in one place" (Acts 2:1). The church is a unity in diversity, a fellowship of faith, hope, and love that binds believers together.

8
PEACE WORK
Peace is not passive; it takes effort. Paul said, "Do your part to live in peace with everyone as much as possible" (Romans 12:18, NLT). Peace is possible, depending on you and on others. You can promote peace, but some people may not live peaceably with you.

SCRIPTURE	CHARACTER OF CHRIST

10

WORTHY VIRTUES
Our society has things backwards, exalting popularity over piety. Contrary to the Sermon on the Mount, the world promotes the mighty over the meek; the rich and famous instead of the poor in spirit; and the perverse of mind rather than the pure in heart. But visibility over virtue has little value.

Matt. 11:29 . . . .

Matt. 21:5 . . . .

Luke 9:41 . . . .

John 13:34-35 . . . .

2 Pet. 3:9 . . . .

10. We have discovered the attributes that reveal how to walk worthy of the Lord: lowliness, gentleness, longsuffering, love, and forbearance. Jesus warned his disciples of competitors to a walk that is worthy of Him. Read the following verses and underline the elements that cause your walk to lose its worth: "He who loves father or mother more than Me is not worthy of Me. And he who loves son or daughter more than Me is not worthy of Me. And he who does not take his cross and follow after Me is not worthy of Me. He who finds his life will lose it, and he who loses his life for My sake will find it" (Matthew 10:37-39).

If the worth of your walk with Jesus has been diminished by any of the distractions above, journal a prayer of repentance to God. Tell Jesus how He is worth more than anything in the world to you.

. . . .

. . . .

. . . .

. . . .

11. John the Baptist challenged the religious leaders of his day to "bear fruits worthy of repentance" (Matthew 3:8). To have a worthy walk we must not only get rid of negative behaviors but adopt positive ones as well. Which of the characteristics of Christ from question 1 are lacking in your life?

. . . .

Journal a prayer to God asking Him to plant these character traits deep in your heart so that they may blossom and bring forth good fruit.

. . . .

. . . .

. . . .

. . . .

After inheriting the throne, Boleslaus, king of Poland, carried a picture of his father in his pocket. Before beginning any great work, he would look at the picture and pray that he would do nothing unworthy of his father's name.

In the same way, God's children should honor their heavenly Father's name. Before beginning any work, it would be wise to look at this prayer that is a picture of your Father's heart: "Our Father in heaven, may your name be honored. May your Kingdom come soon. May your will be done here on earth, just as it is in heaven" (Matthew 6:9-10, NLT). Growing up in Christ means you become aware that your actions can either bring disgrace or distinction to your Lord's family name.

DAY 2 ALL IN THE FAMILY

"Hurry up! The prayer's at noon, and they won't wait for us!" Every Christmas for as long as I (Penny) could remember, my mother would urge us to move faster so we could get to the annual family reunion. Upon arrival my mother would whisper, "Put your hands behind your back so you won't break your aunt's pretties." We'd walk with hands behind our backs, listening impatiently to the phrase "Look how grown up you are!" But we knew better. If we were so grown up, why did we have to sit at the kids' table?

Years have passed, but we still have reunions at my aunt's house. Now *I* call out, "Hurry kids! The prayer's at noon, and they won't wait!" I'm the one telling them to put their hands behind their backs, and now I sit at the grown-up table as my children grudgingly head for the kids' table. Once my aunt brought me to the living room and whispered, "Honey, I want to keep these treasures in the family. Why don't you pick one?" My eyes welled up with tears as I chose a beautiful antique plate to take home. I realize that being a member of my family carries great blessings—from a faithful heritage to family heirlooms.

God is calling to each of us, "Hurry up, my Son's wedding supper can't wait!" As mature members of His family, we've been invited to sit at the Lord's table. He also wants to give us treasures from heaven—to keep it all in the family.

exploration

Yesterday we read Paul's plea for believers to walk worthy of their calling. Today we learn that unity in the body of Christ is based on seven spiritual elements.

Review Ephesians 4, then focus on verses 4-6.

There is one body and one Spirit, just as you were called in one hope of your calling; . . . Ephesians 4:4

1. What is the first element for unity listed here?. . . . .

. . . .

2. Based on previous lessons, to what does "one body" refer?

. . . .

3. What is the second element needed for unity?. . . . .

. . . .

4. What is the third element, "one hope," based upon? . . . .

. . . .

. . . one Lord, one faith, one baptism; . . . Ephesians 4:5

5. To whom does the fourth element of our unity refer? . . . .

. . . .

6. The fifth aspect of unity is one faith. According to Romans 10:8-9, what is the "word of faith"?

. . . .

7. List the sixth element for unity in the body of Christ.

. . . .

a. Read Acts 2:38. What is the requirement for baptism?

. . . .

b. In whose name are we baptized?

. . . .

c. What is the promise we receive?

. . . .

explanation

3

HOLY SPIRIT
The Spirit's power is how believers come to Christ and see with new eyes of faith. "He is closer to us than we are to ourselves. Like the eyes of the body through which we see physical things. . . . He is the one through whom all else is seen in a new light."

7

ONE BAPTISM
Baptism without repentance is like doing laundry without using detergent. You may get wet but you won't get clean. "Preach the baptism of repentance for the remission of sins" (Mark 1:4, KJV). Don't get caught in the "sin cycle."

GOD OF ALL
C. S. Lewis said, "We may ignore, but we can nowhere evade, the presence of God. The world is crowded with him. He walks everywhere incognito." The psalmist said, "I can never escape from your spirit! I can never get away from your presence!" (Psalm 139:7, NLT).

. . . one God and Father of all, who is above all, and through all, and in you all. Ephesians 4:6

8. What is the seventh and final element Paul said would give us unity?

. . . .

a. Which phrase speaks of God's sovereignty?

. . . .

b. Of God's ability to work out His purposes?

. . . .

c. Of God indwelling believers?

. . . .

transformation

9. Unity happens when two or more people join together for a common purpose. Check the groups you are currently joined with in some way. Then write the name of that group and how you fit in.

___ Family name: (Example: Jane Doe, sister, wife, and daughter) . . . .

___ Ethnic background: . . . .

___ Political party: . . . .

___ Church denomination: . . . .

___ Club or Society: . . . .

Reflect on one of these groups to which you belong. What things promote unity in that group? What kinds of things cause disunity or problems? Journal your thoughts.

. . . .

. . . .

. . . .

. . . .

10. This week we've examined seven elements that unite all Christians. Place a check next to the ones that you have experienced thus far in your own faith journey. Then briefly write what your experience has been.

____ One Lord: (Example: I accepted Jesus as Lord in 1992.) . . . .

____ One Body: . . . .

____ One Spirit: . . . .

____ One Hope: . . . .

____ One Faith: . . . .

____ One Baptism: . . . .

____ One Father: . . . .

 11. Christians are to unite together into "one body" as completely as the Father, the Son, and the Holy Spirit are joined as "one Lord" in the Trinity. Jesus prayed, "Holy Father, keep them and care for them—all those you have given me—so that they will be united just as we are" (John 17:11, NLT).

Reflect about a situation where the modern-day church has been fractured by disunity (Example: the conflict between the Catholic and Protestant churches in Ireland). Rewrite Jesus' prayer into your own petition for your brothers and sisters in Christ who are in conflict.

. . . .

. . . .

. . . .

. . . .

United we stand, divided we fall. It is estimated that if the thirteen American colonies had been more unified at the time of the American Revolution, they could have won the war for independence in one year. Instead, because of division, it took eight bloody years of battle. As Christians, we're in a battle for souls, and the tragedy is that we fight one another instead of our common enemy. Imagine what the world would be like if the body of Christ would keep the unity and join forces for the kingdom of God.

ONE ANOTHER
There's another "one" we shouldn't miss—one another. Why? Because you're not the only one in the body. The Bible teaches us to love, care, admonish, and pray for one another. "Be kindly affectionate to one another with brotherly love, in honor giving preference to one another" (Romans 12:10).

ONE LORD
The Lord God is the "one Lord." He's One in quantity—unlike the numerous idols the pagans worshiped. He's One in quality— a cut above the rest. He's One in unity— the triune God. "Hear, O Israel: The Lord our God, the Lord is one!" (Deuteronomy 6:4).

contemplation
When men are animated by the love of Christ, they feel united, and the needs, sufferings, and joys of others are felt as their own.
Pope John XXIII

DAY 3 — DUES PAID

My father is a podiatrist; he heals hurting feet for a living. When I was in college, I needed to earn some money, so Dad invited me to come work in his office for the summer. I pictured myself happily typing letters, answering phones, and taking long lunches. Instead, I was given the unpleasant tasks of washing dirty feet and clipping gnarly toenails. As if that wasn't enough, my dad also expected me to show up early to wash windows and clean toilets—something the other office girls never did. "Don't they have janitors for that sort of thing?" I argued, thinking I was above that job. I guess my father wanted me to learn that I had to pay my dues in the work world so I'd grow into a productive adult.

God the Father created heaven and earth, and He heals hurting hearts for a living. His Son wanted to join the family business, and do you know what? He washed feet, too! And He touched lepers. Slept without a bed. And if that were not enough, He endured the shame of the Cross, descended to the lower parts of the earth, and then ascended far above the heavens. Jesus paid the dues for all of humanity's sin so we could grow into mature Christians.

exploration

In these verses Paul reveals the price Christ had to pay so each of us could be given the free gift of grace.

Review Ephesians 4, then focus on verses 7-10.

> *But to each one of us grace was given according to the measure of Christ's gift.* Ephesians 4:7

1. Who is Paul addressing here? . . . .

. . . .

2. What has been given to each one of us?. . . . .

. . . .

3. How is this grace given? . . . .

. . . .

> *Therefore He says: "When He ascended on high, He led captivity captive, and gave gifts to men." Ephesians 4:8*

4. To where did Christ ascend?. . . . .

. . . .

 5. What two things did His ascension accomplish? . . . .

. . . .

> *(Now this, "He ascended"—what does it mean but that He also first descended into the lower parts of the earth? He who descended is also the One who ascended far above all the heavens, that He might fill all things.)* Ephesians 4:9-10

6. According to verse 9, to where did Christ descend?. . . . .

. . . .

7. What was His purpose for ascending far above the heavens?

. . . .

transformation

8. Christ has set us free from the captivity of sin. Yet Paul warned the Galatians of the danger of falling back into a lifestyle of bondage, "Stand fast therefore in the liberty by which Christ has made us free, and do not be entangled again with a yoke of bondage" (Galatians 5:1). What is a sinful habit you have conquered in the past but have fallen into once again? (Example: smoking, swearing, or gossiping)

. . . .

5
CONQUERING CHRIST
Paul used military terms to depict Christ as a conquering hero returning from battle. In ancient times the victor rode triumphantly through the city leading his victorious army, the bounty of war, and the shackled captives. An ancient ticker-tape parade!

8
CAPTIVES
The phrase "led captivity captive" in Ephesians 4:8 is quoted from Psalm 68:18 and means having conquest over your enemies, specifically those who had taken you captive. Being held captive can also refer to our spiritual enemies: Satan, sin, the world, and our flesh. Jesus conquered those spiritual enemies who had conquered us.

9

DOWN, NOT OUT
There are ups and downs in each of our lives. When King David was down, he didn't let it take him out. Instead he prayed, "From the end of the earth I will cry to You, when my heart is overwhelmed; lead me to the rock that is higher than I" (Psalm 61:2).

Journal about how you got trapped by this habit again. What triggered it? How could you have avoided its snare? What can you do in the future to stay clear?

. . . .

. . . .

. . . .

. . . .

Rewrite the following verse into a personal prayer. Make a fresh confession and commitment to Jesus, who will set you free and help you find victory over this habit. "Let us lay aside every weight, and the sin which so easily ensnares us, and let us run with endurance the race that is set before us, looking unto Jesus, the author and finisher of our faith" (Hebrews 12:1-2).

. . . .

. . . .

. . . .

9. We've learned that Jesus descended to the lower parts of the earth and ascended far above all the heavens to set you free. He went low to bring you up. List things that make your heart sink and things that cause your spirit to soar.

MAKES YOU SINK	HELPS YOU SOAR
(Example: fear)	(Example: friends)

. . . .

. . . .

. . . .

. . . .

. . . .

10. Jesus meets us where we are; then He uses us to meet others who are sinking and lift them up. Think of someone who is overwhelmed and seems to be going down for the count.

> Journal a prayer asking God to bring that person up out of despair and into His glorious light.

. . . .

. . . .

. . . .

. . . .

. . . .

10
UPLIFTING
Don't throw drowning people a rock or they'll sink. Instead lighten their load, and lift them up. Those drowning in a sea of sin need uplifting, not rock throwing. "If another Christian is overcome by some sin, you who are godly should gently and humbly help that person back onto the right path. . . . Share each other's troubles and problems" (Galatians 6:1-2, NLT).

I love a parade. It doesn't have to be Macy's Thanksgiving Day extravaganza; it can be a neighborhood pet parade or a high school homecoming march. They all have the same effect on me: misty eyes and a runny nose. I'm hopelessly sentimental. It all began in my hometown, Ludington, Michigan, with the annual Fourth of July parade—a tradition that would make Norman Rockwell proud. The whole community gathers curbside to watch the action and wave Old Glory. Every emergency vehicle in the county roars by with lights flashing and sirens blaring. Closely behind follow tractors and trailers decorated like floats, carrying the Queen of Asparagus and the Cherry Queen. High school bands march in full regalia, and anyone with a horse rides proudly down the street. The entourage is sprinkled with children riding festive bicycles and senior citizens rolling along in wheel chairs, crepe paper streaming in the wind.

There's a grand parade coming in the future that I can't wait to be a part of. I will stand at attention with my banner raised high as Jesus, the King of kings, rides his white horse through heaven, crowned with glory. The hosts of heaven will cheer for the victory He's won over death and hell. Jesus invites all who will believe in Him to get in on the action. Don't let His parade pass you by.

contemplation

In his life, Christ is an example, showing us how to live. In his death, he is a sacrifice, satisfying for our sins. In his resurrection, he is a conqueror. In his ascension, he is a king. In his intercession, he is a high priest.
Martin Luther

DAY 4 FULLY EQUIPPED

When he was only six, our son Nathan thought his Uncle Mike was the coolest guy to walk the earth. Mike could pitch an 80-mile-an-hour baseball, beat Nate at Super Mario Brothers, and play ice hockey with an attitude. Nathan was putty in his hands. It was no surprise the day he walked in the door and said, "Uncle Mike signed me up for hockey at the ice arena. Can I play?"

"Sure, Nate," I said, completely ignorant of the details. I soon learned that first off he needed skating lessons. As the other kids glided and twirled past us, Nathan came shuffling by, clutching onto a chair so he wouldn't fall. Ice fees to cover practice and playing time cost $200. Hockey requires more pads than football, and those rental fees were about $100. Of course, he needed skates, and we found a used pair at a swap meet for $75. Nate shot with his left hand so a special stick was purchased for $45. Joining the hockey team was much more than signing on the dotted line: it required talent, teamwork, and tons of equipment and money!

When you join God's team, there are no hidden costs. God supplies everything you need. He assigns positions, gives you the necessary talents or gifts, and fully equips you for your place on the team.

exploration

We explored the depths and heights Christ went to in order to set us free. Now we will study some of the spiritual gifts He gives.

Review Ephesians 4, then focus on verses 11-13.

> *And He Himself gave some to be apostles, some prophets, some evangelists, and some pastors and teachers, . . .*
> Ephesians 4:11

1. Match the gifts listed in verse 11 with the proper definitions.

    A_____: "one who is sent with a commission"

    P_____: "one who proclaims the Word of God"

    E_____: "bearers of the gospel, the Good News"

    P_____: "one who shepherds God's people"

    T_____: "a shepherd who feeds the flock the
                          Word of God"

2. Paul's list here is not exhaustive. Fill in the chart below to discover the other spiritual gifts mentioned in Scripture.

SCRIPTURE	GIFTS
Rom. 12:6-8	
1 Cor. 12:4-11	
1 Cor. 12:28	

3. What word repeated in Ephesians 4:11 shows that not everyone receives the same spiritual gifts?

. . . .

> *. . . for the equipping of the saints for the work of
> ministry, for the edifying of the body of Christ, . . .*
> Ephesians 4:12

4. Name two reasons why spiritual gifts are given. . . . .

. . . .

5. According to Paul, what will spiritual gifts equip believers to do?

. . . .

> *. . . till we all come to the unity of the faith and of the
> knowledge of the Son of God, to a perfect man, to the
> measure of the stature of the fullness of Christ; . . .*
> Ephesians 4:13

6. What two things did Paul pray will be the result of the ministry of these gifts?

. . . .

GIFT GIVER
God is not like a great Sears & Roebuck catalog in the sky. We don't order what we want. He chooses what gifts to give us—with a no-exchange policy. Paul lists not only the gifts but the gifted *people* of God. The next time you listen to your pastor, remember the Giver who gifted *him*.

SPIRITUAL GIFTS
A spiritual gift is a God-given ability to serve God and others so that Christ is glorified and believers are edified. Have you received God's spiritual gifts for you?

EQUIPPED TO WORK
God's gifts aren't toys to play with; they're tools to build with. These "power tools" must be taken out of God's toolbox, plugged into His Spirit, and put to work in each believer's life and in ministry. "Do not neglect the spiritual gift you received" (1 Timothy 4:14, NLT).

PERFECT IN FAITH
When Mary Poppins pulled out a ruler to measure herself, she came up "Practically Perfect in Every Way." We all know that the only perfect man was Jesus Christ. But Paul uses the word *perfect* to mean spiritually mature and Christlike. How do you measure up?

EQUAL GIFTS
What's the best shoe? It depends. Sneakers are best for athletics, but high heels are best for the prom. What's the best spiritual gift? Teaching if you're a pastor, mercy if you're a counselor, or hospitality if you entertain. "You should desire the most helpful gifts" (1 Corinthians 12:31, NLT).

GIFT OR TALENT?
A spiritual gift is an extraordinary faculty operating for the benefit of the church. Gifts are given by the grace of God through the power of the Spirit to believers, whether the Holy Spirit imparts entirely new powers or stimulates those already existing to higher power or activity. With the touch of God's Spirit something ordinary becomes extraordinary!

7. According to verse 13, what is the standard by which we measure our spiritual lives?

. . . .

transformation

8. God gives to His children diverse gifts that are appropriate for the ministry to which He has called them. With this in mind, complete the journal exercise below.

    a. List the areas of ministry you are currently fulfilling as well as those you feel God is calling you to in the future.

    . . . .

    . . . .

    b. Review the list of the gifts of the Holy Spirit found in question 2. Which of these gifts would enable you to fulfill your ministry with supernatural power?

    . . . .

    Write a prayer asking God to empower you with the gifts you need to serve Him.

    . . . .

    . . . .

    . . . .

9. Some of our abilities come naturally and others come supernaturally. With this in mind, complete the journal exercises below.

    a. List some of the natural talents you possess. (Example: I'm a good cook; I am very sympathetic; I'm organized.)

    . . . .

    . . . .

    . . . .

b. Reviewing the list of the gifts of the Spirit, which of your natural talents might be a manifestation of God's gifts? (Example: When I cook for others, I am offering hospitality. Caring and listening to others is being merciful.)

. . . .

. . . .

> Write a prayer offering God your natural talents, and ask Him to transform them into supernatural abilities through the power of the Holy Spirit.

. . . .

. . . .

. . . .

10. Gifts are good, but *love* is better. Listed below are the attributes of love described in 1 Corinthians 13. Place a ✔ by the ones you have and a ✘ by the ones you need.

___ Patient	___ Kind	___ Not Proud
___ Not Jealous	___ Not Boastful	___ Not Rude
___ Undemanding	___ Not Irritable	___ Forgiving
___ Rejoices in Truth	___ Enduring	___ Hopeful
___ Believes	___ Not Selfish	___ Faithful

A church in Strasbourg, Germany, was destroyed during World War II. After the bombing, the members went to see what was left and found the entire roof caved in. Much to their surprise, a statue of Christ with outstretched hands was still standing. It was intact, except a falling beam had sheared off both hands. The people asked a sculptor if he could replace the hands on the statue. He was willing, and he even offered to do the work for nothing. The church officials met to consider the sculptor's proposition but decided not to accept his offer. Why? Because they felt that the statue without hands would be the greatest message possible that God's work is done with human hands through His people.

God gives gifts to believers so we can be His hands, His feet, and His mouth, fully equipped "for the work of ministry, for the edifying of the body of Christ" (Ephesians 4:12).

DAY 5 ALL GROWN UP

preparation

Father, please don't allow me to settle for the comfort of narrow surroundings or stunted growth. Stir up my heart and open the way to new horizons and greater growth in You. Amen.

GROWING UP

We always thank God for you, as is right, for we are thankful that your faith is flourishing and you are all growing in love for each other.
2 Thessalonians 1:3

I read about a guy who catches live exotic fish for aquarium owners. His top-selling fish is the shark. He explained that if you catch a small shark and confine it to an aquarium, it would only grow in proportion to its environment. A shark can be a mere six inches long and still be an adult. Its growth is stunted by its surroundings. But if you turn that dwarfed shark loose in the ocean, he'll grow to his normal length of nearly eight feet.

The same thing can happen to Christians. I've seen some of the cutest little Christians who swim around in a little puddle of self-centeredness. They stay small and immature in their faith. But place them into a larger arena—the vastness of the body of Christ—and they can reach their full potential and "grow up in all things into Him who is the head—Christ" (Ephesians 4:15).

exploration

This week we have learned about some of the gifts given by Christ to the church. Today we learn how this supernatural equipping brings about spiritual maturity.

Review Ephesians 4, then focus on verses 14-16.

> *. . . that we should no longer be children, tossed to and fro and carried about with every wind of doctrine, by the trickery of men, in the cunning craftiness of deceitful plotting, . . .* Ephesians 4:14

1. Paul gave another reason for becoming mature in faith. What was it?

. . . .

2. What two phrases describe the instability of these children?

. . . .

3. What influences can cause us to be carried about?

With . . . .

By . . . .

In . . . .

> *. . . but, speaking the truth in love, may grow up*
> *in all things into Him who is the head—Christ—. . .*
> Ephesians 4:15

4. What type of speech is a sign of maturity? . . . .

. . . .

5. What are we to grow "into"? . . . .

. . . .

6. From our past study, of what is Christ the head? (See Ephesians 1:22.)

. . . .

> *. . . from whom the whole body, joined and knit together*
> *by what every joint supplies, according to the effective*
> *working by which every part does its share, causes*
> *growth of the body for the edifying of itself in love.*
> Ephesians 4:16

7. How does each part of the whole body work together most effectively?

. . . .

8. What is the end result of this type of cooperation, according to verse 16?

. . . .

explanation

2

TOSSED ABOUT
To be tossed to and fro means to fluctuate or roll up and down with the waves. Following a prevailing current will take you places you never intended to go—from bell-bottoms to bad behavior. Children get caught in the undertow of peer pressure. Maturity equips us to go against the flow!

4

TRUTH IN LOVE
Truth without love is brutality—love without truth is hypocrisy. Maturity blends both to lead others to Christ. The truth? "All have sinned; all fall short of God's glorious standard" (Romans 3:23, NLT). The love? "God showed his great love for us by sending Christ to die for us while we were still sinners" (Romans 5:8, NLT).

Milk does His body good. God wants His children to be well-fed so they can grow up into His image. If you're spiritually malnourished, open God's Word and drink up. "As newborn babes, desire the pure milk of the word, that you may grow thereby" (1 Peter 2:2).

transformation

9. This week we've learned some traits of childishness, but Jesus taught the value of being childlike: "Whoever does not receive the kingdom of God as a little child will by no means enter it" (Mark 10:15). In the appropriate columns below, place the following attributes: unstable, honest, gullible, trusting, boastful, humble, naive, eager, greedy, imitator, teasing, vulnerable, tender, weak, enthusiastic, impatient, teachable

CHILDLIKE   CHILDISH

. . . .

. . . .

. . . .

. . . .

. . . .

. . . .

. . . .

10. Paul said, "When I was a child, I spoke and thought and reasoned as a child does. But when I grew up, I put away childish things" (1 Corinthians 13:11, NLT). With this Scripture verse in mind, work through the exercise below.

> Review the columns above and examine your own life. Circle the childish attributes that you tend to display. Journal about how you can begin to turn these childish behaviors into more mature ones.

. . . .

. . . .

. . . .

Some of us mistakenly put away our childlike *hearts* with our childish behavior. What childlike attitudes do you need to keep?

. . . .

11. Mature believers develop mature speech by "speaking the truth in love." With this in mind, complete the journal exercise:

Write about a time someone told you the cold, hard truth about yourself. How did it hurt?

. . . .

. . . .

. . . .

Write about a time someone told you the loving reality about yourself. How did it help?

. . . .

. . . .

. . . .

TRUTH HURTS
Truth hurts when someone who doesn't love you tells you your failures hoping to make you bitter. Truth heals when someone who loves you tells you your flaws hoping to make you better. "Open rebuke is better than love carefully concealed. Faithful are the wounds of a friend, but the kisses of an enemy are deceitful" (Proverbs 27:5-6).

What is the one thing every mother wants for her children? To grow up! Picture your preschool child twenty years in the future. He or she has gone off to college or to begin a career. One day there's a knock at the door. When you open it, there stands your fully grown adult child, and the first thing out of his or her mouth is, "Mama, Dada, I want my baba." Your heart would drop, and tears would come at the tragedy of your child growing old without growing up.

Life is about progression. Plants mature from seedling to sapling. Musicians progress from chopsticks to Chopin. Human beings grow from childhood to adulthood. Spiritual maturity, like physical maturity, is a growth process. Born-again believers are babies who must grow up.

Preacher and evangelist Leonard Ravenhill told a story about a group of tourists visiting a picturesque village. They walked by an old man sitting beside a fence, and in a rather patronizing way one tourist asked, "Were any great men born in this village?"

The old man replied, "Nope, only babies."

A frothy question yielded a profound answer. There are no instant adults either in this world or in the kingdom of God. Growth takes time.

contemplation
Although we become Christians instantaneously by faith in Christ, knowing God and developing faith is a gradual process. There are no shortcuts to maturity. It takes time to be holy.
Erwin W. Lutzer

Dress for Success

ABC News reports that Imelda Marcos's legendary shoe collection has grown to nearly 3,000 pairs since her strongman husband was driven from his presidency. At the height of their power, Mrs. Marcos became known for lavish living despite extreme poverty in the Philippines. When Ferdinand and Imelda Marcos escaped the islands during a "people power" revolt, she left 1,220 pairs of shoes behind at the presidential palace—including one pair with lights that blinked when she danced. Her shoe collection, containing expensive foreign-made brands, astounded the world and became a symbol of excessive living.

By the world's standards, if anyone was dressed for success, it was Imelda Marcos. Apparently no one ever told her that clothes don't make the woman. While the palace, presidency, and power crumbled all around her, she continued to buy more shoes. The Marcoses became exiles, literally fulfilling the saying, "All dressed up with no place to go."

This week Paul lets us know that God is more concerned with godly behavior than gorgeous attire. God's standard for success looks different from the world's. Christian living is not about your shoes or the clothes you wear, but about the way you walk in holiness.

DAY 1
Walking Shoes

DAY 2
Mirror, Mirror

DAY 3
*Off with the Old,
On with the New*

DAY 4
*Clean Out
Your Closet*

DAY 5
Dressed for Success

DAY 1 WALKING SHOES

preparation

God, forgive me when I try to clothe myself in my own righteousness. I know that in Your eyes it is just filthy rags. Clothe me in Your righteousness so I can make Your best-dressed list. Amen.

MAKEOVER

I am overwhelmed with joy in the Lord my God! For he has dressed me with the clothing of salvation and draped me in a robe of righteousness.
Isaiah 61:10, NLT

explanation

3

FUTILITY

Futility is to be full of emptiness, worthlessness, or vanity. A futile mind is full of nothing. Picture a hamster running on a wheel. It thinks it is going somewhere, and it is— nowhere fast. In their ignorance, unbelieving Gentiles were busy performing pagan religious rituals that would lead them nowhere. Paul wanted them to stop running around and start wising up.

exploration

Paul continues his teaching on how Christians ought to walk by contrasting fleshly vices and godly virtues. He uses negative examples to encourage positive action. Today we are reminded of how sinful our lives are without Christ.

Read through Ephesians 4 several times to remember the tone, language, and content of this chapter, then focus on verses 17-19.

> *This I say, therefore, and testify in the Lord, that you should no longer walk as the rest of the Gentiles walk, in the futility of their mind, . . .* Ephesians 4:17

1. What phrase did Paul use to emphasize the importance of what he is saying?

. . . .

2. Whom should the Ephesians no longer emulate?. . . . .

. . . .

3. What phrase did Paul use to describe how the Gentiles (unbelievers) walk?

. . . .

> *. . . having their understanding darkened, being alienated from the life of God, because of the ignorance that is in them, because of the blindness of their heart; . . .*
> Ephesians 4:18

4. What is the result of their understanding being darkened?

. . . .

5. What two things cause their alienation from God?. . . . .

. . . .

> *. . . who, being past feeling, have given themselves over to lewdness, to work all uncleanness with greediness.*
> Ephesians 4:19

6. What is the emotional consequence of ignorance and hard-heartedness?

. . . .

7. What do those who are "past feeling" give themselves to?

. . . .

transformation

8. Paul said that to walk with God means to walk in the opposite direction of the "Gentiles," or the world. Draw a line *away from* the specific ungodly behavior *over to* the opposite way we can walk with God.

WALK LIKE GENTILES	WALK WITH GOD
Futility of mind	United in Christ
Darkened understanding	Wise
Alienated from God	Valuable ideas
Ignorant	Generous
Blind hearted	Washed by the blood
Past feeling	Set apart for godliness
Given over to lewdness	Enlightened insight
Unclean	Sensitive to the Spirit
Greedy	Sees clearly

4
DARKENED MINDS
Darkness is the absence of light. It is associated with the chaos before creation. It became a symbol of evil, afflic-tion, or death. In hell there is only darkness. Darkness symbolizes man's ignorance of God's will and is associ-ated with sin. "If the light you think you have is really darkness, how deep that dark-ness will be!" (Matthew 6:23, NLT).

7
LEWDNESS
A preoccupation with sex and sexual desires leading to indecent and disgraceful behav-ior. Those who have "given themselves over to lewdness" have recklessly abandoned themselves to sensual pleasure. Think of Sodom and Gomorrah, Studio 54, or Mardi Gras.

8
WALK THE LINE
Johnny Cash sang, "Because you're mine, I walk the line." For us as Christians, because we're His, we walk the line. "He tells us every-thing over and over again, a line at a time, in very simple words!" (Isaiah 28:10, NLT).

CHANGING HABITS

Bad habits are hard to break. The best way to beat a bad habit is to begin a good one. Don't just stop swearing, start sharing your faith with others. Instead of yielding to fear, give way to faith. "Hold on to what is good. Keep away from every kind of evil" (1 Thessalonians 5:21-22, NLT).

9. From the list above, circle one way you used to walk like the Gentiles. Then check below how God intersected your path to bring about change.

___ Stop sign
___ Dangerous Curve Ahead
___ Children at Play
___ Reduce Speed
___ Yield
___ Bump in the Road

Journal about your experience of God's work in your life. (Example: My greed made me a spendaholic until God put up a Reduce Speed sign in my life.)

. . . .

. . . .

. . . .

. . . .

. . . .

10. God is giving you a green light to let you know it's time to move forward.

Journal about the steps you will now take to begin walking God's way in this area. (Example: God showed me it wasn't enough to stop spending on my own pleasures; I needed to generously invest in His kingdom.)

. . . .

. . . .

. . . .

. . . .

. . . .

The most unattractive part of the body has to be the foot. Thus, fashion designers throughout history have unleashed their imaginations in creating fanciful footwear to transform your body's greatest deficit into an asset. Elvis was protective of his blue suede shoes. In Oz, Dorothy walked the yellow brick road in her ruby red pumps. Cinderella left a glass slipper as her calling card. My personal favorites were a pair of white go-go boots my dad bought me during the mod 1960s. They were more than a fashion statement—they symbolized action. Nancy Sinatra's anthem said it all: "These boots were made for walking, and that's just what they'll do."

I guess that's the point; shoes must be practical, not just pretty. Feet were made for walking and so should your shoes. Isaiah, the prophet, reveals God's plan to beautify your less than lovely feet, and it's not with a new pair of shoes: "How beautiful on the mountains are the feet of those who bring good news of peace and salvation, the news that the God of Israel reigns!" (Isaiah 52:7, NLT). Paul wants believers to put their best foot forward. Instead of telling them to change their shoes, he asks them to walk in a different direction, out of the darkness and into God's wonderful light.

contemplation
If I walk with the world,
I can't walk with God.
Dwight Lyman Moody

DAY 2 MIRROR, MIRROR

preparation

Father, help me see myself as You see me. I know the changes You make are more than skin deep. Transform me from the inside out. Amen.

HIS REFLECTION

Now we see things imperfectly as in a poor mirror, but then we will see everything with perfect clarity. All that I know now is partial and incomplete, but then I will know everything completely, just as God knows me now.
1 Corinthians 13:12, NLT

explanation

1

BUT YOU

Mothers hear the *but* word a lot: "But the other kids do it." "But everyone has one." Even God's kids justify inappropriate behavior. "But that movie won the Academy award." "But all the cute guys go to the dance club." Paul gives us a great comeback: "But you have not so learned Christ." No ifs, ands, or buts.

Mirrors don't lie—they merely reflect the truth. In the morning when the alarm sounds, I stumble to the bathroom, turn on the light, and take a good, long look in the mirror. Ughhh! It faithfully displays every flaw from wrinkles to warts. My mirror has neither chided me on a bad-hair day nor cheered me for having a beaming suntan. It's nothing personal—the mirror simply reveals the truth. After looking, I have the golden opportunity to *do something* about the truth staring back at me in the mirror.

The Bible says that Jesus is the Truth. When we take a good long look at Him, our impure thoughts, unbecoming attitudes, and inappropriate actions are exposed as glaring imperfections. Let's take advantage of this golden opportunity to look the Truth—Jesus Christ—in the face and do something about it. As you look in the mirror of God's Word, make it your goal to wear a beaming Son-tan.

exploration

We've seen that walking in spiritual ignorance results in grave emotional, physical, and spiritual consequences. Now it's time to look in the mirror of God's truth.

Review Ephesians 4, then focus on verses 20-21.

> **But you have not so learned Christ, . . .** Ephesians 4:20

1. *"But you"* are words that mark a contrast from the previous verses. Reflect on yesterday's lesson (Ephesians 4:17-19). Who were the Ephesians contrasted with?

. . . .

2. What would the Gentiles see if they looked honestly in the mirror of God's truth?

. . . .

3. What had the Ephesians learned that the Gentiles had not?

. . . .

> *. . . if indeed you have heard Him and have been taught by Him, as the truth is in Jesus: . . .* Ephesians 4:21

4. Paul dissects the elements necessary to learn Christ. Which of the five senses must we utilize in learning Christ?

. . . .

5. What else is required to learn Christ? . . . .

. . . .

6. What phrase in verse 21 reveals that what we have heard and been taught is true?

. . . .

transformation

7. We've seen that it's easy to justify inappropriate behavior using a "but" mentality. Look in the mirror of your life, and circle the excuses you've used for making bad choices.

But . . . .
But I can handle it.
But my friends do it.
But they might reject me.
But I've always done it.
But it's not that bad.
But my husband doesn't pay attention.
But it's just this once.
But no one will see.
But it's just the way I am.
But it's because of hormones.

4
EARS TO HEAR
There are none so deaf as those who will not hear. The first martyr, Stephen, wanted Saul and his countrymen to hear about Jesus but "they put their hands over their ears, and drowning out his voice with their shouts, they rushed at him" (Acts 7:57, NLT). It took the audible voice of God on the Damascus Road to give Saul ears to hear.

6
TRUTH OR LIE?
Who is Jesus? To the Jews a prophet. To Muslims the son of Abraham. To New Agers a miracle worker. None of them admit the whole truth—Jesus is God! Paul wrote, "Let God be true but every man a liar" (Romans 3:4). The truth doesn't change because skeptics don't believe it. Jesus said, "I am the Truth."

7
EXCUSE ME
Human beings have been making excuses and shirking responsibility since time began. God wanted to know who was to blame for eating forbidden fruit. Adam's excuse? "It's Eve's fault." Eve's excuse? "The snake made me do it!" Jesus told the truth: "They have no excuse for their sin" (John 15:22).

BREAK THE SILENCE
By remaining silent, many Christians take only part of Solomon's advice, "There is . . . a time to be quiet and a time to speak up" (Ecclesiastes 3:1-7, NLT). Paul urges us to speak up and share the gospel: "How can they hear about him unless someone tells them?" (Romans 10:14, NLT). Let's break the silence!

Now that you've reflected on the ways in which you justify wrong behavior, you have the opportunity to make some improvements. Journal an "exchange" prayer in which you trade in one of your bad excuses for a better response. (Example: God, just because I'm hormonal doesn't mean I can treat people horribly. May Your holiness control my hormones.)

. . . .

. . . .

. . . .

. . . .

8. Today we discovered that the first step in learning Christ is to hear about Him.

Journal some of the different ways you've heard about Christ. (Example: I watched a Billy Graham Crusade; a friend became a "Jesus freak"; I went to church, etc.)

. . . .

. . . .

. . . .

. . . .

. . . .

9. Paul reminds us that we must not only hear of Christ, we must also be taught by Him. Which of the following tools has He used to teach you?

___ His Word	___ Adversity
___ His Holy Spirit	___ Success
___ Christian literature	___ His people
___ Joy	___ Mistakes
___ My pastor	___ Sunday school

Reflect on one of these items and journal about how God used it to teach you the truth.

. . . .

. . . .

. . . .

. . . .

. . . .

. . . .

Recently I read about a woman who, on the advice of her doctor, went to see a pastor to talk about joining the church. She had recently had a face-lift, and when her doctor dismissed her, he gave her this advice. "My dear, I have done an extraordinary job on your face, as you can see in the mirror. I have charged you a great deal of money, and you were happy to pay it. But I want to give you some free advice. Find a group of people who love God and who will love you enough to help you deal with all the negative emotions inside of you. If you don't, you'll be back in my office in a very short time with your face in far worse shape than before."

What happens on the outside is only a reflection of what's occurring on the inside. A face-lift won't disguise a faulty heart. Solomon said, "As a face is reflected in water, so the heart reflects the person" (Proverbs 27:19, NLT). God sees past your face and into your heart.

DAY 3 — OFF WITH THE OLD, ON WITH THE NEW

POSSIBILITIES
Jesus looked at them intently and said, "Humanly speaking, it is impossible. But not with God. Everything is possible with God."
Mark 10:27, NLT

Human beings are creatures of habit. I'm no exception to the rule. In grade school I choked down my first cigarette, trying to look cool. By my senior year I was blowing smoke on a daily basis. It's my belief that if you've got a habit, you should be the one paying the price—no bumming cigarettes or matches. I told my friends, "If you want to smoke, buy your own. I'm not sharing." That philosophy worked well until the day I needed a smoke. My friends threw my attitude back at me. "If you want to smoke, Lenya, then get your own." Then it occurred to me: *I don't want to smoke; it's not cool, it's a nasty habit.*

Mark Twain said, "A habit cannot be tossed out the window; it must be coaxed down the stairs a step at a time!" Old habits—especially sinful ones—are hard to break. Paul teaches an all-important lesson: replace bad habits with good ones. My new philosophy is, "Off with the old, and on with the new."

exploration

Yesterday we learned to look at the truth found in Christ. Today we learn that once we know the truth, we must be willing to make some other changes.

Review Ephesians 4, then focus on verses 22-24.

> *. . . that you put off, concerning your former conduct, the old man which grows corrupt according to the deceitful lusts, . . .* Ephesians 4:22

1. Since we have learned about Christ, what else are we to do?

. . . .

2. What name did Paul give to describe this former conduct?

. . . .

3. How does our old nature grow? According to what? . . . .

. . . .

> *. . . and be renewed in the spirit of your mind, . . .*
> Ephesians 4:23

4. After putting our old nature to death, what is an important part of our growing process as Christians?

. . . .

5. Where do we become renewed? . . . .

. . . .

> *. . . and that you put on the new man which was created according to God, in true righteousness and holiness.*
> Ephesians 4:24

6. What are we to "put on"?. . . . .

. . . .

7. Who was responsible for this new creation? . . . .

. . . .

8. What are the two outstanding characteristics of the new man?

. . . .

transformation

9. Paul made it clear that our dirty old natures must be put to death. Have you tried to resuscitate your "old man" by falling back into old habits?

explanation

2

THE OLD MAN
This term refers to our sinful nature—the flesh. Putting off the old man is not deferring it for another day; it means putting it to death. "Our old sinful selves were crucified with Christ so that sin might lose its power in our lives" (Romans 6:6, NLT).

4

BE RENEWED
This phrase, *be renewed*, means "to make young or recent" (Vine's Expository Dictionary). Retin A, face-lifts, and derma-brasion promise to peel away wrinkles; God's renewal plan offers a spiritual lift. "If anyone is in Christ, he is a new creation; old things have passed away; behold, all things have become new" (2 Corinthians 5:17).

9

BATTLING SIN
Don't be discouraged if the old sin nature makes you feel defiled; Paul had the same struggle. "Oh, what a miserable person I am! Who will free me from this life that is domi-nated by sin? Thank God! The answer is in Jesus Christ our Lord" (Romans 7:24-25, NLT).

10

A NEW YOU

God is not satisfied with outward, superficial change. He wants you to be completely transformed: to experience a new birth, take on a brand-new nature, and become a new you. Think of the difference between a snake and a caterpillar. A snake who sheds his skin is still a snake; but a caterpillar who sheds his cocoon becomes a butterfly.

Journal about any bad habits that are trying to come back to life. (Example: I was getting up early to have quiet time, but lately I've been sleeping in.)

. . . .

. . . .

10. The only way to become a new person is to be born again through faith in Jesus.

If you have not placed your faith in Jesus, journal a prayer asking Him to forgive you of your sins and to make your life new in Him. If the "new man" in you is growing old, ask God to revive you.

. . . .

. . . .

11. Being renewed in the spirit of your mind begins by challenging negative thoughts with positive input. Follow the exercise below to discover ways to overcome negative thoughts with good ones.

a. Ask God to reveal to you a thought or thought pattern that is not pleasing to Him. Write it down. (Example: I'm afraid of the future, so I don't sleep at night.)

. . . .

b. Using Philippians 4:8, write out biblical truths that will replace this unpleasing thought or pattern with a renewed spirit that exhibits your new, godly character.

. . . .

. . . .

"Whatever things are true": (Example: God holds my future in His hands. I can rest in Him.)

. . . .

"Whatever things are noble": (Example: I will look forward to a future with Christ by my side.)

. . . .

"Whatever things are just":

. . . .

"Whatever things are pure":

. . . .

"Whatever things are lovely":

. . . .

"Whatever things are of good report":

. . . .

"If there is any virtue":

. . . .

"If there is anything praiseworthy":

. . . .

Two children, a boy and a girl, played together a great deal. One summer they attended a local Vacation Bible School, where they both accepted Jesus as their Savior. One day the boy told his mother, "Mom, I know for sure that Emily's a Christian."

"How do you know?"

"Because she plays like a Christian. If you take everything she's got, she doesn't get mad. Before she was selfish. If she didn't get her way, she'd say, 'I won't play with you; you're an ugly little boy.'"

What an amazing promise that you are made new—He removes your ugliness and gives you His righteousness. What a mighty God who recreates His people. "Then He who sat on the throne said, 'Behold, I make all things new'" (Revelation 21:5).

No man can create faith in himself. Something must happen to him which Luther calls "the divine work in us," which changes us, gives us new birth, and makes us completely different people in heart, spirit, mind, and all our powers.
Nikolaus Ludwig von Zinzendorf

DAY 4 CLEAN OUT YOUR CLOSET

preparation

Lord, what do You see when You look inside the closet of my life? Are there things that don't coordinate with Your Holy Spirit? Help me to do spring cleaning and clear away the clutter. Amen.

UNCLUTTERED
So give to the needy what you greedily possess, and you will be clean all over.
Luke 11:41, NLT

Everything I ever wanted to know about my friends, I learned by looking in their closets. Patty, the prayer warrior, has a closet that would rival Martha Stewart's, organized by color, season, and occasion. "A place for everything and everything in its place" is her motto. Penny says, "If it's fun, then I'll do it." Looking in her closet is like going on safari, seeking out the next conquest—dressing is an adventure. Our women's ministry storage closet, tucked up in the rafters of our church building, is a scary place. Rats have been heard gnawing, boxes have mysteriously disappeared, and grown men have been known to say, "I'm not going in there!" What would I learn about *you* if I peeked inside your closet?

My personal philosophy of closet maintenance is simple: when I get a new item, I give away an old one. I can remain current but uncluttered. In the same way, the apostle Paul teaches us to keep our spiritual lives uncluttered. In the Christian life, before you can put on new actions that please God, you must strip away outdated, sinful habits. It's time to clean out your closets!

exploration

Paul tells us we must not only *put on* the new man but we must also *put away* sinful vices. Today we examine four of these sins and the reasons Paul gives for clearing away the clutter.

Review Ephesians 4, then focus on verses 25-29.

> *Therefore, putting away lying, "Let each one of you speak truth with his neighbor," for we are members of one another.* Ephesians 4:25

1. What are we to put away? . . . .

. . . .

2. What should we do instead, and what should be our motivation?

. . . .

"Be angry, and do not sin": do not let the sun go down on your wrath, nor give place to the devil. Ephesians 4:26-27

3. Verse 26 gives some do's and don'ts. We can be _____ as long as we don't_____.

4. What time limit did Paul give for dealing with anger? . . . .

. . . .

5. How can sinful anger give place to the devil?. . . . .

. . . .

Let him who stole steal no longer, but rather let him labor, working with his hands what is good, that he may have something to give him who has need. Ephesians 4:28

6. Stealing was another item on Paul's "don't do" list.

a. Rather than stealing, what two things should thieves do instead?

. . . .

b. How does this benefit others? . . . .

. . . .

Let no corrupt word proceed out of your mouth, but what is good for necessary edification, that it may impart grace to the hearers. Ephesians 4:29

7. What should *not* come out of the mouth of a believer?

. . . .

explanation

1

THE WHOLE TRUTH
"The essence of lying is in deception, not necessarily in words; a lie may be told by silence, by equivocation, by the accent on a syllable, by a glance of the eye attaching a peculiar significance to a sentence" (John Ruskin).

3

ANGER AND SIN
Anger in itself is not a sin since "God is . . . angry with the wicked every day" (Psalm 7:11). Anger is sinful when it flares without reflection; when it is disproportionate to the offense; when it lasts too long and becomes revengeful (*New Unger's Bible Dictionary*).

6

WORKING HARD
Humanity was sentenced to life with hard labor. "I have placed a curse on the ground. All your life you will struggle to scratch a living from it" (Genesis 3:17, NLT). But God turns curses into blessings. Hard work pays off with status, satisfaction, and sleep.

GOOD WORDS
Our words should be good, necessary, edifying, and gracious to those who hear them. THINK before you speak, and ask yourself: Is it *True*, is it *Humble*, is it *Inspirational*, is it *Necessary*, is it *Kind*? "May the words of my mouth . . . be pleasing to you" (Psalm 19:14).

10
FAMILY LIES
The Day America Told The Truth reveals that 69 percent of Americans lie to their spouse. A lie is a statement or act designed to deceive others. People lie to inflict pain or to protect themselves, usually out of fear or pride. "Do not lie to one another, since you have put off the old man with his deeds" (Colossians 3:9).

12
TRUE CONFESSIONS
Biblically, there are two types of confessions: admission of sins and profession of belief. Believers must not only confess what they've done wrong; they must proclaim what they know is right. "If you confess with your mouth that Jesus is Lord and believe in your heart that God raised him from the dead, you will be saved" (Romans 10:9, NLT).

8. What *should* proceed out of our mouths? . . . .

. . . .

9. What does this kind of speech offer people who hear it?

. . . .

transformation

10. This passage has exhorted us to stop lying and start telling the truth to our neighbors and fellow believers. Your closest "neighbor" may live in your own home. With that in mind, how have you compromised the truth with someone close to you recently?

___ pretending   ___ withholding information
___ hiding bad habits   ___ spending secretly
___ shading the truth   ___ looking the other way
___ exaggerating   ___ denying reality
___ blaming others   ___ other_____

11. To whom did you lie, and what were your reasons?

. . . .

. . . .

12. John gives the remedy for lying (as well as any other sin): "If we confess our sins, He is faithful and just to forgive us our sins and to cleanse us from all unrighteousness" (1 John 1:9). With this in mind, complete the following exercise.

Journal a prayer confessing your sin of lying to God.

. . . .

. . . .

. . . .

. . . .

Ask God for the strength to go to the person you lied to and seek forgiveness.

. . . .

. . . .

. . . .

. . . .

Journal a prayer asking God to lead you to another Christian to whom you can confide your weaknesses and who can pray with you. "Confess your sins to each other and pray for each other so that you may be healed" (James 5:16, NLT).

. . . .

. . . .

. . . .

. . . .

A woman was married to a miserly man. One day she was going window-shopping, and he told her, "Look, but don't buy." A few hours later she came home with a new dress. Her husband said, "I thought I told you to look but not buy." She explained, "I saw this dress and thought I'd try it on. When I did, the devil said, 'It sure looks good on you.'" "Right then you should have told him, 'Get thee behind me, Satan!'" her husband exclaimed. "I did," she answered, "but when he got behind me, he said, 'It looks good from the back, too.'"

Comedian Flip Wilson used to say, "The devil made me do it," as a way of excusing sinful behavior. Satan will take advantage of every opportunity to promote sin. Lying, anger, stealing, and corrupt communication leave the door of our hearts wide open to Satan's influence—they "give place to the devil." Don't give Satan a foothold in your life by allowing him to influence what goes into the closet of your heart. Instead, put away the old sinful behaviors and put on the characteristics of the new person God created you to be!

contemplation
Temptation is the devil looking through the keyhole; yielding is opening the door and inviting him in.
Billy Sunday

DAY 5 DRESSED FOR SUCCESS

TRANSFORMATION
Don't copy the behavior and customs of this world, but let God transform you into a new person by changing the way you think. Then you will know what God wants you to do, and you will know how good and pleasing and perfect his will really is. Romans 12:2, NLT

Parading down the red carpet of the annual Academy Awards, Hollywood's "royalty" are always dressed in hopes of success. These days every star has a team of stylists and designers for Oscar night, and the stars' fashions can be fabulous. Jane Fonda never looked better in her platinum colored gown by Vera Wang, with matching gloves and pearls. But Hollywood fashion can also be fickle. Recently Uma Thurman arrived in a stunning lilac slip dress by Prada. The next year there wasn't a slip dress in the crowd. Even those who were dressed in the height of fashion seemed outdated by the time the show was over. It's all about appearances, and if you didn't like this year's fashion look, don't worry; it's changed by now.

When the prophet Samuel was choosing a king for Israel, God gave him some good advice, "Do not look at his appearance or at the height of his stature. . . . For the Lord does not see as man sees; for man looks at the outward appearance, but the Lord looks at the heart" (1 Samuel 16:7). Examine the inward attire of your heart. Are you a fashion victim adorned with bitterness, anger, and malice, or are you dressed for success in robes of kindness, tenderness, and forgiveness?

exploration

This week we have examined some of the attitudes and actions we should "put off" and "put on" as Christians. Now we discover that our sins hurt God as well as others.

Review Ephesians 4, then focus on verses 30-32.

> ***And do not grieve the Holy Spirit of God, by whom you were sealed for the day of redemption.*** Ephesians 4:30

1. What did Paul warn against? . . . .

. . . .

2. According to this verse, what has the Holy Spirit done for you?

. . . .

Let all bitterness, wrath, anger, clamor, and evil speaking be put away from you, with all malice. Ephesians 4:31

3. Name the six sins Paul listed. . . . .

. . . .

. . . .

4. What did Paul urge us to do with these sins? . . . .

. . . .

5. How much of these sins should be put away? . . . .

. . . .

And be kind to one another, tenderhearted, forgiving one another, just as God in Christ forgave you. Ephesians 4:32

6. What three virtues does Paul encourage among believers?

. . . .

. . . .

7. Why should we exhibit these virtues to one another? . . . .

. . . .

transformation

8. We have discovered that the Holy Spirit is a person who has feelings, including grief. Fill in the chart below to discover some other personality traits of the Holy spirit.

GRIEVING THE SPIRIT
To grieve means to distress, make heavy-hearted, or cause sadness. The Holy Spirit is a person who has feelings, intellect, and will. Whatever is unholy—contrary to the will of God—grieves the Holy Spirit. Every sin hurts God, but sin in His children breaks His heart.

TENDERHEARTED
This means to be easily moved by another's distress, or to feel a gnawing pain in empathy for another's suffering. The Greek word for *tenderhearted* literally means "having strong, kindly bowels." In the Bible the bowels are regarded as the source of kindness.

PERSONALITY
The Holy Spirit has a great personality, but this Person is God. The Spirit (1) is called God; (2) exhibits divine attributes such as omniscience and omnipresence; (3) performs divine works such as creation and the new birth; (4) is offered worship and homage which belong only to God. "Now, the Lord is the Spirit" (2 Corinthians 3:17, NLT).

THICK SKIN
Here's a wise rule for living: "Learn to be thick-skinned while remaining tender-hearted." Developing thick skin in a world full of sharp tongues is essential for survival. However, thick-skinned people can be insensitive; a tender heart is imperative for revival.

Mark 13:11 . . . .

Luke 12:12 . . . .

Acts 9:31 . . . .

Acts 15:28 . . . .

Acts 16:6 . . . .

9. In which of the above ways has the Holy Spirit interacted with you this week? How have you responded?

. . . .

10. In order to please God, Paul exhorts us to put away *all* bitterness. *Bitterness* means "to cut or to prick." It is literally translated "pointed, sharp, or keen" *(Vine's Expository Dictionary)*. In other words, our words can cut like a knife.

Write about a time when someone pierced your soul with bitter words. How did it make you feel?

. . . .

. . . .

. . . .

. . . .

Describe a situation when your bitter words stung another's heart. How did it make them feel?

. . . .

. . . .

. . . .

. . . .

Take the time now to ask God through prayer and forgiveness to cut away the root of bitterness from your life and the lives of those you've injured.

. . . .

. . . .

11. To be tenderhearted means to be moved by another's distress—to feel another's pain.

   a. Think of someone in your life who is in pain (physical, emotional, or spiritual). Write what you know about the situation that is causing their pain.

   . . . .

   . . . .

   b. Ask God to help you be tenderhearted and bear this person's burden through prayer. Write down a tangible way you can show you care this week.

   . . . .

   . . . .

Before Louis XII of France came to power, he had been thrown into prison and kept in chains. Later when he became king, he was urged by others to seek revenge on those who imprisoned him. But he refused and instead prepared a scroll listing the names of all those who had perpetrated crimes against him. Next to each person's name he placed a cross in red ink. When the guilty people heard about this, they fled in fear for their lives. Then the king explained that the cross he had drawn beside each name was not a sign of punishment but a pledge of forgiveness extended for the sake of the crucified Savior, who upon His cross forgave His enemies and prayed for them.

Kindness, tenderheartedness, and forgiveness don't come naturally; they are acquired supernaturally through the redeeming power of the Cross. King Louis XII had been completely transformed. Outwardly his clothes were upgraded from prison rags to palace robes, and inwardly his attitude toward his enemies changed from bitterness to blessing. He was dressed for success.

Do not keep the alabaster boxes of your love and tenderness sealed up until your friends are dead. Fill their lives with sweetness. Speak approving, cheering words while their ears can hear them and while their hearts can be thrilled by them.
Henry Ward Beecher

In My Father's Footsteps

Bible teacher E. Stanley Jones told the story of a missionary who got lost in an African jungle. There was nothing around him but thick bush and a few cleared spaces. He came upon a local village and asked one of the men if he could lead him out of the jungle. When the native agreed, the missionary said, "Well, show me the way." The African man responded, "Walk." So they walked and hacked their way through unmarked jungle for more than an hour. The missionary began to get worried. "Are you sure this is the right way? Where is the path?" The man said, "Friend, in this place there is no path. I am the path."

It *is* a jungle out there—from pop culture to pop psychology, the path of life is overgrown with too many options and too little time. It's hard to see the forest for the trees. We need clear direction. Jesus said, "I am the light of the world. He who follows Me shall not walk in darkness, but have the light of life" (John 8:12). Jesus walked in His Father's footsteps, illuminating a path for others who desire to find their way. This week you will discover three ways to walk in His footsteps: in love, in the light, and in wisdom.

DAY 1
Walk in Love

DAY 2
Dangerous Detours

DAY 3
Out of Bounds

DAY 4
Walk in Light

DAY 5
Walk Wisely

DAY **1** WALK IN LOVE

preparation

Lord, hold my hand as I walk in this world. Guide my footsteps so I can go where You lead and walk as You walk. Keep me on Your path. Amen.

WALK WITH GOD
God said: "I will live in them and walk among them. I will be their God, and they will be my people." 2 Corinthians 6:16, NLT

explanation

IMITATING GOD
To *imitate* means to mimic or to act as. Children like to play dress-up and pretend they are adults like Mom or Dad. Christians should not pretend but actually *become* like our heavenly Dad. Imitation is the sincerest form of flattery.

exploration

Over the last few weeks we have learned to walk worthy of our high calling in Christ. We have also been challenged to no longer walk as the Gentiles walk. This week Paul shows us how to walk in godliness and in love.

Read through Ephesians 5 to get a feel for the tone, language, and content of this chapter, then focus on verses 1-2.

> **Therefore be imitators of God as dear children.** Ephesians 5:1

1. Who are we to imitate? . . . .

. . . .

2. What relationship compels us to become imitators of God?

. . . .

> **And walk in love, as Christ also has loved us and given Himself for us, an offering and a sacrifice to God for a sweet-smelling aroma.** Ephesians 5:2

3. How are we to walk as believers? . . . .

. . . .

4. Whose love are we to model ourselves after? . . . .

. . . .

5. What did Christ give to show His love for us? . . . .

. . . .

6. In what two ways did Christ give Himself to God? . . . .

. . . .

7. Fill in the chart below to discover how Jesus fulfilled Old Testament requirements of an acceptable sacrifice.

REQUIREMENT	FULFILLMENT
Without blemish = 1 Pet. 1:19	
Outside camp = John 19:17	
With free will = John 10:18	
Perfect = 2 Cor. 5:21	

transformation

8. Today we discovered that our goal as believers is to imitate God—to become like our heavenly Father. In order to become like Him, we must understand what He is like. Draw a line linking the attributes of God with the appropriate Scriptures.

GOD IS:	SCRIPTURE:
Faithful	Deuteronomy 4:31
Good	Psalm 145:17
Holy	Psalm 100:5
Just	Psalm 71:19
Love	Psalm 99:9
Merciful	1 Thessalonians 5:24
Righteous	1 John 4:8

9. Which of the attributes of God listed above has been difficult for you to imitate?

. . . .

5

REAL LOVE
Love is not about getting, but giving. True love the God kind is sacrificial. When God showed His love, He gave His Son. When Christ showed His love, He gave His life. For God so loved the world that he gave his only Son (John 3:16, NLT).

6

SWEET AROMA
In the Old Testament, the Levitical sacrifices were a sweet savor to God. In the New Testament, Christ s sacrifice was a sweet-smelling aroma. In heaven, the prayers of the saints are like incense ascending to the throne of God. I will fr eely sacrifice to You; I will praise Your name, O Lord, for it is good (Psalm 54:6).

8

GOD IS
God is called the great I AM because whatever you need, He *is*. If you need forgiveness, God is merciful. If you need discipline, God is just. Even if you are faithless, God is faithful. God is everything that is good and nothing that is bad. He is the Lord God Almighty, Who was and is and is to come! (Revelation 4:8).

COSTLY LOVE
King David's philosophy was, "Give until it hurts." God told David to build Him an altar on Araunah's threshing floor. Araunah offered to donate the land, but David said, "I cannot present burnt offerings to the Lord my God that have cost me nothing" (2 Samuel 24:24, NLT).

Write a prayer asking God to help you become like Him in this area of your life.

. . . .

. . . .

. . . .

. . . .

. . . .

. . . .

10. Paul revealed that one specific way to imitate God is to love as Christ loved—sacrificially.

Journal about a time when someone sacrificed something to show his or her love for you.

. . . .

. . . .

. . . .

. . . .

. . . .

Write about a time when you have loved someone sacrificially. What was the circumstance, and what did it cost you?

. . . .

. . . .

. . . .

. . . .

. . . .

11. We should not only love others sacrificially, we should also love God sacrificially. Choose one of the following ways to pour out a sweet-smelling sacrifice to your heavenly Father. Describe how you will follow through this week.

Fasting: I will fast from _____ so I can feed on God's Word.

Money: I will tithe $ _____ to support God's work.

Intercessory Prayers: I will pray for _____ to show God's love.

Time: I will offer time to _____ to be God's hands on earth.

Pleasure: I will abstain from _____ to obey God's commands.

Friendships: I won't call _____, so I can talk to God instead.

Love is the gift of oneself! I experienced a wonderful illustration of this truth. In 1984 my husband and I traveled to India with Gospel for Asia to train indigenous pastors and their wives. Nothing could prepare me for the experience. To know India is to smell its pungent aroma, to wilt in its humid air, to be overwhelmed walking its congested streets, and to see its slum villages drowning in poverty. Although the nation is poor economically, the people I met were rich in good deeds.

Finding food and drink that wouldn't upset our stomachs was challenging. We had been warned, "Don't drink the water, and limit your diet to foods cooked thoroughly and to fruits that have to be peeled." In one jungle village there was no bottled water, so a native climbed a coconut palm and gave us milk to drink from the shell. One morning we were served the sweetest pineapple. I gushed, "It's better than pineapple in Hawaii!" Incredibly, our host sent his son on a day's journey to pick another pineapple for dinner. When I learned of the boy's hike, I said, "You didn't have to walk so far for me." The boy smiled and said, "Long walk part of gift!"

Love prompted God to send His Son, Jesus, on the long walk from heaven to earth to give you the best gift you could ever receive—Himself.

contemplation
True love is always costly.
Billy Graham

DAY 2 DANGEROUS DETOURS

Hugh Hefner, founder of the Playboy empire, once said in an interview, "If Christ were here today and had to choose between being on the staff of one of the joy-killing, pleasure-denying churches [and *Playboy*], he would, of course, immediately join us." He went on to declare, "We reject any philosophy which holds that a man must deny himself for others." The Playboy organization holds that we all should love ourselves preeminently and pursue our own pleasure constantly. Nowhere is the clash between Playboyism and the ways of Jesus any sharper than over how the good life is to be achieved. Hugh Hefner tells us to get all we can. Jesus tells us to give all we can (*Bible Illustrator*).

Hefner's views are nothing new, but they will take you off course. Jesus said, "You can enter God's Kingdom only through the narrow gate. The highway to hell is broad, and its gate is wide for the many who choose the easy way. But the gateway to life is small, and the road is narrow, and only a few ever find it" (Matthew 7:13-14, NLT). It's important to avoid the dangerous detours found on the path of life and stick to God's righteous road instead.

exploration

Yesterday we learned to walk in love. Today, we learn to distance ourselves from sinful desires.

Review Ephesians 5, then focus on verses 3-4.

> *But fornication and all uncleanness or covetousness, let it not even be named among you, as is fitting for saints; . . .* Ephesians 5:3

1. What three sins did Paul warn against here? . . . .

. . . .

2. What phrase cautions believers not to even speak of, much less participate in, these sins?

. . . .

3. According to this verse, why should the saints abstain from these sins?

. . . .

> *. . . neither filthiness, nor foolish talking, nor coarse jesting, which are not fitting, but rather giving of thanks.* Ephesians 5:4

4. What are the next three sins Paul warned against in verse 4?

. . . .

5. What area do these particular sins deal with? . . . .

. . . .

6. What reason did Paul give for avoiding these sins? . . . .

. . . .

7. Rather than using our mouths in filthiness, foolishness, and coarseness—sinful speech—what should we be doing?

. . . .

transformation

8. Paul exhorted believers to abstain from fornication, uncleanness, or covetousness. Read the definitions, then journal in the space provided.

explanation

1

BAD FRUIT
The way to heaven is too straight for a person who wants to walk the crooked road of unclean living. A crooked walk exposes a person who is bent on sin. "You will know them by their fruits. . . . Every good tree bears good fruit, but a bad tree bears bad fruit" (Matthew 7:16-17).

5

BAD LANGUAGE
Filthiness refers to obscenities; foolish talking implies silliness or buffoonery; coarse jesting portrays a person who uses vulgar repartee or witticism. A good indication of a person's character is what makes him laugh. "Let your speech always be with grace" (Colossians 4:6).

8

SAFE SEX?
Sex-education classes teach kids that condoms and contraceptives make having sex anytime safe. This philosophy is full of holes. In God's Word, we discover that abstinence is the best policy until sex is in its safest context: the marriage of one man and one woman for a lifetime.

Fornication: any sexual relationship outside the bond of marriage; unchastity. If you are currently engaged in sexual behavior that is unfitting for a saint, journal a prayer of repentance to God.

. . . .

. . . .

. . . .

Uncleanness: physical or moral impurity. If you have become defiled sexually, write a prayer asking God to wash you clean with His blood, making you white as snow.

. . . .

. . . .

. . . .

Covetousness: an intense desire to possess something or someone that belongs to another person. If you have been coveting something or someone who belongs to another, pray that God will help you change your thoughts and seek first His kingdom.

. . . .

. . . .

. . . .

9. People who have base appetites usually develop disgraceful speech and humor. The Bible says to replace gross speech with giving thanks. Meditate on the following Scripture verses, then write prayers of thanksgiving.

"He has removed our rebellious acts as far away from us as the east is from the west" (Psalm 103:12, NLT). Journal your thanks to God that your rebellious acts can cease once and for all.

. . . .

. . . .

"No matter how deep the stain of your sins, I can remove it. I can make you as clean as freshly fallen snow. Even if you are stained as red as crimson, I can make you as white as wool" (Isaiah 1:18, NLT). Give thanks that the stain of sin can be removed completely.

. . . .

. . . .

. . . .

"Restore to me again the joy of your salvation, and make me willing to obey you" (Psalm 51:12, NLT). Thank God that He can miraculously restore your joy.

. . . .

. . . .

. . . .

Author and speaker Josh McDowell often speaks about sexual purity. He believes that in these last decades, contrary to popular opinion, we have been through not a sexual revolution but a revolution in the search for intimacy. He observes, "Most of our young people do not want the physical aspect of sex, they want someone who cares. They want to be able to care. They want intimacy. We have allowed our culture to dictate to us that the only way you find intimacy is through the physical—and that's an absolute lie!"

Too many people get detoured by the idea that intercourse creates intimacy. One-night stands breed insecurity since there's no commitment for the future. But Scripture reveals that true intimacy is found in the bond of holy matrimony, not just the bedroom. "A man shall leave his father and mother and be joined to his wife, and the two shall become one flesh" (Matthew 19:5). When sex is on track with God's plan, it is beautiful. When it bypasses the bounds of marriage, it is sinful.

contemplation
Things are seldom what they seem; that's why people mistake education for intelligence, wealth for happiness, and sex for love.
Anonymous

DAY 3 OUT OF BOUNDS

BOUNDARY LINES
The boundary lines have fallen for me in pleasant places; surely I have a delightful inheritance.
Psalm 16:6, NIV

Boundaries—in or out? The whistle blows when the football player runs out of bounds. The baseball player hits one outside the lines and hears, "Foul ball!" When snow skiing, out of bounds is a dangerous place to go. You might come face-to-face with a tree or be swept away in an avalanche. Boundaries are our friends—they keep us safe.

In the film series Focus on the Family, James Dobson told about a group of educators who decided to remove the chain-link fences from around the school playgrounds. They believed the fences promoted feelings of confinement and restraint. However, as soon as the fences were removed, the children huddled in the center of the playground to play. Conclusion: Children need boundaries.

Adults need boundaries, too. God has set loving parameters for His people, and those who choose to live "out of bounds" will find themselves outside of His kingdom.

exploration

This week we have received firm instruction concerning God's holy boundaries. Now we read about the consequences of purposefully, perpetually walking in disobedience.

Review Ephesians 5, then focus on verses 5-7.

> ***For this you know, that no fornicator, unclean person, nor covetous man, who is an idolater, has any inheritance in the kingdom of Christ and God.*** Ephesians 5:5

1. List the three kinds of sinful people Paul named here.

. . . .

2. The person who practices these sins is an _____.

3. What is the consequence of engaging in these sinful lifestyles?

. . . .

> **Let no one deceive you with empty words, for because of these things the wrath of God comes upon the sons of disobedience.** Ephesians 5:6

4. What type of words is used to deceive believers?. . . . .

. . . .

5. What sinful "things" mentioned in this week's lesson bothered Paul?

. . . .

6. What is the consequence for participating in these things?

. . . .

. . . .

7. Who experiences God's wrath? . . . .

. . . .

> **Therefore do not be partakers with them.** Ephesians 5:7

8. How should we respond to the deceit of the sons of disobedience?

. . . .

transformation

9. Paul taught that what a person does reveals who a person worships—creature or Creator. Fill in the chart below to learn more about the futility of idol worship in contrast to the fulfillment of worshiping God.

IDOLARY
Idolatry is worshiping or paying divine honor to something created instead of the Creator. Idolatry may involve the worship of these things: graven images or inanimate objects, animals, nature, people, and ideals. In Ephesus, the primary idol was Diana, a multibreasted fertility goddess.

GOD S WRATH
God s wrath is the manifestation of God s holy indignation against sin. God s wrath Is not irrational or malicious. Rather, it is the just and proper expression of His righteousness. God offset wrath with love by sending His Son.

DON T MIX
To partake means to join in partnership or cooperate with in an activity. Don t team up with those who are unbelievers. How can goodness be a partner with wickedness? (2 Corinthians 6:14, NLT). Like oil and water, some things just don t mix.

10

SONS OF
DISOBEDIENCE
Sons of disobedience
habitually sin and
encourage others to sin.
Children of God are to
be the opposite—obey
God and help others
obey. "We can tell who
are children of God
and who are children
of the Devil. Anyone
who does not obey
God's commands and
does not love other
Christians does not
belong to God" (1 John
3:10, NLT).

SCRIPTURE	CHARACTERISTICS OF IDOLS	CONTRAST TO GOD
Deut. 4:15-19		
Ps. 135:5-7; 15-18		
Hab. 2:18-20		
Rom. 1:20-25		

Take the time to name some forms of modern idol worship. (Example: anything that you give devotion to, from cars to stars). Journal about a situation in your life where you worshiped and served a created thing more than the Creator. What was the result?

. . . .

. . . .

. . . .

. . . .

10. Paul warned that the "sons of disobedience"—unbelievers— will try to deceive believers with empty words. Fill in the chart with ways you have been led astray by enticing propaganda. If these sources have been saturating you with fast talk, it's time to talk back. This week as you encounter any lies the media spouts, stand up and shout, "That's a lie, and I don't believe it!"

SOURCE	SPECIFICS	SOLICITATION
Ad Campaign	Ford/GMC	New car = fulfillment
Ad Campaign		
TV series		
Movie		
Printed material		

11. Review the previous chart. Write down the ways this enticing propaganda has failed to deliver what was promised. (Example: My new car didn't bring fulfillment; instead it brought debt and dents.)

. . . .

. . . .

12. Bible teacher Warren Wiersbe says, "A Christian is not *sinless*, but he does *sin less*—and less—and less!"

Journal about a time when you became aware of buying into a lie propagated by the world. How did you replace the lie with the truth? What was the result?

. . . .

. . . .

. . . .

. . . .

12
SIN LESS
Less is more. When we sin less, we become more like Christ. "As the Spirit of the Lord works within us, we become more and more like him and reflect his glory even more. And so . . . we never give up" (2 Corinthians 3:18–4:1, NLT).

A teenage girl wanted to join her friend's church. The pastor asked, "Were you a sinner before you received the Lord Jesus into your life?"

"Yeah, and it got me into lots of trouble," she replied.

"Well, are you still a sinner?" he asked.

The girl replied, "To tell you the truth, I think I'm a bigger sinner now than I ever was."

"So what difference has Christ made in your life?" the pastor responded.

She said, "I used to be a sinner running *after* sin, but now that I'm saved, I'm a sinner running *away* from sin!"

We all used to be sons or daughters of disobedience, running after sin. Learning to run away from sin is the right thing to do. However, sometimes we must learn to run away from sinners as well. Paul warned, "Do not be deceived: 'Evil company corrupts good habits'" (1 Corinthians 15:33). Peer pressure is a powerful thing, for good or for evil. If you're running with the wrong crowd, perhaps it's time to turn around and "run with endurance the race that is set before us" (Hebrews 12:1).

contemplation
Idolatry: trusting people, possessions or positions to do for me what only God can do.
Bill Gothard

DAY 4 WALK IN LIGHT

Years ago the Denver city zoo was offered the gift of a beautiful polar bear. Unfortunately there was no room for the animal. At the time of the gift the board of directors was in the middle of a fund-raising campaign to renovate the zoo. They changed the plans to include a magnificent habitat for the polar bear. In the meantime the bear was put in a temporary cage. The space was so small and cramped that it could only take three steps, turn around, and walk three steps back.

Due to countless delays the construction took three years, but the bear's new home was filled with waterfalls, caves, and lots of space. The bear entered its new home, looked around, took three steps, turned around, and took three steps back.

Like the polar bear given a new habitat, the Christian has entered a new realm too. You have been transported from darkness into His wonderful light. Now you must break out of your old habits, explore your new terrain, and learn how to walk as a child of the light.

exploration

Walking on God's path means walking away from sin's path. Let's examine yet another aspect of the Christian journey—walking as children of light.

Review Ephesians 5, then focus on verses 8-14.

> *For you were once darkness, but now you are light in the Lord. Walk as children of light . . .* Ephesians 5:8

1. How did Paul contrast our lives before and after salvation?

. . . .

2. How, then, should we walk? . . . .

. . . .

> *. . . (for the fruit of the Spirit is in all goodness, righteousness, and truth), finding out what is acceptable to the Lord.* Ephesians 5:9-10

3. According to verse 9, what three types of "soil" does the fruit of the Spirit grow well in?

. . . .

4. What should children of light be seeking? . . . .

. . . .

> *And have no fellowship with the unfruitful works of darkness, but rather expose them. For it is shameful even to speak of those things which are done by them in secret.* Ephesians 5:11-12

5. What two things are believers to do about unfruitful works of darkness?

. . . .

6. What is shameful to speak of? . . . .

. . . .

> *But all things that are exposed are made manifest by the light, for whatever makes manifest is light. Therefore He says: "Awake, you who sleep, arise from the dead, and Christ will give you light."* Ephesians 5:13-14

7. What happens to all things that are exposed? . . . .

. . . .

8. Paul gave a symbolic gospel message to unbelievers.

a. What two things did God exhort the unbeliever to do? Why?

. . . .

4

ACCEPTABLE
Acceptable is finding what is agreeable or well pleasing to God. Humans were created with a purpose. "Our purpose is to please God, not people" (1 Thessalonians 2:4, NLT). Crowd pleasers are often contrary to God pleasers. "Pilate, anxious to please the crowd, released Barabbas to them. He ordered Jesus flogged, . . . then turned him over . . . to crucify him" (Mark 15:15, NLT).

8

RISE AND SHINE
To sinners lulled to sleep by the dark world Christ says, awake! Spiritual awakening is to recognize and repent of sin. To those who are dead in trespasses, Jesus says, arise! Spiritual resurrection means to be born again. "The day is at hand. Therefore let us cast off the works of darkness, and let us put on the armor of light" (Romans 13:12).

CHILDREN OF LIGHT

"God is light" (1 John 1:5). God is not a light or the light, but God is light. The Greek word indicates that God in His very essence is light, making Him the true source of illumination. When we reflect His glory, we become children of light. "You are the light of the world, . . . let it shine for all" (Matthew 5:14-15, NLT)

MANIFEST

Manifest means to make visible, uncover, lay bare, or reveal. Light and darkness are mutually exclusive; they can't coexist. It's either one or the other. "For everyone practicing evil hates the light and does not come to the light, lest his deeds should be exposed. But he who does the truth comes to the light, that his deeds may be clearly seen" (John 3:20-21).

b. What condition are sinners in before they know Christ?

. . . .

transformation

9. We are to walk as children of light. Fill in the following chart to discover how.

SCRIPTURE	HOW TO WALK
Deut. 8:6 . . . .
Isa. 30:21 . . . .
John 12:35-36 . . . .
Rom. 6:4 . . . .
Rom. 13:13 . . . .

10. Light exposes or manifests the things that are in darkness. With this in mind journal through the steps below.

Step One: List some dark places in the world around you. (Example: adult bookstores, nightclubs, Internet sites, etc.)

. . . .

. . . .

Step Two: Imagine you've been given a powerful, portable spotlight. What would happen if you directed its beam on the dark places listed above? How would the people in those places respond?

. . . .

. . . .

. . . .

. . . .

Step Three: Rewrite this passage into a prayer for people dwelling in darkness: "The people who sat in darkness have seen a great light. And for those who lived in the land where death casts its shadow, a light has shined. From then on, Jesus began to preach, 'Turn from your sins and turn to God, because the Kingdom of Heaven is near'" (Matthew 4:16-17, NLT).

. . . .

. . . .

11. The apostle John warned that children of light can become blinded when they hate or reject other Christians: "Anyone who loves other Christians is living in the light and does not cause anyone to stumble. Anyone who hates a Christian brother or sister is living and walking in darkness. Such a person is lost, having been blinded by the darkness" (1 John 2:10-11, NLT).

Name Christians you have trouble getting along with. How have you rejected them in word or deed? Write a prayer asking God to help you shine the light of His love on them instead.

. . . .

. . . .

. . . .

Rose Crawford, who had been blind for fifty years, was recovering from a delicate eye surgery. "I just can't believe it!" she gasped as the doctor lifted the bandages from her eyes. She wept for joy when a beautiful world of form and color came into focus for the first time. The amazing thing about this story, though, is that twenty years of her blindness had been unnecessary. She didn't know it, but surgical techniques had been developed, and she could have had her sight restored much earlier.

Are there any Rose Crawfords in your life—people who are blinded by sin and have not yet heard that there is a cure in Christ? As a child of the light, reflect His glory to the dark world around you.

11

NOW I SEE
Saul of Tarsus was blind with rage, seeking to imprison Christians. After the Lord appeared to him on the road to Damascus, he was blinded by God's light. It took the prayer of one of his enemies to help him see with new eyes. "Receive your sight and be filled with the Holy Spirit" (Acts 9:17).

contemplation
A single sunbeam is enough to drive away many shadows.
Francis of Assisi

193

LESSON 9 - DAY 4

DAY 5 WALK WISELY

preparation

Father, help me to slow down so that I can consider what steps to take. Lead me in paths of righteousness for the sake of Your name. Amen.

PRUDENCE
The prudent carefully consider their steps.
Proverbs 14:15, NLT

At one time our neighborhood was infested with pigeons— flying rodents, I called them. As I racked my brain thinking of ways to rid our roof of them, my son, Nathan, was making plans to capture one. One day we were bird-watching from the front porch and just burst out laughing at the way pigeons walk. They waddle from side to side like Charlie Chaplin, heads jerking back and forth like Egyptian dancers'. "Why do pigeons walk so funny?" Nathan asked me. I read an article explaining that a pigeon walks that way so it can see where it's going. Apparently it can't adjust its focus as it moves, so the pigeon brings its head to a complete stop between steps in order to refocus. The bird waddles along: head forward, stop, head back, stop, and so on.

It made me stop and think. In our spiritual walk we can learn something from the pigeon. Human beings can be haphazard, moving at a pace that blurs our vision. We should stop between steps to refocus on the Word of God so we can walk in the will of God.

exploration

We are called to walk in love and in the light of God's Word. Now we see how to be wise in our steps as well.

Review Ephesians 5, then focus on verses 15-17.

> **See then that you walk circumspectly, not as fools but as wise, . . .** Ephesians 5:15

1. Paul begins verse 15 with the exhortation "see then." What did we learn in yesterday's lesson that makes it possible for Christians to see?

. . . .

2. As children of light, how are we to walk and how are we not to walk?

. . . .

3. Fill in the following sentence based on verse 15: When I walk _____, God considers me to be

_____.

> . . . *redeeming the time, because the days are evil.*
> Ephesians 5:16

4. What is one way to walk wisely? . . . .

. . . .

5. Why is it important for believers to redeem the time?

. . . .

> *Therefore do not be unwise, but understand what the will of the Lord is.* Ephesians 5:17

6. What are believers cautioned not to be?. . . . .

. . . .

7. What should the believer understand?. . . . .

. . . .

transformation

8. Fill in the chart below to discover some characteristics of a spiritually foolish person. Then write a brief note evaluating whether or not you are exhibiting these.

CIRCUMSPECT
Circumspect means to look around and walk carefully. The Greek word carries the idea of precision and accuracy. In other words, we should walk carefully or with exactness. Paul said, "But you have carefully followed my doctrine, manner of life, purpose, [and] faith" (2 Timothy 3:10).

GOD'S WILL
God's will is two-sided. One side shows what His will *is;* the other side reveals what His will *is not.* Peter taught, "The Lord is . . . not willing that any should perish but that all should come to repentance" (2 Peter 3:9). Not in His will? Are you willing to repent?

8
FOOLISH
Fool in Scripture refers more to moral than to intellectual deficiencies. The "fool" does not lack mental powers but misuses them. He does not lack the ability to reason but reasons wrongly. The "fool" primarily casts off the fear of God and acts as if he could safely disregard the eternal principles of God's righteousness *(New Unger's Bible Dictionary).*

WISE PERSON
Jesus told of two builders: one wise and one foolish. Both built homes, endured storms, and heard God's Word. The difference? Obedience. It changes a fool into a scholar! "Whoever hears these sayings of Mine, and *does* them, I will liken him to a wise man" (Matthew 7:24, italics added).

SCRIPTURE	FOOLISH CHARACTERISTIC	SELF-EVALUATION
Ps. 14:1		
Prov. 10:18		
Luke 24:25		
Gal. 3:1-3		
1 Tim. 6:9		

In which of these areas do you need to wise up? Journal your thoughts.

. . . .

. . . .

. . . .

9. Fill in this chart to find some of the ways you can walk wisely, and evaluate whether or not you are exhibiting these.

SCRIPTURE	WISE CHARACTERISTIC	SELF-EVALUATION
Prov. 9:10		
Prov. 14:1		
Rom. 16:19		
2 Tim. 3:14-15		
James 1:5		

In which of these areas do you need to gain more insight? Journal your thoughts.

. . . .

. . . .

. . . .

. . . .

10. Moses wrote this prayer, "So teach us to number our days, that we may gain a heart of wisdom" (Psalm 90:12).

Reword Moses's prayer into your personal prayer.

. . . .

. . . .

. . . .

. . . .

Imagine that you and Jesus are taking a walk. His footprints go consistently, rarely varying. But your footprints are a stream of zigzags. Gradually your footprints come alongside His—you and Jesus are walking side by side! As you continue, your footprints begin to fit precisely in His—you and He are becoming one. This goes on for many miles. But suddenly your footprints are back and it seems worse than before! Zigzags everywhere. Stops. Starts. Deep gashes in the sand.

Puzzled, you say, "Lord, I understand that at first You taught me to walk with You."

"That's true," He replies.

"And when my footprints were inside of Yours, I was learning to walk in Your steps—becoming one with You, right?" I ask.

"You've understood everything so far," He says and smiles.

"So, Lord, did I blow it or something? Why did the footprints separate?"

There is a long pause before the Lord explains, "Didn't you know? We were dancing."

God made people with hearts as well as minds. A wise mind will walk circumspectly; a happy heart will dance with joy. The wise King Solomon ruled with his intellect. The passionate King David ruled as a man after God's heart. "David danced before the Lord with all his might" (2 Samuel 6:14, NLT). It's wise to walk with the Lord; it's wonderful to dance with Him.

10

REDEEM THE TIME
Redeeming the time means taking advantage of or buying up the opportunity. If you're thirty-five, live a normal life span, subtract time for sleep, work, hygiene, chores, eating, traveling, and such activities, in the next thirty-six years you'll have about 500 days left to live! Life is short, so spend your time wisely.

contemplation
A fool wanders; the wise man travels.
Unknown

Change of Heart

*T*hink of the heart. It weighs less than a pound, but it has a lot of work to do. On average, it pumps 100,000 times every day, circulating 2,000 gallons of blood through 60,000 miles of arteries, capillaries, and veins. This hollow muscular organ forces blood through the circulatory system, pumping life through every organ. However, when the arteries become clogged or the heart becomes diseased, there is a very real danger of heart failure and loss of life.

But the heart is more than an organ. The biblical meaning for *heart* represents our inner self—the source of emotions and deepest feelings. The inner heart, when clogged and sickened by sin, can lead us into spiritual danger. Scripture tells us, "The human heart is most deceitful and desperately wicked" (Jeremiah 17:9, NLT). There is only one cure—heart surgery. God says, "I will give you a new heart with new and right desires, and I will put a new spirit in you" (Ezekiel 36:26, NLT).

This week we discover that God wants to replace our spiritually diseased hearts with Spirit-filled ones: hearts full of praise, thanksgiving, submission, respect, love, and unity. As you study this lesson, ask God to give you a new heart that is strong and ready to carry on the work of His kingdom.

DAY 1
Spirit-Filled Heart

DAY 2
Heart of Submission

DAY 3
Heart of Respect

DAY 4
Heart of Love

DAY 5
Heart of Unity

DAY 1 SPIRIT-FILLED HEART

preparation

Father, the only way for my heart to be strong is to be filled with Your Spirit. Don't let me settle for worthless substitutes; instead, fill me to overflowing with Your Spirit. Amen.

HEART OF PRAISE

O Lord, you alone can heal me; you alone can save. My praises are for you alone! Jeremiah 17:14, NLT

explanation

DISSIPATION
Dissipation means "indulgent or wasteful living, especially excessive drinking." People who live to "get wasted" end up wasting their lives like the Prodigal Son, who "packed all his belongings and took a trip to a distant land, and there he wasted all his money on wild living" (Luke 15:13, NLT).

exploration

For the past few weeks we have studied what it means to live out our calling in Christ. This week we examine the inner heart attitudes that influence our outward actions. God wants us to be filled with His Holy Spirit and to exhibit hearts of praise and thanksgiving.

Read through Ephesians 5 to get a feel for the tone, language, and content of this chapter, then focus on verses 18-20.

> **And do not be drunk with wine, in which is dissipation; but be filled with the Spirit,** . . . Ephesians 5:18

1. What negative command did Paul give here?. . . . .

. . . .

2. Why should believers not be drunk with wine?. . . . .

. . . .

3. Rather than being filled with wine, what are believers to be filled with?

. . . .

> . . . *speaking to one another in psalms and hymns and spiritual songs, singing and making melody in your heart to the Lord,* . . . Ephesians 5:19

4. We have been commanded to be filled with the Spirit. In what three ways are believers to speak to one another?

. . . .

5. Where does this singing take place, and to whom do we sing?

. . . .

> *. . . giving thanks always for all things to God the Father in the name of our Lord Jesus Christ, . . .* Ephesians 5:20

6. What are we to be doing and how often?. . . . .

. . . .

7. For what and to whom are we to give thanks?. . . . .

. . . .

8. In whose name are we to give thanks?. . . . .

transformation

9. God wants us to be filled with the Holy Spirit rather than with artificial stimulants. Write down the name of a prodigal person who has filled his or her life with drugs or alcohol:

. . . .

Journal a prayer asking God to bring them to their senses. Rewrite the following verses into a prayer: "When he finally came to his senses, he said to himself, . . . 'I will go home to my father and say, "Father, I have sinned against both heaven and you"'" (Luke 15:17-18, NLT).

. . . .

. . . .

. . . .

. . . .

3
SPIRIT-FILLED
Filled has three meanings (1) *Filled:* As wind fills a ship's sail, so God's Spirit fills us with power and direction; (2) *Permeated:* As salt permeates food with flavor and preserves, so God's Spirit provides us with zest and permanence; (3) *Controlled:* As one reins in a horse with a bit, so the Spirit guides and controls a life surrendered to Him.

6
ALL THINGS
Give thanks *always* in *all ways.* At work, give thanks for provision; at home, give thanks for family; on the road, give thanks for the occasion to practice patience with strangers. In all you say and do, let your life be a thank-you note to God.

8
IN JESUS' NAME
Shakespeare said, "A rose by any other name would smell as sweet." But there is no name sweeter than the one given by God to His only Son. "You are to name him Jesus, for he will save his people from their sins" (Matthew 1:21, NLT). What's in *His* name? The sweetness of salvation!

FILLED
The Greek word for *filled* means to keep on being filled. The indwelling of the Holy Spirit is a one-time experience, but the filling of the Holy Spirit is an experience where believers are continually filled. There are two prerequisites for being filled with the Spirit: repentance of sin and yielding to God.

10. Fill in the chart below to discover people in the Bible who were filled with the Holy Spirit.

SCRIPTURE	WHO WAS FILLED	WHAT THE SPIRIT PROVIDED
Exod. 28:2-3		
Exod. 31:2-4		
Luke 1:67		
Luke 4:1		
Acts 4:31		
Acts 7:55, 59		
Acts 13:52		

11. Paul's instruction to be filled with the Spirit applies to *you* too. Before you can be filled with God, you must be emptied of self. Listed below are some of the "works of the flesh" and also the "fruit of the Spirit" taken from Galatians 5:19-23. Draw a line through the works of the flesh of which you need to be emptied. Then circle the fruits of the Spirit with which you desire to be filled.

WORKS OF FLESH	FRUIT OF THE SPIRIT
Hatred	Love
Fits of Rage	Joy
Envy	Peace
Drunkenness	Patience
Hostility	Kindness
Jealousy	Goodness
Quarreling	Faithfulness
Selfish Ambition	Gentleness
Divisions	Self-control

12. With the Holy Spirit's help, you can possess the graces of praise and thankfulness in the midst of difficult circumstances.

> Journal about a time when you were able to praise the Lord or offer Him thanks *only* through the power of the Holy Spirit.

. . . .

. . . .

. . . .

. . . .

. . . .

. . . .

12
PRAISE AT MIDNIGHT
Spirit-filled Paul could sing praises when the night was dark and the walls were closing in. "Around midnight, Paul and Silas were praying and singing hymns to God. . . . Suddenly, there was a great earthquake, and the prison was shaken to its foundations" (Acts 16:25-26, NLT). When you want to shake things up, sing songs of praise.

In the late 1970s I was a preppie coed. Disappointment over my parents' divorce had made my heart calloused. Control became my way of coping. I controlled my appearance, every hair in place. I controlled my emotions with artificial stimulants, partying instead of pain. And I controlled my relationships, dates but no commitments. Then my dad was saved and invited me to attend Calvary Chapel in Costa Mesa, California.

Pastor Chuck Smith reflected God's love as he entered the sanctuary. His Spirit-filled words disarmed my heart. His service ended with an invitation for prayer. I wanted to go forward, but I was terrified to relinquish control. The Holy Spirit compelled me to let go.

I told Pastor Malcolm Wild, "I believe in Jesus and I've been coming to church, but something's missing." He asked, "Have you repented of sin?" I had no idea what he meant. He explained, "Repentance means to have a change of heart, to turn from sin and toward God. Sin separates you from God, but confession brings forgiveness."

As he spoke, tears ran down my face. My "in control" veneer melted away. He led me in a prayer that changed my life, repenting and asking God to fill me with His Holy Spirit. I sighed with relief. At last God was in control!

If your life is controlled by *you* instead of by God's Spirit, maybe it's time to let go and let God take charge.

contemplation
A man should never give all his heart to anything which will end when his life ends.
C. S. Lewis

HEART OF SUBMISSION

You're in the army now! God has enlisted you "as a good soldier of Jesus Christ" (2 Timothy 2:3). The army, like the body of Christ, has a chain of command. Each member under the chain of command is equal in quality but differs in position. Generals are not better people than privates; generals just have a star instead of a stripe on their shoulders.

General Eisenhower once rebuked an officer for calling a soldier "just a private." Eisenhower thought the army could operate better without its generals than without its foot soldiers. "If this war is won," he said, "it will be won by privates." In the same way, simple Spirit-filled saints are the core of the church. Gifted evangelists run crusades; pastors lead large and small congregations; and parachurch ministries are headed up by charismatic leaders. But, if God's work is to be accomplished, if the great commission is to be fulfilled, it will be the "ordinary" Christians who will do it.

There are no "ordinary" Christians in God's army. He has developed an extraordinary chain of command in which we all submit to one another. The difference between human armies and the Lord's armies is that God, not the president, is *the* Commander in Chief. Soldiers surrender their will, serving their president out of compulsion. Christians surrender their hearts, serving their God out of love. Where do you fit in God's army? Have you gotten your marching orders from your Commander in Chief?

exploration

We have found that the mark of a Spirit-filled believer is a heart of praise and thanksgiving. Today we find that God insists that believers possess a heart of submission to God and to others.

Review Ephesians 5, then focus on verse 21.

> *. . . submitting to one another in the fear of God.*
> Ephesians 5:21

1. To whom are believers to submit? . . . .

. . . .

2. Fill in the chart to discover some "one anothers" we all must submit to.

SCRIPTURE	SUBMIT TO
1 Cor. 16:16	
James 4:7	
1 Pet. 2:13-14	
1 Pet. 2:18	
1 Pet. 5:5	

3. How does the definition of submission given in the sidebar influence or change your view of submission?

. . . .

4. What actions or attitudes are the opposite of the definition above?

. . . .

5. According to verse 21, how should we submit to one another?

. . . .

6. To discover more about the fear of the Lord, fill in the chart below.

SCRIPTURE	RESULTS OF FEAR OF THE LORD	HAVE YOU EXPERIENCED IT?
Deut. 10:12-13		
Prov. 1:7		
Prov. 8:13		
Mal. 2:5		

---

explanation

1
ALL SUBMIT
Submission is not just for women. "One another" includes both sexes. Male children as well as female children are to honor their parents. Both genders are commanded to obey governing authorities.

2
BIBLICAL SUBMISSION
The word *submission* means "humble obedience to another's will" (*Nelson's Quick Reference Topical Bible Index*). This word in the original Greek denotes the idea of military ranking, to arrange in order. Biblically, submission means willingly relinquishing one's rights to another person based on the order God, in His wisdom, has established.

5
FEAR OF GOD
To fear the Lord means to stand in awe of him. Awe combines honor, fear, and respect before someone of superior office or action—primarily God. "Let everyone in the world fear the Lord, and let everyone stand in awe of him" (Psalm 33:8, NLT).

GOD'S ORDER
Submission isn't personal; it's practical. At creation, God subdued the elements, bringing order out of chaos (Genesis 1:1-3). At the Fall in the Garden of Eden, God established submission of wives to their husbands (Genesis 3:16). Part of submission is recognizing God's order of things—His chain of command. Are you the missing link?

CIVIL DISOBEDIENCE
Chinese Christians disobey their government's ban on having Bibles. Israeli Christians disobey the official ban on evangelism. Commentator William Barclay writes, "The Christian has a higher obligation than even his obligation to the state. While he must render to Caesar the things which are Caesar's, he must also render to God the things which are God's." When society's laws conflict with God's law, Christians must "obey God rather than men."

7. How has your fear of the Lord enabled you to submit to others?

. . . .

transformation

8. When you hear the word *submit*, how do you respond?

___ "Submit on the outside, not the inside."

___ "I'll submit *if* _____."

___ "I'm willing to do that."

___ "You can't make me!"

___ "Women have been liberated."

___ "I'll submit joyfully."

Journal about your responses to question 8. What makes you respond that way? What do you need to change?

. . . .

. . . .

Write a prayer asking God to supernaturally enable you to submit—to Him first of all, and then to one another. Confess and repent of the sin in your life that keeps you from submitting.

. . . .

. . . .

9. Submission and obedience to God are related. In Acts 5:24-32 the disciples found themselves in a situation where submission to God took precedence over submission to other people. Read this passage and answer the following questions.

a. Who took the apostles captive? (v. 26)

. . . .

b. Before whom were they put on trial? (v. 27)

. . . .

c. What did the authorities command the apostles *not* to do and why? (v. 28)

. . . .

d. How did Peter and the apostles respond and why? (v. 29)

. . . .

Journal about a time when you or someone you love felt compelled to obey God rather than other people. What were the circumstances? What was the result?

. . . .

. . . .

. . . .

On a thirty-six-hour train ride from Beijing to Guangzhou, Vic and Colette Jury broke the law. They were traveling with a group of smugglers carrying illegal imports: over two tons of Bibles and gospel tracts. While the armed guards turned their backs to check travel documents, these "outlaws" extended their hands to pass out life-giving literature. In the dark of the night, a young woman covertly read the forbidden pamphlet, and the light of salvation broke through as she accepted the Lord. She became a lawbreaker too, acting as interpreter for this band of believers and recruiting other Chinese nationals to act as lookouts. Throughout the long journey, she whispered the Good News to anyone who would listen. Eventually, she helped lead several others to faith in the Lord on this "gospel train," bound for glory!

What made Vic and Colette act in civil disobedience to China's governing authority at the risk of punishment or deportation? They realize a higher authority—Christ—governs them. He commanded, "Go into all the world and preach the Good News to everyone, everywhere" (Mark 16:15, NLT).

Does this *true* story of civil disobedience imply that the Jurys don't know how to submit to "one another" as Paul instructed us? Definitely not! In our church I've seen them model humility and respect toward their pastor and the church leadership. Vic has generously submitted his time, energy, and support for worldwide missions. The key to godly submission is recognizing *who* to submit to and *when* to submit.

contemplation

In submission we are free to value other people. Their dreams and plans become important to us. We have entered into a new, wonderful, glorious freedom, the freedom to give up our own rights for the good of others. . . . We discover that it is far better to serve our neighbor than to have our own way.

Richard J. Foster

BEAUTIFUL WOMEN
That is the way the holy women of old made themselves beautiful. They trusted God and accepted the authority of their husbands.
1 Peter 3:5, NLT

explanation

SUBMIT AS EQUALS
Wives aren't commanded to obey their husbands in the same manner as children obey their parents or slaves their masters. Submission may require obedience, but submission is not servitude. A wife should not be treated as a child, but an equal—bone of bones and flesh of flesh (see Genesis 2:23).

When a man entered the hospital for tests, he never would have guessed what the doctors would find. At first they thought the X-ray technicians had put the film in backward. But then they discovered that nothing was wrong with the X rays; there was something wrong with the patient. The man's heart was in a reversed position. What was supposed to be on the left side of the man's chest was on the right side, and vice versa. He had a rare reversed-organ condition. His heart was not where it should be.

In many homes, women's hearts are not where they should be, either. Instead of respecting their husbands, they are ruling the roost. The diagnosis? A reversed-*order* condition—role reversal where husbands and wives have gotten things backward. The cure? A heart of respect helps women turn their hearts and homes around.

exploration

We now move into the realm of the marriage relationship, showing us that the Spirit-filled home is a picture of the Spirit-filled church. Today we get some practical instruction concerning God's requirements for the wife in marriage.

Review Ephesians 5, then focus on verses 22-24 and also verse 33.

> **Wives, submit to your own husbands, as to the Lord.**
> Ephesians 5:22

1. To whom should wives submit? . . . .

. . . .

2. With what attitude are they to submit? . . . .

. . . .

> *For the husband is head of the wife, as also Christ is head of the church; and He is the Savior of the body.* Ephesians 5:23

3. What further reason did Paul give for the wife to submit to her husband?

. . . .

4. Whose headship is the husband's role compared to? . . . .

. . . .

5. How else did Paul describe Christ, the head of the church?

. . . .

> *Therefore, just as the church is subject to Christ, so let the wives be to their own husbands in everything.* Ephesians 5:24

6. How should a wife mirror the church? . . . .

. . . .

7. In how many areas should the wife submit to her husband?

. . . .

> *Nevertheless let each one of you in particular so love his own wife as himself, and let the wife see that she respects her husband.* Ephesians 5:33

8. How does a wife exhibit a submissive heart toward her husband, and what does he do to make it easy for her to submit?

. . . .

. . . .

3

HEADSHIP
The *head* is one who is "chief or exalted above." As the head governs the physical body, so Christ, the "head of the church," governs His body, the church. "The head of every man is Christ, the head of woman is man, and the head of Christ is God" (1 Corinthians 11:3).

6

SUBJECT TO
Subjecting and *submitting* are similar terms meaning to relinquish one's rights. *Relinquish* means to yield, release, or surrender. In a healthy marriage the act of submission is not demanded by the husband; rather the wife freely offers it as a response to his love. Giving up rights isn't wrong.

8

LOVE AND RESPECT
"Each one of you" implies a universal duty from which no husband or wife is exempt. It applies to *every* (not some) Christian wife regardless of age, occupation, or spiritual maturity. It includes *all* (not a few) Christian husbands no matter their intelligence, character, or upbringing.

9

R-E-S-P-E-C-T

Respond prayerfully instead of reacting poorly. **E**xhibit compassion instead of contempt. **S**peak words of support instead of sabotage. **P**lace his needs first instead of last. **E**xpect God to intervene instead of taking things into your own hands. **C**ast all your cares on the Lord instead of complaining to others. **T**rust God to change your husband's heart instead of hardening your own.

10

RESPECT THE UNRESPECTABLE

The head of the home is a God-given office. The person who holds that office deserves respect. A citizen of the U.S. can respect the position of the president even if the person in the Oval Office is unrespectable. A wife can respect the position given to her husband even if he's an unrespectable man.

transformation

9. R–E–S–P–E–C–T, find out what it means to *you*. It means a lot to your heavenly Head, Christ, and to your earthly head, your husband. Using the word *HEAD* as an acrostic, describe four qualities you respect about your husband. Then write him a note telling him of your respect for him, and give it to him this week.

H (Example: Helps with the kids)

. . . .

E (Example: Earns a living)

. . . .

A (Example: Always remembers my birthday)

. . . .

D (Example: Draws near to God)

. . . .

Author and theologian John Stott says, "People have equal dignity . . . but different God-appointed roles." Journal about how you have found dignity and fulfillment in your role as a submissive wife.

. . . .

. . . .

. . . .

. . . .

10. Respecting someone who is not respectable isn't easy, but it is possible. David is an example of this. Saul deserved respect from David because he was David's father-in-law and the king. Yet Saul was a proud, bitter, and vengeful man who attempted to murder David and who gave his wife to another man. Read 1 Samuel 26:7-11, 21, then answer the questions.

a. What opportunity did David have? (v. 8)

. . . .

b. What did David do with his opportunity and why? (vv. 9, 11)

. . . .

c. How did David trust God to take care of Saul? (v. 10)

. . . .

d. How did Saul respond to David's show of respect? (v. 21)

. . . .

e. How did Saul describe David's respect? (v. 21)

. . . .

I love submission! You may think I'm outdated or crazy, but I've learned that when I obey God's Word by relinquishing my rights to my husband, Skip, it gives God the opportunity to accomplish His will in my husband's heart. Submission means I get out of the way so God can get in the loop.

If Abraham is the "father of faith," then Sarah is the "mother of submission." She was willing to submit to Abraham, trusting God to get her husband's attention. Genesis 12 tells us that Sarah was beautiful to behold. Abraham knew foreign dignitaries would covet her and threaten his life, so he asked Sarah to bend the truth by telling them she was his sister. Genesis 20 reveals that she was his half sister—the daughter of his father but not his mother. Sarah submitted, and as a result a king took her into his harem. Sarah let her husband make a bad decision, knowing God would hold Abraham accountable. And He did. God tormented the king with nightmares and threatened him with death if he touched Sarah. All's well that ends well: Sarah remained chaste, Abraham was chastened for his lack of faith, and the king was restored.

When a wife doesn't submit, it's like a tug-of-war—husband on one end and wife on the other—both pulling with all their might. When a wife submits, she lets go and places her end of the rope in God's hands. No one wins in a tug-of-war against God—the person just gets dragged through the mud.

contemplation
Respect a man; he will
do the more.
James Howell

DAY 4 HEART OF LOVE

USA Today reported the story of a 700-pound lovesick moose that was courting a cow on a farm in Vermont. The Hereford cow apparently accepted the moose. "They've nuzzled like they're kissing, but I ain't seen no action,'" said the owner, Larry Carrara. Curious spectators from all over have parked cars and pickups in front of the farmhouse to watch the strange affair. Can they mate? Yes, and fertilization is even possible. But reproductive physiologists say there would be no offspring because their chromosome numbers don't match.

A cow has a face only a mother cow could love, but somehow a tall, dark, and handsome moose fell head over hooves for Mr. Carrara's Hereford. The attraction compelled him to abandon his roguish moose ways for domestic bliss. It was a match made in green pastures. Today we learn about a match made in heaven. Jesus came to earth to find an unlikely bride—the church—and make her His own. He teaches men to leave their selfish ways and to love their wives the way He loves His church—by laying down their lives.

exploration

We have learned about the submissive role of the wife in the home. Now we turn our attention to the husband's role to love sacrificially.

Review Ephesians 5, then focus on verses 25-28.

> **Husbands, love your wives, just as Christ also loved the church and gave Himself for her, . . .** Ephesians 5:25

1. What does God command husbands to do?. . . . .

. . . .

2. Whose love should husbands model their own after? . . . .

. . . .

3. How did Christ show His love for the church? . . . .

. . . .

> *. . . that He might sanctify and cleanse her with the washing of water by the word, . . .* Ephesians 5:26

4. What two things did Christ do for the church by giving Himself?

. . . .

5. How does He sanctify and cleanse the church? . . . .

. . . .

> *. . . that He might present her to Himself a glorious church, not having spot or wrinkle or any such thing, but that she should be holy and without blemish.* Ephesians 5:27

6. To whom did Christ present the church?. . . . .

. . . .

7. What kind of church did Christ desire to present to Himself?

. . . .

> *So husbands ought to love their own wives as their own bodies; he who loves his wife loves himself.* Ephesians 5:28

8. How are husbands to love their wives?

. . . .

explanation

1

UNCONDITIONAL LOVE
The Greek word for *love* here is *agape*, a love which is the antithesis of selfishness. Husbands should love wives under one condition—*unconditionally!*—regardless of how she looks, acts, or submits. God loves the unlovely: "God showed his great love for us by sending Christ to die for us while we were still sinners" (Romans 5:8, NLT).

4

SANCTIFY
Sanctify means to separate or set apart; to separate from the sinful in order to set apart for a sacred purpose. "May the God of peace Himself sanctify you completely; and may your whole spirit, soul, and body be preserved blameless" (1 Thessalonians 5:23).

8

LOVE AS HIMSELF
The true spirituality of a husband is measured not by his church attendance or tithe record but by the way he treats his wife at home when no one else is around. The man who lacks love and care for his wife is guilty of self-neglect and spiritual fraud.

transformation

9. Actions speak louder than words. Jesus told us how to measure love: "Here is how to measure it—the greatest love is shown when people lay down their lives for their friends" (John 15:13, NLT). Your husband may be a man of few words, but his sacrificial actions can speak volumes. Check off the ways your husband has shown his love for you.

____ Coaches the team   ____ Pays the bills
____ Helps with chores   ____ Maintains the vehicles
____ Works in the yard   ____ Disciplines the kids
____ Does household repairs   ____ Manages crises
____ Protects the home   ____ Prays for the family
____ Gives me free time   ____ Plans for the future

10. Today we learned that husbands should love their wives as they love themselves. This type of love needs to be reciprocal in marriage. List a few things that you do for yourself (Example: exercise, eating, or entertainment).

. . . .

. . . .

Journal about a way that *you* can sacrifice one of these things to show your "better half" that you care for *him* as much as for yourself. (Example: Cancel your workout time to free him up to go fishing.)

. . . .

. . . .

. . . .

. . . .

11. Husbands are to give their wives tender love and physical affection. Has your husband been trying to warm up to an iceberg? If you have been giving your husband the cold shoulder, it's time to open your arms for a warm embrace.

Draw a line to discover how to replace cold treatment with warm response.

COLD	WARM
Silent treatment	Tender touch
Cold shoulder	Warm embrace
Icy glare	Sweet nothings in his ear
Walking on thin ice	Glowing eyes
Pointing the finger	Paths of pleasure

Theologian Charles Spurgeon retold a story about the deep love French soldiers had for Napoleon Bonaparte. It wasn't uncommon for a soldier on his deathbed to prop himself up and proclaim allegiance to his much-admired general. If the dying man happened to see Napoleon nearby, he would cry out, *"Vive l'Emprereur!"* One of the most moving declarations of love came from the mouth of a soldier who'd received a critical chest wound. As the surgeon desperately attempted to remove the fatal bullet, the dying man whispered, "If you go much deeper, doctor, you'll come to the Emperor!"

The husband is the head of his wife, but she is his heart of hearts. The two have become one flesh. To injure one is to inflict pain on the other. No healthy human would intentionally harm himself. No healthy husband should ever intentionally wound his soul mate—it will cause heart damage.

DAY 5   HEART OF UNITY

preparation

Lord, thank You for cementing my marriage together. Keep my heart inextricably bound to the husband You've given me. Don't allow any outside influence to corrode our commitment to one another. Amen.

HEARTS ENTWINED
Since they are no longer two but one, let no one separate them, for God has joined them together. Matthew 19:6, NLT

It's been said that there's "chemistry" involved in finding the right spouse. In chemistry when two different yet compatible elements are mixed together, a whole new substance is created. Marriage is much the same: the blending of a man who is completely different yet wholly compatible with a woman creates a new compound— one flesh.

I read about a scientist in the field of chemistry who said that if you mix hydrogen and oxygen, the well-known components of water, you would get no chemical reaction and no water! But if you add a small amount of platinum to this stable mixture, things start to happen quickly. The hydrogen and oxygen begin to unite as a chemical change occurs, producing H_2O. Marriages, like chemical reactions, require an extra element for unification. In a Christian marriage that extra element is God, the strongest bonding agent known. Two becoming one is good, but three bound together is better. Solomon said, "A threefold cord is not quickly broken" (Ecclesiastes 4:12). The chemical compound for water is H_2O (two parts hydrogen plus one part oxygen), while the designation for a strong marriage is HWC (*husband* plus *wife* plus *Christ*). The new compound created is two hearts beating as one— a heart of unity!

exploration

We have learned how a husband must love his wife both unconditionally and sacrificially. Now we discover that the bond between a man and a woman is meant to reflect the unity between Christ and His church.

Review Ephesians 5, then focus on verses 29-32.

For no one ever hated his own flesh, but nourishes and cherishes it, just as the Lord does the church.
Ephesians 5:29

1. Yesterday we learned that a husband must love his wife as his own body. What reason does Paul give for this?

. . . .

2. In what two ways should a husband show he loves his wife as his own flesh?

. . . .

3. What perfect example should the husband follow? . . . .

. . . .

For we are members of His body, of His flesh and of His bones. Ephesians 5:30

4. Why does the Lord nourish and cherish the church?. . . . .

. . . .

5. What is Christ's body made of? . . . .

. . . .

"For this reason a man shall leave his father and mother and be joined to his wife, and the two shall become one flesh." Ephesians 5:31

6. What are the two steps a man should take in the marriage process?

. . . .

7. What supernatural event occurs between husband and wife?

. . . .

This is a great mystery, but I speak concerning Christ and the church. Ephesians 5:32

---

explanation

2

NOURISH AND CHERISH
To nourish is to provide for someone's needs and give what is necessary for growth and maturity. To cherish is to give tender love and physical affection with warmth, comfort, protection, and security. While some view nourishing and cherishing as feminine traits, these responsibilities are primarily directed to the husband for his wife.

7

BECOMING ONE
Becoming one flesh is a process: leaving and cleaving. Leaving means you detach yourself from your parents in order to attach yourself to a marriage partner. Cleaving means to cement together in a permanent, unbreakable bond. This bond is a spiritual mystery and a physical reality from the bedroom to the birthing room.

MARRIAGE VOWS
Couples recite the familiar vows: "For better, for worse; for richer, for poorer; in sickness and health; to love and to cherish, until death us do part." Some people selectively hear "better, richer, and healthy." They ignore the "worse, poorer, and sickness" parts. Couples who cherish each other will take the bad, nourishing it until it becomes better.

8. What great mystery does marriage depict?

. . . .

transformation

9. Review the sidebar that defines *nourishing* and *cherishing*. List the qualities that define each trait:

Nourish: . . . .

. . . .

Cherish:. . . . .

. . . .

Journal about a specific situation in which your husband has demonstrated these qualities toward you.

. . . .

. . . .

. . . .

. . . .

10. Fill in the chart below to discover how God displays these same traits toward His loved ones.

SCRIPTURE	TRAITS OF NOURISHING AND CHERISHING
Ps. 32:7-8	
Ps. 61:3-4	
Ps. 103:4-5	
Isa. 66:13.	
Phil. 4:19	
James 1:2-4	
1 Pet. 2:2-3	

Journal a prayer asking God to help you see the ways He has nourished and cherished you. Thank Him for His tender care in your life.

. . . .

. . . .

. . . .

11. Becoming one flesh in marriage is a two-step process: leaving and cleaving. Before you can firmly hold on to your spouse, you must let go of your parents. List the things you need to release and those you need to hold on to.

THINGS I MUST LET GO (LEAVE)	THINGS I MUST HOLD ON TO (CLEAVE)
. . . .	. . . .
. . . .	. . . .

HANDS OFF
Marriage is the birth of a family. The new couple releases old family ties in the realm of authority and responsibility. Leaving parents doesn't mean dishonoring them. Parents are to be respected, but after marriage they no longer exercise control over their children's lives. "Honor your father and your mother, so that you may live long." (Exodus 20:12, NIV).

When Kerry and I (Penny) were first married, we didn't know that things would get *worse* before they got *better*. As newlyweds we experienced the *poorer* part when we were devastated by a lawsuit that cost us everything. As new parents we began to struggle with the *sickness* part when I began to suffer from debilitating migraines.

That's when the *nourishing* and *cherishing* parts of our vows were put to the test. Kerry felt like a failure because we had to file for bankruptcy. I let him know that success in my eyes was measured by his godly attitude, not a giant bank account. At his lowest point, he confessed to me, "I don't know what to do." I lovingly embraced him and said, "We're in this together, Baby; God will take care of us." Kerry has nourished me in physical struggles. Countless times I've interrupted his sleep groaning, "Honey, we need to go to the ER. My head's killing me." When the migraines come, he cooks, cleans, and cares for me.

It's a mystery to me how deeply a married couple can feel and heal one another's deepest needs. But Paul revealed a greater mystery still: the bond between husband and wife reflects the bond between Christ and the church, His bride. He feels our pain and went to the Cross to heal our wounds.

contemplation
There can be no unity, no delight of love, no harmony, no good in being, where there is but one. Two at least are needed for oneness.
George Macdonald

Work Ethic

The book *The Day America Told the Truth* by James Patterson and Peter Kim claims, "The so-called Protestant ethic is long gone from today's American workplace.

"Workers around America frankly admit that they spend more than 20 percent (seven hours a week) of their time at work totally goofing off. That amounts to a four-day week across the nation.

"Almost half of us admit to chronic malingering, calling in sick when we are not sick, and doing it regularly.

"One in six Americans regularly drink or use drugs on the job.

"Only one in four give work their best effort; only one in four work to realize their human potential rather than merely to keep the wolf from the door. . . .

"About one in four expect to compromise their personal beliefs in order to get ahead on their current job."

Why the decline of the honorable work ethic in the United States? This week we will discover that honor and duty are learned long before a job interview. The Bible encourages parents to train their children in "Word ethics" that will influence their "work ethics." Though there are no guarantees, children trained up in biblical values are more likely to become productive employees and employers, filling the work force with men and women who can be trusted.

DAY 1 ACCOUNTABILITY

preparation

Father, thank You for my parents. Give me the wisdom to honor them in all that I say and do. Amen.

ACCOUNTABILITY
A wise child accepts a parent's discipline; a young mocker refuses to listen. Proverbs 13:1, NLT

explanation

OBEDIENCE
To be obedient is to carry out the word and will of another person. "Obedience is a positive, active response to what a person hears." There are three signs of disobedience: (1) delayed obedience, (2) partial obedience, and (3) resentful obedience.

exploration

Having examined the marriage relationship in lesson 10, we turn our attention on the attitudes and actions of Spirit-filled believers at home and work. Today we look at the God-given responsibilities of Christian children.

Read through Ephesians 6 to get a feel for the tone, language, and content of this chapter, then focus your attention on verses 1-3.

> *Children, obey your parents in the Lord, for this is right.*
> Ephesians 6:1

1. What are children commanded to do? . . . .

. . . .

2. How are children to obey their parents? . . . .

. . . .

3. Why are children to obey? . . . .

. . . .

> *"Honor your father and mother," which is the first commandment with promise: . . .* Ephesians 6:2

4. Describe the attitude children are to exhibit toward their parents.

. . . .

5. What Old Testament law did Paul quote? . . . .

. . . .

6. What accompanied this commandment? . . . .

. . . .

> *. . . that it may be well with you and you may live long on the earth.* Ephesians 6:3

7. What two things does God promise as a result of keeping this commandment?

. . . .

. . . .

8. Read Exodus 20:12. How did Paul change the wording of this commandment to include Gentile believers in the promise?

. . . .

. . . .

transformation

9. Listed below are the three signs of disobedience found in today's lesson. Journal about a time when your children fell into each of these dishonoring behaviors. How did you discipline them?

Delayed obedience:

. . . .

. . . .

. . . .

4

HONOR
Honor is respect mingled with reverence and love. Honor is more than obedience. Obedience is action-oriented; honor is attitude-oriented. As a child Jesus honored and obeyed his parents. "He returned to Nazareth with them and was obedient to them; . . . Jesus grew both in height and in wisdom, and he was loved by God and by all who knew him" (Luke 2:51-52, NLT).

6

REINFORCEMENTS
God the Father promises either a positive or a negative reinforcement to train His kids. "I am giving you the choice between a blessing and a curse! You will be blessed if you obey the commands of the Lord. . . . You will receive a curse if you reject the commands of the Lord" (Deuteronomy 11:26-28, NLT)

BETTER TO OBEY
Peter's betrayal of Jesus was one of the worst forms of disobedience. "Jesus' words flashed through Peter's mind: 'Before the rooster crows, you will deny me three times.' And he went away, crying bitterly" (Matthew 26:75, NLT). Disobedience to God is a crying shame. But when godly sorrow leads to repentance—He'll wipe away your tears.

Partial obedience:

. . . .

. . . .

. . . .

Resentful obedience:

. . . .

. . . .

. . . .

10. Reflect on a time when *you*, as a child of God, fell into similar dishonoring behaviors in your journey of faith. Journal about how you disobeyed and how God corrected you.

Delayed obedience:

. . . .

. . . .

. . . .

Partial obedience:

. . . .

. . . .

. . . .

Resentful obedience:

. . . .

. . . .

. . . .

11. Disobedience leads to God's loving discipline. The writer of Hebrews wrote encouraging words for Christians who are going through a season of discipline from the Lord. Rewrite these verses into a personal prayer to your heavenly Father, thanking Him for His loving correction: "Have you entirely forgotten the encouraging words God spoke to you, his children? He said, 'My child, don't ignore it when the Lord disciplines you, and don't be discouraged when he corrects you. For the Lord disciplines those he loves, and he punishes those he accepts as his children'" (Hebrews 12:5-6, NLT).

. . . .

. . . .

. . . .

. . . .

11
CONSEQUENCES
Sin has consequences: some are natural, and others are supernatural. Natural consequences are simple: touch a fire you'll get burned. Supernatural repercussions are certain: "You can't ignore God and get away with it. You will always reap what you sow! Those who live only to satisfy their own sinful desires will harvest the consequences of decay and death" (Galatians 6:7-8, NLT).

"How do you honor a dishonorable parent?" a young woman asked me in hushed tones. Though she was shy and fragile, with patient coaxing, her story took shape. "My mother's not normal. She's mentally ill, and for as long as I can remember, I've been embarrassed by her. I never brought friends home from school. If she wouldn't go away, then I would disappear into a place of quiet shame. But now I'm grown with kids of my own. It's her birthday this week. Do I have to go? I'm a new Christian. How do I honor my mother?"

I ached for her lost childhood and longed to somehow make it better. I encouraged her, "You can't change *her*, but God can change *you*, from resentful to respectful. You can honor your mother's role as a parent without approving of her inordinate behavior. Focus on appreciating *who* she is instead of *what* she's done. She gave you life; you can offer her love—God's unconditional love. God loved us while we were inordinate, and He can teach you how to love her even if you can't change her. Go to her birthday and offer her the gift of a blessing instead of a curse."

Honoring your parents is not a divine suggestion but one of the Ten Commandments. When you honor your earthly parents, it reflects a heart that honors your Heavenly Parent. Obedience and honor bring great rewards: blessings on earth and treasures in heaven.

contemplation
To "honor" our parents means much more than simply to obey them. It means to show them respect and love, to care for them as long as they need us, and to seek to bring honor to them by the way we live.
Warren Wiersbe

DAY 2 ADMONITION

A cartoon showed a father scowling over his son's bad report card. His son asked, "What do you think it is, Dad? Heredity or environment?" This kid was no dummy. Either way, the father would be forced to take the blame if his son didn't make the grade. What impact *does* a father have on his child? Consider the results of a study done on these contrasting parenting philosophies.

Max Jukes was a New Yorker who didn't believe in Christ or Christian training. He never took his children to church. He has had over 1,000 descendants. Of these 300 were sent to prison; 190 were public prostitutes; 680 were alcoholics. So far his family has cost the state an excess of $420,000. They've made no noticeable contribution to society.

Jonathan Edwards lived in the same state at the same time as Jukes. He loved the Lord and saw that his children attended church every Sunday. He has had over 1,000 descendants. Of these, 430 were ministers; 86 became university professors; 13 became university presidents; 75 authored books; 7 were elected to Congress. One became vice president. At the time of this study his family hadn't cost the state one dime but had contributed immeasurably to society.

We know that not all children with good fathers become pastors or presidents, nor do all offspring of wicked fathers become pushers or parolees. Yet, dads who provide a loving home where the Bible is taught and prayer is offered give their children everything they need to succeed.

exploration

So far we have seen God's requirements for Spirit-filled husbands, wives, and children. Now we examine God's requirements for Spirit-filled parents.

Review Ephesians 6, then focus on verse 4.

> **And you, fathers, do not provoke your children to wrath, but bring them up in the training and admonition of the Lord.** Ephesians 6:4

 1. What negative command for fathers is given here? . . . .

. . . .

2. How do children respond to being provoked? . . . .

. . . .

3. According to Colossians 3:21, what is another consequence of provoking children?

. . . .

4. Rather than provoking their children, how should parents bring them up (Ephesians 6:4)?

. . . .

 5. According to Proverbs 22:6, what is the promise for parents who train their children as God prescribes?

. . . .

6. Read Deuteronomy 6:6-9.

   a. What is the prerequisite for parents in teaching their children God's Word?

. . . .

   b. How thorough should parents be when teaching God's Word to their children?

. . . .

. . . .

explanation

1

PROVOKING
When you provoke someone, you stir up that person, making him or her bitter and angry. The term implies a long-term, repeated pattern of treatment that slowly forms a latent anger and resentment eventually manifesting itself in outward hostility.

3

DAD OR DICTATOR?
A dictator uses his authority to throw his weight around, regardless of the feelings of others. An ideal dad throws his weight behind God's Word, elevating his children to greater heights, encouraging their emotional well-being.

5

TRAIN A CHILD
Training: using fair, consistent discipline to raise children in a godly manner. "What son is there whom a father does not chasten? No chastening seems to be joyful for the present, but painful; nevertheless, afterward it yields the peaceable fruit of righteousness to those who have been trained by it" (Hebrews 12:7, 11).

7.

ENCOURAGING
WORDS
Children, like tender
seedlings, need to be
fertilized with your favor,
watered with your words
of praise, and exposed
to the light of your love.
Overexposure to hot
tempers, blustery atti-
tudes, and cutting
words makes them wilt.
Encouragement is Mira-
cle-Gro for the soul.

transformation

7. From the following list of words and phrases, separate those
that tend to *provoke* children from those that *encourage* them:
praise, favoritism, criticism, unconditional love, unfulfilled
promises, acceptance, physical abuse, compliments, blaming,
hugs, perfectionism, conditional love, comparisons, unfair
punishment, consistent discipline, high standards, affection,
undivided attention. Add your own words to each list.

PROVOKES   ENCOURAGES

Examine the list of provoking behaviors. Is there some
way you are provoking your children? How is God asking
you to change? Journal your thoughts.

. . . .

. . . .

. . . .

. . . .

Examine the list of encouraging behaviors. Choose two
ways to encourage your children this week, and journal
about what you will do.

. . . .

. . . .

. . . .

8. God wants His plan and His Word to be passed on to your children and the next generation.

Journal a prayer asking God to help you pass on His Word and His ways to the next generation.

. . . .

. . . .

. . . .

9. What wrong things may you have been telling your children while showing them by your actions that they're all right?

. . . .

. . . .

How can you undo your hypocrisy? Journal a prayer asking God to help you be more consistent in these areas.

. . . .

. . . .

. . . .

. . . .

9
SAYING AND DOING
Parenting balances words and deeds. As the father of the Gentile church, Paul was a good parent whose works and words matched up. "I have brought the Gentiles to God by my message and by the way I lived before them" (Romans 15:18, NLT). Do what you say in order to bring your children to God.

In this passage the apostle Paul affirmed a father's authority in the home. He also warned that fathers who abuse their authority raise anger-filled children. Godly parenting can be a balancing act—seesawing between looking the other way and overlooking a child's feelings.

A 1986 Stanford University study of 7,836 high school students and 3,500 parents in the San Francisco area showed that children with either permissive *or* authoritarian parents tended to earn lower grades. However, parents who encouraged their children and were communicative enabled their children to get higher grades. Parents who balance punishment with praise really do make the grade!

contemplation
Correction does much, but encouragement does more. Encouragement after censure is as the sun after a shower.
Goethe

DAY 3 ATTITUDE

preparation

Father, when I am asked to serve You by serving others, help me to follow through with a sincere heart. Give me the strength to work faithfully until You return. Amen.

SINCERITY

That you may approve the things that are excellent, that you may be sincere and without offense till the day of Christ. Philippians 1:10

"My boss is such a slave driver!" Oh, really? Roman slaves were treated with brutality. They had no legal rights and were treated like expendable commodities: bought, sold, traded, and discarded as if they were used cars. One Bible commentary notes that the Roman statesman Cato said, "Old slaves should be thrown on a dump, and when a slave is ill do not feed him anything. It is not worth your money. Take sick slaves and throw them away because they are nothing but inefficient tools."

Unlike employees today, slaves had no coffee breaks, no paid vacations, no insurance plan, and no profit sharing. Their hours were 24/7, not 9 to 5. They worked hard for no money. They were the exclusive property of real slave drivers and had no rights to complain of wrong treatment.

Paul told the Ephesian slaves suffering under terrible tyranny to obey their masters as they would obey their Lord. If slaves could adopt a Christ-centered attitude in their work, so can you. Your boss is no slave driver to expect reasonable work for fair wages. Maybe *you* need a perspective check. Diligently work for your earthly employer, knowing the Supreme Supervisor will give you an eternal promotion.

exploration

We shift our focus from relationships in the home to relationships in the workplace. Though Paul addresses this section of Scripture to "bondservants" or slaves, we can logically apply his teaching to today's business relationships. Let's look at how Christian workers ought to respond to their "masters" or bosses.

Review Ephesians 6, then focus on verse 5.

Bondservants, be obedient to those who are your masters according to the flesh, with fear and trembling, in sincerity of heart, as to Christ; . . . Ephesians 6:5

1. How should bondservants respond to their masters? . . . .

. . . .

2. Masters maintain authority according to what? . . . .

. . . .

3. With what two attitudes should servants approach their masters?

. . . .

4. In what condition should their heart be? . . . .

. . . .

5. How should workers submit to their masters? . . . .

. . . .

6. The best masters lead by example. Our Master, Jesus, knew what it was like to be a servant during His earthly ministry. Read Philippians 2:5-9 to discover the example He set for all believers.

   a. Before He became a man, what form did Jesus have and to whom was He equal? (v. 6)

   . . . .

   b. Jesus emptied Himself of the prerogatives of His deity at the incarnation. What three transformations took place to make this possible? (v. 7)

   . . . .

   c. What two attributes made His transformation into a bond-servant possible? And to what extent did He take on the role of servant? (v. 8)

   . . . .

---

explanation

1

BONDSERVANT

A bondservant is a person who is bound to service without wages. Kids don't say, "When I grow up, I want to be a slave and earn no money." Yet, Peter, Paul, and James aspired to be "bondservants" of Christ, to be like Christ. "I, the Son of Man, came here not to be served but to serve others" (Matthew 20:28, NLT).

4

SINCERITY

The word *sincere* comes from two Latin words meaning "without wax." Ancient potters repaired flawed statues by filling in cracks with wax, lowering their value. A perfect piece was labeled "sincere," meaning it was genuine, without pretense.

6b

POURED OUT

"Made Himself of no reputation," from the Greek, means, "He emptied Himself." Literally, Jesus emptied Himself of self! He poured out the full benefits of Deity, limiting Himself to flesh and bones, time and space. Jesus had all the rights of Deity, yet during His incarnation He surrendered His right.

d. How did God reward Jesus for His humble obedience? (v. 9)

. . . .

transformation

7. Fill in the chart to discover who called themselves servants
and how these servants of Christ behaved.

SCRIPTURE	SERVANT'S NAME	SERVANT'S BEHAVIOR
1 Sam. 3:9-10		
Ps. 78:70-72		
Gal. 1:10		
Col. 4:12		

8. Today we discovered that a bondservant is one who works
without wages. The Bible teaches that all who call on the Lord
become His slaves. "If you were a slave when the Lord called
you, the Lord has now set you free from the awful power of sin.
And if you were free when the Lord called you, you are now a
slave of Christ" (1 Corinthians 7:22, NLT).

a. What have you done for Christ without receiving monetary
compensation?

. . . .

b. What are you willing to do for Him without reward or
recognition?

. . . .

9. Slaves are called to serve with "sincerity of heart." We learned
that a "sincere" statue was one without wax covering up
weaknesses—pure and without pretense. Picture yourself as
a statue. Acknowledge below any sinful cracks you may have
covered over with pretense. (Example: Eyes: I act indignant
about pornography but watch inappropriate movies.)

Eyes: . . . .

Ears: . . . .

Mouth:. . . . .

Heart: . . . .

Hands:. . . . .

Feet:. . . . .

> Reword the following psalm into a personal prayer of repentance and restoration: "Oh, give me back my joy again; you have broken me—now let me rejoice. Don't keep looking at my sins. Remove the stain of my guilt. Create in me a clean heart, O God. Renew a right spirit within me." (Psalm 51:8-10, NLT).

. . . .

. . . .

. . . .

. . . .

Franklin Graham, president of the relief and evangelistic organization Samaritan's Purse, encounters people around the world willing to sacrifice the promise of gold for the kingdom of God. In his book *Living Beyond the Limits,* he tells of one such man, Steve Duncan.

"Steve was a well-educated Boston man and a skilled surgeon. He was preparing to leave for Angola as soon as he could raise support and make the logistical arrangements. Steve made quite an impression on me as he told of his desire to serve the Lord in a foreign country. I knew he could be earning enough money to buy anybody's version of the great American Dream. Instead, all he talked about was taking God's gospel to Angola—a country that at the time was in the throes of a particularly vicious and ugly civil war."

Steve, like Paul the apostle, is just one example of a modern-day bondservant of Christ. He works long hours in a dangerous place without financial compensation. He has given up boardrooms and surgical suites for bunkers and grass huts, living for eternal rather than temporal rewards.

Where is God calling you to work for Christ instead of cash?

contemplation
The average church member would do well to look in his concordance and see how many columns it takes to list all the "serve," "servant," and "service" references.
Vance Havner

DAY 4 ACTIONS

"When the cat's away, the mice will play." When I was in high school, I worked at the local drugstore with two good friends. When the boss was gone, we goofed off: trying on the latest lipstick, reading magazines, and spiking our sodas on Friday nights. My friends and I were living proof that the Protestant work ethic was dying.

God breathed new life into my personal work ethic when I was born again. Later, on my first professional job at McLain Development Company in Newport Beach, if the boss wasn't around I could be found doing the right thing. When my duties were done, I would offer to help my coworkers finish their work or straighten up the lunchroom. I never called in sick if I wasn't and didn't take long lunches.

How did I go from goof-off to Goody Two-Shoes? It was through the influence of my pastor, Chuck Smith, who has the most amazing work ethic of anyone I know. He taught me that even when my boss didn't see me, God did. My work then became an act of worship. Your work should be worship as well: your actions and attitudes at work reflect your service to God.

exploration

Yesterday we looked at the godly attitudes of the Christian worker. Today we explore the righteous actions of Christian workers on the job.

Review Ephesians 6, then focus on verses 6-8.

> *. . . [be obedient] not with eyeservice, as men-pleasers, but as bondservants of Christ, doing the will of God from the heart, . . .* Ephesians 6:6

1. What phrase lets you know that servants should not just be obedient only when the boss is watching?

. . . .

2. Whom do those who work with eyeservice seek to please?

. . . .

3. In contrast, how are believers to work, and what does this accomplish?

. . . .

4. From where does the desire to do God's will come?

. . . .

> *. . . with goodwill doing service, as to the Lord, and not to men, . . .* Ephesians 6:7

5. What heart attitude should characterize our serving?

. . . .

6. Once again, Paul reminds us that our service should be conducted as to _____ and not _____.

> *. . . knowing that whatever good anyone does, he will receive the same from the Lord, whether he is a slave or free.* Ephesians 6:8

7. What does God promise Christian workers for the good they do?

. . . .

8. What phrase lets you know that God rewards believers with servant hearts regardless of their position?

. . . .

explanation

1

EYESERVICE
Eyeservice is working only under the "master's eye"; performance when the boss is looking, but neglect in the boss's absence. Out of sight, out of mind? While your boss is out of sight, you still have to mind because "the eyes of the Lord watch over those who do right" (1 Peter 3:12, NLT).

3

GOD'S WILL
Some Christians are obsessed with knowing the will of God and not concerned with doing the will of God. But when you actively do God's will, you'll automatically know God's will. "Continue to do God's will. Then you will receive all that he has promised" (Hebrews 10:36, NLT).

8

SLAVE OR FREE
People may play favorites, but God levels the playing field. He treats all who follow Him with equality. "In this new life, it doesn't matter if you are a Jew or a Gentile, circumcised or uncircumcised, barbaric, uncivilized, slave, or free.

transformation

9.

9. Rather than trying to please people on the job, we must strive to please God. Fill in the chart below to discover some of the things that are pleasing to God.

SCRIPTURE	WHAT PLEASES GOD
Ps. 69:30-31	
Col. 1:10	
1 Thess. 2:4	
Heb. 11:6	
1 John 3:22	

Journal about when you know that you are pleasing God (based on the above passages). Then write about how you will try to please God in the areas where you fall short.

. . . .

. . . .

. . . .

10. In Matthew's Gospel, Jesus named three ways His disciples could express their devotion to God in a secret way, not to please people but to please God. How will you offer something in secret to God this week? Journal about how you will follow through.

Financial Giving: "Give your gifts in secret, and your Father, who knows all secrets, will reward you" (Matthew 6:4, NLT).

. . . .

. . . .

9.

FOR HIS PLEASURE
Pleasing others is not the Christian's aim. It can, however, become the means to an end. Pleasing others in order to please God puts you right on target. "Exhort bondservants . . . to be well pleasing in all things, not answering back, not pilfering, but showing all good fidelity, that they may adorn the doctrine of God our Savior in all things" (Titus 2:9-10).

10.

SECRET CHARACTER
Reputation and *character* are different. Reputation is achieved in public—what others see. Character is cultivated in private—what God sees. Reputation is fleeting, for people are fickle. Character is forever, for God rewards the faithful.

Praying: "When you pray, go away by yourself, shut the door behind you, and pray to your Father secretly. Then your Father, who knows all secrets, will reward you" (Matthew 6:6, NLT).

. . . .

. . . .

Fasting: "No one will suspect you are fasting, except your Father, who knows what you do in secret. And your Father, who knows all secrets, will reward you" (Matthew 6:18, NLT).

. . . .

. . . .

11. We also discovered that pleasing God takes more than eye-service—it takes service from the heart. In which of the following ways will you, with goodwill, serve someone this week?

____ Do my chores singing praise songs

____ Pay the bills with thanksgiving in my heart

____ Season dinner with love and serve it with kindness

____ Bless a fellow employee by pitching in and offering praise

____ Take my boss to an appreciation lunch

One day a defiant child talked back to his mother when she asked him to do his chores. His dad scolded him and said, "Son, go sit in time-out for fifteen minutes." The strong-willed lad refused, clenching his fists and digging in his heels. His father insisted and threatened to take away TV privileges if he didn't get in that chair *now!* The little boy slumped, dragged himself to the chair, and sat down with a moan. As he crossed his arms he muttered, "I may be sitting down on the outside, but I'm standing up on the inside."

When your boss asks you to do your work, do you talk back? "That's not my job." Do you comply on the outside but complain on the inside? "I'll do it but I don't have to like it." Your actions and your attitudes are inseparable—your heart and hands must work together to get the job done or, in God's eyes, it's not a job well done.

contemplation
There is no work better than another to please God; to pour water, to wash dishes, to be a cobbler, or an apostle, all is one; to wash dishes and to preach is all one, as touching as the deed, to please God.
William Tyndale

DAY 5 AUTHORITY

My husband is one of the best examples of a servant-leader I know. We moved from the sunny beaches of California to the desert sands of New Mexico to start a new church. When Calvary of Albuquerque began, Skip wore many hats: leading worship, keeping the financial records, and moving sound equipment, as well as teaching and counseling. As the church staff has grown, Skip has never lost his servant's heart. You can still find him picking up trash, clearing tables, or mopping floors.

As a boss, he responds to the needs of his staff. When one staff member's wife was diagnosed with breast cancer, Skip gave him time off and the church paid some of their bills. When an employee's daughter couldn't afford her cheerleading uniform, Skip pitched in what was needed. One employee observed, "Working for Skip is a great adventure because of his predictable unpredictability. He's a visionary who encourages others to excel." A former youth director went to lead a Christian rock band. Several assistant pastors have gone on to pastor their own churches. Church secretaries have gone overseas to become missionaries. Skip's employer philosophy is simple: "Release people to reach their God-given potential."

You don't have to be a pastor to be a good employer. The book of Ephesians shows us that God sets high standards for all Christian employers.

exploration

We have seen how slaves or Christian employees ought to respond to those God has placed in authority over them. Today we examine the responsibility of masters—Christian employers.

Review Ephesians 6, then focus on verse 9.

And you, masters, do the same things to them, giving up threatening, knowing that your own Master also is in heaven, and there is no partiality with Him. Ephesians 6:9

1. Paul told masters to do the same things to their slaves and servants. What things was Paul referring to (see vv. 6-8)?

. . . .

2. What are employers to give up?. . . . .

. . . .

3. According to Colossians 4:1, how are masters to treat their bondservants?

. . . .

4. According to Colossians 4:1 and Ephesians 6:9, why should masters treat their servants well?

. . . .

5. Fill in the chart below to discover how masters acquired their slaves in ancient times.

SCRIPTURE	BECAME SLAVES BY . . .
Gen. 37:28 . . . .
Exod. 21:2, 4 . . . .
Lev. 25:39-40 . . . .
Josh. 9:23-27 . . . .

6. Read Matthew 20:25-28. How was Jesus' standard for authority contrary to the world's view of authority?

. . . .

7. Who did He give as an example of leading through serving?

. . . .

explanation

1

SAME WORK
What's good for the goose is good for the gander. If employees must work sincerely, so must employers. If slaves were to be God-pleasers rather than men-pleasers, so should masters. Both blue- and white-collar workers should work with good will in their hearts.

4

GOD THE MASTER
The buck stops here? Corporate executives, presidents, and managers may think they are the top dogs, but in fact, God is King of the hill—the Master of the universe. With God, you don't climb the corporate ladder, you meet on common ground—common people serving an uncommon God.

7

BECOME A SERVANT
If you're an employer, maybe you should institute "Show and Tell" at your place of business. The most effective bosses are those who are willing to roll up their sleeves and get their hands dirty. Are you willing not only to *tell* people what to do but to *show* them how to do it?

8. According to Ephesians 6:9, what two things do earthly masters know about their heavenly Master?

. . . .

transformation

9. Christian employers ought to serve their employees, not threaten them. List some ways that employers in today's workforce might threaten their employees.

. . . .

. . . .

10. Fill in the chart below to discover three ways to serve those over whom you have some form of authority. In the space provided, journal about how you will serve someone under your authority this week (i.e., children, employees, ministry workers, etc.).

SCRIPTURE	HOW TO SERVE	HOW I WILL SERVE
Luke 12:35-37		
Rom. 1:9		
Gal. 5:13		

We've seen that Christian employers should treat their employees as God treats us, without partiality. Journal about a time when you played favorites or when someone played favorites with you. How did it make you feel?

. . . .

. . . .

. . . .

. . . .

11. Based on your experience, why are you grateful God doesn't play favorites?

. . . .

. . . .

. . . .

The legend is told of a desert wanderer who found a clear, fresh, crystal spring. The water was so pure he decided to bring some to his king. Hardly satiating his own thirst, he filled a leather bottle and carried it many days through the hot desert until he reached the palace. When he finally offered the king his gift, the water had become stale and rancid. But the wise king did not reveal to his faithful servant that it was unfit to drink. He sampled it with expressions of gratitude and delight, and the wanderer went his way, filled with gladness. After he had gone, others asked why the king pretended to enjoy the bitter water. "Ah!" said he. "It was not the water I tasted, but the love that brought the offering." Frequently our service is tainted by imperfections, but our Master sees our motives and says, "It is good."

This week we have learned that our motivation in serving others stems from our love for God and our desire to please Him. When you serve others—husbands, children, employers, employees—as you would serve Him, you can know that one day you will hear your heavenly Master say, "Well done, my good and faithful servant. You have been faithful in handling this small amount, so now I will give you many more responsibilities. Let's celebrate together!" (Matthew 25:23, NLT).

NO FAVORITES
"Mom always liked you best." Comedian Tommy Smothers always got a laugh with this famous line to his brother. But partiality is no joke. God doesn't play favorites; He likes *all* of His children best. "There is no iniquity with the Lord our God, no partiality" (2 Chronicles 19:7).

contemplation
A leader is one who knows the way, goes the way, and shows the way.
John Maxwell

Stand Your Ground

Once upon a time in a distant kingdom, there lived a dreadful dragon. Its great wings could be heard flapping for miles around, striking terror in the hearts of the people throughout the countryside. With a single blow its terrible claws could kill an ox. Its nostrils billowed clouds of smoke and flame, bringing death to anyone who encountered the beast.

Each year a young girl was chosen as an offering to appease the dragon. One year the lot fell to the beautiful daughter of the king. Just as the dragon swooped in on the fair damsel, a valiant knight in shining armor rode to her rescue. Brandishing his gleaming sword, he struck the monster a mighty blow, wounding it so badly that the princess was able to wrap her sash around its head and lead it to the marketplace of her village. There amidst the cheering throngs, the knight slew the fearsome dragon. And they all lived happily ever after.

That story may be just a fairy tale. But the real story is that your heavenly Knight in shining garments has come to *your* rescue, delivering you from sin and transforming you from victim to victor. You are no longer a damsel in distress but have been clothed in His shining armor, ready to deliver others from Satan, the fire-destined dragon. This week you will learn about the dragon's devices, how to deploy your armor and artillery against him, and how to defend your spiritual treasures by standing your ground.

DAY 1
Be Powerful

DAY 2
Be Protected

DAY 3
Be Prepared

DAY 4
Be Prayerful

DAY 5
Be Peaceful

exploration

In our exploration of Ephesians we have learned about the heavenly treasures God has in store for His children. Throughout the study we have learned to walk worthy of our position as His spiritual heirs. Now we come to the end of our journey, where we learn to stand "in the power of His might" against the enemies who would rob us of our inheritance. Today we learn how to stand powerfully against our spiritual enemies as we gain insight into God's battle plan.

Read through Ephesians 6 to get a feel for the tone, language, and content of this chapter, then turn your attention to verses 10-13.

> *Finally, my brethren, be strong in the Lord and in the power of His might. Put on the whole armor of God, that you may be able to stand against the wiles of the devil.*
> Ephesians 6:10-11

1. As Paul draws his letter to a close, what two things does he urge his brethren to be strong in (v. 10)?

   . . . .

2. What equipment should the Christian "put on" in order to be strong in the Lord?

   . . . .

3. What parts of God's armor can you leave off? . . . .

   . . . .

preparation

God, thank You for making me aware of the fact that I have an enemy. Help me to be alert to his tactics and vigilant in my stand against him. Amen.

VIGILANCE
Be careful! Watch out for attacks from the Devil, your great enemy. He prowls around like a roaring lion, looking for some victim to devour.
1 Peter 5:8, NLT

explanation

POWERFUL GOD
Christians shouldn't rely on their own strength but must tap into the mighty power of the Lord. Human strength is impotent in opposing our supernatural enemy, the devil. With the omnipotent God as our power source, even a little strength is sufficient for victory. "Remember that it is the Lord your God who gives you power" (Deuteronomy 8:18, NLT).

4. Why do we need God's armor? . . . .

. . . .

For we do not wrestle against flesh and blood, but against principalities, against powers, against the rulers of the darkness of this age, against spiritual hosts of wickedness in the heavenly places. Ephesians 6:12

5. Paul acknowledges that we are in a battle.

a. What phrase lets you know that our battles are not physical in nature?

. . . .

b. What four enemies do we war against? . . . .

. . . .

. . . .

c. Complete the phrases describing where these enemies are deployed.

"of the darkness of _____ "

"hosts of wickedness in _____ "

Therefore take up the whole armor of God, that you may be able to withstand in the evil day, and having done all, to stand. Ephesians 6:13

6. What will we be able to do by taking up the armor of God? (Compare with Ephesians 6:11 above.)

. . . .

7. When will we need to stand strong? . . . .

. . . .

8. Paul gives assurance that, "having done all," we will not fall in battle. What is God's part in this? What is our part?

. . . .

. . . .

4
DEVIL'S SCHEMES
The word *wiles* refers to schemes or devices to deceive or ensnare; it is often used of predatory animals who cleverly stalk and suddenly pounce on their victims. *Devil* literally means slanderer and refers to the personal supreme spirit of evil; tempter of humanity; and leader of apostate angels.

5
RULERS OF DARKNESS
Principalities, powers, rulers, and spiritual hosts describe the different ranks of Satan's minions. The devil's army is extremely organized and prepared for devastating battle. Their demonic influence spans time, from past to present, and space, from heaven to earth.

6
STAND STRONG
God wants you to be able to *withstand* and *stand* against the devil's onslaught. To withstand means to resist or oppose an evil influence. To stand is to take a prolonged stance, to continue to hold up under pressure. Withstand for the moment; stand for a lifetime.

10

NO CONDEMNATION
The difference between condemnation and conviction? The Spirit convicts of sin to bring forgiveness and fellowship. Satan condemns already confessed sin to bring shame and separation. But, "there is no condemnation for those who belong to Christ Jesus" (Romans 8:1, NLT).

transformation

9. Paul has warned us about the wiles of the devil—his cunningly disguised traps. One of his favorite traps is temptation. Temptation is often an attempt to fulfill our fleshly needs through inappropriate ways. How have you tried to get something right the wrong way?

___ I was hungry, so I stole bread.

___ I felt inferior, so I lied about my past.

___ I needed money, so I cheated the IRS.

___ I was lonely, so I dated an unbeliever.

___ I was depressed, so I drank.

___ I was bored, so I read a trashy novel.

___ I wanted children, so I settled for sex.

___ I wanted friends, so I gossiped about others.

___ Other:_____

10. Once a Christian succumbs to temptation, Satan takes on the role of an accuser, debilitating a Christian with recriminations of shame and guilt. "The Accuser has been thrown down to earth—the one who accused our brothers and sisters before our God day and night" (Revelation 12:10, NLT).

If you have been bullied by Satan's name-calling or buried under his shame, take the time to write out and confess your sins to God. Ask Him to wash your conscience clean with the blood of the Lamb. "They have defeated [Satan] because of the blood of the Lamb and because of their testimony" (Revelation 12:11, NLT).

. . . .

. . . .

. . . .

. . . .

. . . .

. . . .

11. Satan is persistent. If he doesn't get you now, he'll try again later. "Now when the devil had ended every temptation, he departed from Him [Jesus] until an opportune time" (Luke 4:13).

> Journal a prayer asking the Lord to make you strong in the power of His might, so you will be able to resist temptation today, tomorrow, and always. Make sure you are leaning on His everlasting arms.

. . . .

. . . .

. . . .

. . . .

. . . .

. . . .

The city of Pompeii in southern Italy was destroyed in A.D. 79 when Mount Vesuvius erupted and covered the ancient city with molten rock. Pompeii's most amazing spectacle is the remains of a Roman soldier who stood his ground. On the fatal day when Vesuvius shook the earth, the guard kept watch by the gate that faced the burning mountain. Roman sentinels were trained to never abandon their posts unless relieved by a superior. To do so would blemish a soldier's reputation and end his career. This loyal guard was left to choose between death and dishonor. A picture of courage under fire, he stood by his post, slowly covered from sandals to helmet with hot lava.

Christian martyrs who stood against tyrants lost their earthly lives but gained an eternal reward. The Roman soldier who stood against a raging volcano lost his life but gained honor. As a believer, you stand against a formidable foe, and you too can gain ultimate victory in the power of God's might.

contemplation
Stand still . . . and
refuse to retreat.
Look at it as God looks
at it and draw upon
his power to hold up
under the blast.
Charles R. Swindoll

DAY 2 BE PROTECTED

After his butcher shop in Brooklyn was robbed four times in one month, William Levine bought a bulletproof vest. Other business proprietors asked him where they could get a vest like his. Mr. Levine began taking orders. Today Levine is out of the butcher business and full-time president of Body Armor, International. He supplies forty sales representatives across the country and is selling five hundred to six hundred vests a month.

There comes a day when God's children, like William Levine, discover that life on earth can be a spiritual battle, not business as usual. Believers don't often encounter bad guys with bullets; they face Satan's artillery of temptations and accusations. Bill's Body Armor may be an adequate defense against earthly ammo, but God's breastplate of righteousness is what you need to be protected from Satan's spiritual assault. If God is passing out spiritual armor, don't you want to try it on?

exploration

Paul urges us to wear God's armor as we fight against our spiritual enemies. Let's look at three pieces of the armor God provides.

Review Ephesians 6, then focus on verses 14-15.

> **Stand therefore, having girded your waist with truth, having put on the breastplate of righteousness, . . .**
> Ephesians 6:14

1. What equipment is to go around your waist?. . . . .

2. Fill in the following chart to discover where truth is found.

SCRIPTURE	TRUTH FOUND
John 14:6.	
John 16:13.	
John 17:17.	
2 John 4.	

 3. According to verse 14, what is the second piece of equipment believers should put on?

. . . .

4. Read Romans 13:14. What more must we put on in order to wear the breastplate of righteousness?

. . . .

5. According to Isaiah 64:6, what do we wear when we put on self-righteousness rather than the breastplate of righteousness?

. . . .

> *. . . and having shod your feet with the preparation of the gospel of peace*; . . . Ephesians 6:15

6. As Christian soldiers, what should we wear on our feet?

. . . .

7. The gospel is good news for everyone. Read Luke 4:18, and list the five groups of people Jesus reached with the gospel.

. . . .

. . . .

8. We've seen that the belt of truth keeps a Christian soldier from falling down or falling apart. Listening to lies, and not truth, can do damage.

RIGHTEOUSNESS
A Roman soldier's breastplate was made of metal, leather, or animal horns and protected his vital organs. Your spiritual breastplate is impenetrable, made of "the righteousness which is from God by faith" (Philippians 3:9), protecting your soul from the assault of Satan's accusations.

GOSPEL SHOES
To "stand" and "withstand" requires the surefooted shoes of the gospel—the good news about Jesus Christ. The Christian who witnesses is the Christian who wins spiritual battles. Proclaiming the gospel defends your borders and conquers new territory for God's army! "The gospel of Christ . . . is the power of God to salvation for everyone who believes" (Romans 1:16).

RIGHTEOUSNESS
Righteousness is "holy and upright living in accordance with God's standard; it comes from a root word that means 'straightness.' God's character is the definition and source of all righteousness. Therefore, people's righteousness is defined in terms of God's righteousness."

Write down a lie you have been told and believed. (Example: "If you take this pill, you'll lose weight.")

. . . .

. . . .

How did that lie trip you up or make you fall apart? (Example: "I didn't think the pills would keep me awake, make me irritable, and get me hooked.")

. . . .

. . . .

Journal about how finding out the truth helped you get back on your feet or pull it together. (Example: "Those pills are full of caffeine. The healthy way to lose weight is to eat less and exercise more.")

. . . .

. . . .

9. To put on the breastplate is to live in daily obedience to God's Word through practical acts of righteousness. Satan can't bring accusations against a Christian who is living a righteous life. How do your words and deeds promote righteousness? What behaviors give place for Satan to accuse you and make you feel ashamed? Write a few examples of these down in the columns below.

PRODUCES SHAME	PROMOTES RIGHTEOUSNESS
(Example: When I'm petty, criticizing or treating others cruelly)	(Example: When I tell the neighborhood kids about Jesus)
. . . .	. . . .
. . . .	. . . .
. . . .	. . . .
. . . .	. . . .

10. The Christian's feet are to be adorned with "the preparation of the gospel of peace." Are you prepared to preach the gospel? Let's take a walk on the Roman road, learning the steps to help lead others to salvation. Read each passage, and describe the step in the space below. Then underline the passages in your Bible, writing the number of the step it is (1–6) at the beginning of each underlined passage. At the end of each underlined passage, write which passage to turn to next.

Step 1: Rom. 3:10-12

. . . .

Step 2: Rom. 3:23

. . . .

Step 3: Rom. 6:23

. . . .

Step 4: Rom. 5:8

. . . .

Step 5: Rom. 10:9-10

. . . .

Step 6: Rom. 10:13

. . . .

10

GOSPEL OF PEACE
Peace is not the absence of war but the presence of God. Isaiah said Jesus would be called the "Prince of Peace," bringing the gospel of peace. The Bible teaches that we are at war with God. But "there is peace with God through Jesus Christ" (Acts 10:36, NLT). Jesus is God's peace treaty with us.

A brother and sister visited their grandparents on the farm. Johnny was given a slingshot to play with in the woods. He practiced but couldn't hit the target. Discouraged, he headed home, and there he spotted his grandma's pet duck. On impulse, he took out the slingshot and killed the duck. In a panic, he hid the dead duck and then looked up to see his sister, Sandy, watching.

Over the next few days, every time Grandma asked the little girl to do a chore, she'd boldly say, "Oh, Johnny said he'd do it!" then whisper, "Remember the duck?"

After several days of doing both his and Sandy's chores, Johnny had had enough, so he told his grandma about her dead duck. She knelt down, gave him a hug, and said, "Honey, I know; I was standing at the window and saw the whole thing. I forgive you. I just wondered how long you would let Sandy make a slave out of you."

I don't know what sin the enemy keeps accusing you of, causing chinks in your armor. But whatever it is, you need to know something: Jesus is standing at the window and sees the whole thing. But because He loves you, He has forgiven you. Perhaps He's wondering how long you'll let the enemy get past your armor and make a slave out of you.

contemplation
Peace is not made at the council tables, or by treaties, but in the hearts of men.
Herbert Hoover

DAY 3 BE PREPARED

An ancient king of Sparta boasted about his mighty walls, which could thwart any invading army. An ambassador on a diplomatic mission came to view the famous city-state. The reputation of Sparta's strength was acclaimed throughout Greece, so he anticipated seeing great, fortified walls surrounding the town. He was shocked to discover no walls whatsoever. He chided the ruler, "Sir, I've seen no famed walls of defense. Where are they?" "Come with me tomorrow and I will show you the walls of Sparta," replied the king. The next day he led his guest to a field where his army was arrayed in full battle gear, their shields glistening in the sun. Pointing proudly to the columns of soldiers who stood at attention, he said, "Behold the walls of Sparta—10,000 men, and every man a brick!"

The king of Sparta was prepared for battle. He had recruited and trained an army of men, supplying them with shields for defense and swords for combat. God is prepared for the battle of the ages: the forces of light against the powers of darkness. You've been enlisted as a member of His mighty army. You must be prepared for combat; so raise high the shield of faith, and unleash the sword of the Spirit on God's enemies.

exploration

We have studied about three pieces of spiritual equipment necessary for protection during spiritual warfare: the girdle, the breastplate, and the shoes. Paul continues with three more armor pieces necessary for Christians in battle.

Review Ephesians 6, then focus on verses 16-17.

> *. . . above all, taking the shield of faith with which you will be able to quench all the fiery darts of the wicked one.* Ephesians 6:16

1. What are believers to take into battle above all else? . . . .

. . . .

2. In what way does this piece of equipment help us against the wicked one?

. . . .

3. How many fiery darts—attacks—will it quench? . . . .

. . . .

> **And take the helmet of salvation, and the sword of the Spirit, which is the word of God; . . .** Ephesians 6:17

4. What piece of armor should we wear figuratively on our head?

. . . .

5. Read 1 Thessalonians 5:8-10. According to these verses, what additional benefits does the helmet of salvation offer?

. . . .

6. Look back to Ephesians 6:17. What is the sword of the Spirit?

. . . .

7. According to Hebrews 4:12, why is the Word of God such an effective weapon?

. . . .

transformation

8. We read that the shield of faith will quench Satan's fiery darts. Fill in the following table to discover some of the other "arrows" found in Scripture.

explanation

SHIELD OF FAITH
United we stand! Shields in Paul's day had interlocking edges to enable soldiers to become a solid wall of defense. God fortifies Christian soldiers who unite their shields as one. "Where two or three gather together because they are mine, I am there among them" (Matthew 18:20, NLT).

4
SALVATION HELMET
The bronze helmet protected the soldier's head from harm. God's helmet of salvation protects the believer's mind from havoc. The mind controlled by God is safe from Satan's turmoil. "His peace will guard your hearts and minds as you live in Christ Jesus" (Philippians 4:7, NLT).

6
SPIRIT SWORD
The sword of the Spirit is the only piece of equipment used for offense. Metal swords cut the flesh to maim and kill. God's sword, His Word, divides soul from spirit, bringing wholeness and life. Christians are to use this sword to slay God's spiritual enemies, not to hurt one another.

8

GOD'S ARSENAL
The enemy is powerful, but he is not equal to God. God is eternal but Satan is finite. God is omnipotent while the devil is limited. Satan's weapons can wreak havoc, but they're no match for God's invincible arsenal. "We use God's mighty weapons, not mere worldly weapons, to knock down the Devil's strongholds" (2 Corinthians 10:4, NLT).

MIND GAMES
"There is another law at work within me that is at war with my mind" (Romans 7:23, NLT). The enemy uses an arsenal to conquer the believer's mind. *Deception:* to mislead or cause to believe an untruth. *Distraction:* to turn aside or to stir up and confuse with conflicting emotions. *Disillusionment:* to disappoint, to let down, or to dishearten.

SCRIPTURE	ARROW USED BY	ARROW USED TO
2 Kings 13:17		
Ps. 64:7		
Prov. 7:21-23		
Prov. 25:18		
Jer. 9:8-9		
Zech. 9:13-14		

9. A believer's helmet is necessary to guard the mind from dangerous beliefs. Our enemies—the world, the flesh, and the devil—work together to *deceive* with half-truths, *distract* with competing loyalties, or *disillusion* with doubts about God.

Journal about a time when failing to trust in your helmet allowed the enemy to strike a devastating blow that damaged your thought process in one or more of the following ways.

Deception:

. . . .

. . . .

Distraction:

. . . .

. . . .

Disillusionment:

. . . .

. . . .

10. Once you become aware of the mind games your enemies have used against you, God exhorts you to eradicate them with the truth. Journal the following passage into a personal prayer asking God to eliminate destructive thought patterns and to replace them with divine ones: "Do not be conformed to this world, but be transformed by the renewing of your mind, that you may prove what is that good and acceptable and perfect will of God" (Romans 12:2).

. . . .

. . . .

. . . .

. . . .

You wouldn't wear a bikini to the battlefield any more than you'd use a BB gun against a bazooka. A good soldier has the clothes and the gear to get the job done. When my son, Nathan, was small, he loved to dress up as a marine, a gladiator, or a cowboy. He was out to conquer any foe in our neighborhood or his imagination. One night when I came to tuck him in, I felt something hard underneath his covers. As I lifted his blanket, I discovered an arsenal: a plastic sword, a wooden gun, and a leather whip. I asked him, "Why did you bring your weapons to bed?" He grinned and said, "Don't worry, Mommy, I'll protect you if any bad guys break into our house." I smiled, kissed him goodnight, and said, "You're growing up to be such a big boy, but Daddy is bigger, and he'll watch over you while you sleep. And you know what? God is the biggest of all; He'll watch over *all* of us as we sleep."

Isn't it good to know that in battles, seen and unseen, you can rest assured that God is on your side? With His weapons and His wardrobe you are prepared and invincible against the bad guys who go bump in the night.

4 BE PRAYERFUL

preparation

Lord, teach me how to fight the good fight in prayer. Help me to pray for those in battles to be strengthened by Your Spirit and delivered from the evil one. May I see Your mighty hand prevail. Amen.

DELIVERANCE

For I know that as you pray for me and as the Spirit of Jesus Christ helps me, this will all turn out for my deliverance. Philippians 1:19, NLT

Oswald Chambers said, "The armor is for the battle of prayer. . . . Prayer is the battlefield!" My husband, Skip, told me a story from his mission trip to the Philippines about a battle fought and won by prayer. Communist guerrillas in the Philippines, who were violently opposed to Christianity, were threatening and raiding small churches in remote jungle villages. In one village the church was assaulted by a band of armed guerrillas one Sunday during services. They threatened the church members with death if they met the following week. The congregation decided to fight on their knees. All week they prayed, and when Sunday came, they met in church and continued to pray. The services ended without incident. Later the victorious saints discovered that the jeep full of armed rebels had crashed and flipped, defeating their wicked plans.

When you find yourself in a battle, don't just stand there—pray!

exploration

The whole armor of God is needed to stand against the wiles of the devil. Paul reminds us that prayer is the secret weapon behind spiritual victories.

Review Ephesians 6, then focus on verses 18-20.

> *. . . praying always with all prayer and supplication in the Spirit, being watchful to this end with all perseverance and supplication for all the saints—* . . . Ephesians 6:18

1. When should believers pray? . . . .

. . . .

2. How much and what kind of prayer did Paul specify here?

. . . .

3. Which member of the Trinity empowers prayer?. . . . .

. . . .

4. What phrase reveals that we should be alert as we pray?

. . . .

5. What phrase reveals that we should not give up in prayer?

. . . .

6. For whom should we pray? . . . .

. . . .

> *. . . and for me, that utterance may be given to me, that*
> *I may open my mouth boldly to make known the mystery*
> *of the gospel, for which I am an ambassador in chains;*
> *that in it I may speak boldly, as I ought to speak.*
> Ephesians 6:19-20

7. What did Paul ask would be given to him? Why? . . . .

. . . .

. . . .

8. Despite being in prison and in chains, what was Paul's heartfelt desire?

. . . .

transformation

9. There are many ways to pray, and Paul encourages us to use all forms. If you're in a praying rut, perhaps it's time to break free. Check off all the ways you have prayed in the past.

3

IN THE SPIRIT
The Trinity asserts three requirements for prayer: 1) In the name of the Son: "If you ask anything in My name, I will do it" (John 14:14); 2) In the will of the Father: "Your will be done." (Matthew 6:10); 3) In the Spirit's power: "Pray at all times . . . in the power of the Holy Spirit" (Ephesians 6:18, NLT).

5

PERSEVERANCE
To persevere is to continue persistently in a steadfast effort stemming from a faithful trust in God. Remember the poster with a kitten dangling from a bar? It read, "Hang in there, baby!" Persevering prayer is hanging on to God, knowing He won't let go.

9

PRAYER STAIR
If your prayer life is stuck, climb to the next level. Try STAIR. **S**upplication: ask God for what you need. **T**hanksgiving: thank God for what He does. **A**doration: praise God for who He is. **I**ntercession: stand in the gap for someone else. **R**epentance: confess sin.

FORM OF PRAYER	POSTURE	TIME
___ public	___ walking	___ morning
___ private	___ standing	___ noon
___ loud	___ bowing	___ evening
___ silent	___ kneeling	___ in the night
___ structured	___ sitting	___ meal time
___ spontaneous	___ lying down	___ crisis
___ singing	___ hands raised	___ special occasions

Review the columns above. From each column choose an item that you have never experienced before. Journal about how you will incorporate this new method into your life this week. If possible, go ahead and practice this new method of prayer now.

. . . .

. . . .

. . . .

. . . .

10

PATIENT PRAYER
Prayer sows spiritual seed, planting a crop that takes time. The prayer warrior, like the farmer, must practice patience. "See how the farmer waits for the precious fruit of the earth, waiting patiently for it. . . . You also be patient" (James 5:7-8).

10. We are instructed to persevere in prayer—never give up! Name a person or situation about which you have grown discouraged in prayer.

. . . .

Take the time now to tell God about your frustration. Ask Him to fill you with new hope and vision to pray. Begin again by writing a prayer concerning this discouraging situation.

. . . .

. . . .

. . . .

11. Who prays for you on a regular basis? Do you pray for them? If not, return the favor by journaling a prayer on their behalf.

. . . .

. . . .

. . . .

. . . .

Life is full of unsung heroes—men and women who have given of themselves unselfishly for others without receiving recognition. I'd like to sing the praises of one of my heroes of the faith, Kay Smith. As wife of Pastor Chuck Smith from Calvary Chapel in California, she is the great woman behind a great man. An unpretentious woman with an unstoppable prayer life, her time spent on her knees helps others stand on their feet. I've heard many shipwrecked Christians express, "I was down for the count; everyone had given up on me. But Kay Smith never gave up in prayer for me. Through her intercession God rebuilt my broken life."

Southern California in the 1960s was a mecca for longhaired hippies on the pursuit to find themselves. It was a scene that was volatile, sensual, and psychedelic. Kay would drive with her husband down to the Huntington Beach pier and watch the hippies tune in, turn on, and trip out. Her heart was grieved by what she saw, so she began to pray and then found others to pray with her for that lost generation. As a result of their prayers the Jesus Movement took off—a generation of hippies were delivered from drugs and deception to devotion to God.

You, too, can become an unsung hero. Who knows what God will do when you go to the football game, the mall, the beach, the movies—wherever—and pray "always with all prayer and supplication in the Spirit" for this generation?

11
PRAY FOR ME
Paul told the Ephesians, "I have never stopped thanking God for you. I pray for you constantly" (Ephesians 1:16, NLT). Now Paul asks the Ephesians to return the favor. Praying for each other is a duty and a privilege.

contemplation
Satan trembles when he sees the weakest saint upon his knees.
William Cowper

DAY 5 BE PEACEFUL

preparation

Father, I praise You that You are the God of all comfort. I ask You to allow me to comfort others with the comfort I have received. Amen.

COMFORT

"Comfort, comfort my people," says your God.
Isaiah 40:1, NLT

God's people are like sheep. David the psalmist found comfort in knowing that the Lord was his shepherd, who could make him "lie down in green pastures." Modern-day shepherd Phillip Keller wrote in his book *A Shepherd's Look at Psalm 23*, "Freedom of torment from parasites and insects is essential to the contentment of sheep. . . . Sheep can be driven to distraction by . . . flies and ticks. When tormented by pests, it is literally impossible for them to lie down and rest."

In the Christian life our most annoying pest is worry. It can drive us crazy with concern. My mother never slept at night until her three kids were home safe and sound. My son, Nathan, is unsettled at school when his father is traveling overseas. The apostle Paul knew it was natural to worry about those you love, so he wrote to the Ephesians in order to comfort their hearts and give them peace.

exploration

This week we've learned to put on the armor of God and utilize the secret weapon of prayer. As we come to the end of our exploration of the book of Ephesians, let's study Paul's closing words to his friends and his prayer for peace.

Review Ephesians 6, then focus on verses 21-24.

> *But that you also may know my affairs and how I am doing, Tychicus, a beloved brother and faithful minister in the Lord, will make all things known to you; . . .*
> Ephesians 6:21

1. Why did Paul send Tychicus to the Ephesians? . . . .

. . . .

2. How did Paul describe this messenger and his message?

. . . .

> *. . . whom I have sent to you for this very purpose, that you may know our affairs, and that he may comfort your hearts.* Ephesians 6:22

3. What two reasons did Paul give for sending Tychicus? . . . .

. . . .

. . . .

> *Peace to the brethren, and love with faith, from God the Father and the Lord Jesus Christ.* Ephesians 6:23

4. For what two blessings does Paul pray? . . . .

. . . .

5. From whom do these blessings come? . . . .

. . . .

> *Grace be with all those who love our Lord Jesus Christ in sincerity. Amen.* Ephesians 6:24

6. What was Paul's final benediction to the Ephesians? . . . .

. . . .

7. Whom does Paul pray will receive this blessing? . . . .

. . . .

explanation

2

BELOVED BROTHER
As members of God's family, we acquire brothers and sisters, not by physical birth, but by the new birth of the Spirit. Jesus said, "Anyone who does the will of my Father in heaven is my brother and sister and mother!" (Matthew 12:50, NLT). It's all in the family!

3

COMFORT
The Greek word for *comfort* means "to give forth sighs, to call alongside, or to help." The English definition is "to ease, encourage, inspirit, or enliven." Comfort combines encouragement with easing of grief. "God does not comfort us to make us comfortable, but to make us comforters" (John Henry Jowett).

6

GRACE TO YOU
We might close a letter with "Sincerely yours." Paul concludes his letter encouraging us to be "Sincerely His." When we genuinely belong to God, we experience peace, love, faith, and grace "from God the Father and the Lord Jesus Christ." Amen!

9

LETTERS

"She's like a breath of fresh air." Some people have a way of refreshing others. One way to quench a loved one's thirst for encouragement is by writing a letter. "As cold water to a weary soul, so is good news from a far country" (Proverbs 25:25).

10

BENEDICTION

A *benediction* is "a blessing, declaring or wishing God's favor and goodness upon others. Blessing is the good effect of words as well as the power to bring them to pass. Biblically important persons blessed those with less power or influence." "The Lord bless you and keep you; the Lord make His face shine upon you, and be gracious to you" (Numbers 6:24-25).

8. Paul called Tychicus a beloved brother in the Lord. Write down the names of three people who, though not born into your earthly family, have become beloved members of your heavenly family.

. . . .

. . . .

9. Paul sent this letter because he wanted to comfort and encourage the Ephesians. Choose one of the people from your list above, and send that person a letter offering words of comfort or encouragement. Share what you've learned about God and His spiritual treasures from this study in Ephesians.

10. Modeled after Paul's benediction, write a prayer of blessing for your beloved friends.

. . . .

. . . .

. . . .

. . . .

11. In his final words Paul bestowed blessings on his beloved friends: peace, love with faith, and grace.

Journal about which of these things you need most in your life right now. Why?

. . . .

. . . .

. . . .

. . . .

. . . .

Journal about the ways God has blessed you throughout your study of Ephesians.

. . . .

. . . .

. . . .

. . . .

. . . .

The television game show *Who Wants to Be a Millionaire?* has captured network ratings and the hearts of Americans. If this slick show has tapped into the pulse of current society, then we find ourselves living in a world obsessed with material wealth but where many people are spiritually bankrupt. A million dollars sounds great—but you can't take it with you!

Living for the here and now and not for the hereafter is a risky game. Jesus said, "How do you benefit if you gain the whole world but lose your own soul in the process? Is anything worth more than your soul?" (Matthew 16:26, NLT). You're in the hot seat, and you're gambling with your soul. The all-important question is "What will *you* do with Jesus?" Host Regis Philbin offers three flimsy lifelines. Will you risk your spiritual inheritance on a 50/50 chance, the opinion of an audience, or the advice of a friend on the phone? Or will you confess "your faith in the Lord Jesus" (Ephesians 1:15) and be a real winner?

God wants to know, "Is that your final answer?" If you answer the question correctly, you'll inherit much more than a mere million dollars—you'll gain eternal life and spiritual treasures that are "exceedingly abundantly above all that we ask or think" (Ephesians 3:20).

contemplation

To forsake Christ for the world is to leave a treasure for a trifle . . . eternity for a moment, reality for a shadow.
William Jenkyn

Bibliography

The authors have used the following books and electronic sources in preparing the illustrations and sidebar material for this book.

Armstrong, Richard. *Make Your Life Worthwhile,* taken from the *Bible Illustrator Electronic Library.*

Barclay, William. *The Letters to the Galatians and Ephesians.* The Daily Bible Study Series. Philadelphia: Westminster, 1958.

Bible Illustrator for Windows. Parsons Technology, 1997–1998.

Criswell, W. A. *Ephesians: An Exposition.* Grand Rapids: Zondervan, 1974 (out of print).

Graham, Billy. *Just As I Am.* San Francisco: HarperSanFrancisco, 1997.

Graham, Franklin. *Living Beyond the Limits: A Life in Sync with God.* Nashville: Thomas Nelson, 1998.

Halley, Henry H. *Halley's Bible Handbook.* Grand Rapids: Zondervan, 1978.

Harrison, Everett F., and Charles F. Pfeiffer, eds. *The Wycliffe Bible Commentary.* Chicago: Moody Press, 1962.

Henry, Matthew. *Matthew Henry's Commentary on the Whole Bible: One Volume Edition, Complete and Unabridged.* Peabody, Mass.: Hendrickson, 1991.

Hewett, James S. *Illustrations Unlimited.* Wheaton, Ill.: Tyndale House, 1988.

Hodge, Charles. *Ephesians.* The Crossway Classic Commentaries. Edited by Alister E. McGrath and J. I. Packer. Wheaton, Ill.: Crossway, 1994.

INFOsearch™, Illustrations data and database, The Communicator's Companion™, P.O. Box 171749, Arlington, Texas 76003. Web site: <www.infosearch.com>. Search by finding a search word in the illustration.

Larson, Bruce. *There's a Lot More to Health Than Not Being Sick,* taken from the *Bible Illustrator Electronic Library.*

Lockyer, Herbert, ed. *Nelson's Illustrated Bible Dictionary.* Nashville: Nelson, 1986 (out of print, but appears in *The PC Study Bible*).

MacArthur, John. *The MacArthur New Testament Commentary: Ephesians.* Chicago: Moody Press, 1986.

MacArthur, John. *The MacArthur Study Bible.* Nashville: Word, 1997.

McLellan, Vern. *The Complete Book of Practical Proverbs and Wacky Wit.* Wheaton, Ill.: Tyndale House, 1996.

Meyer, F. B. *Devotional Commentary.* Wheaton, Ill.: Tyndale House, 1989.

Morris, Leon. *Expository Reflections on the Letter to the Ephesians.* Grand Rapids: Baker, 1994.

Nelson's Quick Reference Topical Bible Index. Nashville: Thomas Nelson, 1995 (out of print).

Shereos, William C. *Sermons Illustrations.com,* search word: "Ravenhill" then click "Spiritual Maturity."

Simpson, Charles. *Sermon Illustrations.com,* search word: "shark" then click "Growth."

The PC Study Bible for Windows. Biblesoft, Version 3.0. Seattle: Jim Gilbertson, 1999.

Unger, Merrill F., and R. K. Harrison, eds. *The Unger's Bible Dictionary*. Chicago: Moody Press, 1998.

<v-j-enterprises.com/roswell.html>.

Vine, W. E., Merrill F. Unger, and William White Jr. *Vine's Complete Expository Dictionary of Old and New Testament Words*. Nashville: Nelson, 1985.

Walvoord, John F., and Roy B. Zuck, eds. *The Bible Knowledge Commentary: New Testament*. Wheaton, Ill.: Victor, 1987.

Warren Wiersbe. *Be Rich*. Colorado Springs, Colo.: Victor, 1993.

With Gratitude

Lenya—Heartfelt appreciation to my family for imparting faith to me: Thanks to my father, Rod Farley, for introducing me to the faith; to my mother, Helen DeBeck, for her unconditional faithfulness to me; to my husband, Skip, for being an example of unshakable faith; to my son, Nathan, for showing me childlike faith; and to all the Women at Calvary for faithfully serving God side by side with Penny and me.

Penny—Many thanks to those who have shown me such love: Thanks to my parents, Jack and Janelle Pierce, for loving me since I was agleam'; to my husband, Kerry, who loves me even though he knows everything about me; to my children—Erin, Kristian, and Ryan—who fill my heart to overflowing with love; and to the Women at Calvary for loving God's Word.

Thanks from both of us to the talented Tyndale team—Ron Beers, Jon Farrar, Lynn Vanderzalm, Mary Horner Collins, MaryLynn Layman, Timothy Botts, Kelly Bennema, and Gwen Elliott—for embracing our vision and making it a reality.

Lenya Heitzig was headed for a promising career in fashion merchandising when God changed her direction. After a lifetime steeped in agnosticism, Lenya became a Christian in 1978, joining the Jesus Movement in southern California.

Her training for ministry was forged on the anvil of servant leadership. She joined Youth With a Mission (YWAM) in 1980 as a single women's counselor and discovered that ministry is not just telling people how to act but serving them as cook and secretary. Helping to establish a Christian coffeehouse in the red-light district of Honolulu taught her compassion as she shared Christ's love with prostitutes and pimps.

After YWAM, Lenya married Skip Heitzig, a determined California surfer on his own spiritual journey. In 1981 they headed to the Southwest and settled in Albuquerque. Their home Bible study quickly blossomed into Calvary of Albuquerque, a church that now sees over 10,000 people in weekly attendance. The Heitzigs share a passion for world missions, traveling together to Japan, India, Rwanda, Israel, Jordan, Mexico, Honduras, and Europe while spreading the gospel.

Lenya's gift in teaching and communicating truth paved the way for a thriving women's ministry impacting women throughout the Southwest. Lenya served on the executive board for a Billy and Franklin Graham Crusade, and currently directs the Southwest Woman's Festival, sharing the conference podium with such speakers as Kay Arthur, Elisabeth Elliot, Florence Littauer, and Anne Graham Lotz. Lenya speaks regularly for the Women at Calvary and is in demand as a conference speaker for seminars throughout the United States and Europe.

Skip, Lenya, and their son, Nathan, live in Albuquerque and continue to travel this exciting pathway God has set them on.

Penny Pierce Rose was raised in a loving Christian home and heard God call her by name while attending church camp at the age of nine. During high school and college she wandered off the straight-and-narrow path. Soon after marriage and motherhood she became discontent with her life and grudgingly attended a Bible Study Fellowship meeting with her persistent mother. God's Word inspired her to renew her relationship with God. Not long afterward, her husband, Kerry, followed in the footsteps of faith, bringing salvation to their household.

Penny graduated from Texas Tech University with a degree in political science. After seven years in Bible Study Fellowship, Penny joined the leadership team of the Women at Calvary, where she serves as writer-in-residence. She has served in other capacities including Kid's Crusade Coordinator for Harvest Crusade with Greg Laurie, and secretary for the Women's Committee of New Mexico Festival '98 with Franklin Graham. Her writing has appeared in *Why Fret That God Stuff?* and *God's Little Rule Book*. She continues to write and speak at conferences and retreats. Her fervent desire is to minister to women by teaching them to study God's Word, apply the truths to their daily lives, and embrace the Christian life as a grand adventure. She and her husband have three children: Erin, Kristian, and Ryan.